The Full English

The Ways We Eat and Why

Lewis Bassett

VERSO
London • New York

First published by Verso 2026

The manufacturer's authorized representative in the EU for product safety (GPSR)
is LOGOS EUROPE, 9 rue Nicolas Poussin, 17000, La Rochelle, France
contact@logoseurope.eu

1 3 5 7 9 10 8 6 4 2

Verso
UK: 6 Meard Street, London W1F 0EG
US: 207 East 32nd Street, New York, NY 10016
versobooks.com

Verso is the imprint of New Left Books

ISBN-13: 978-1-83674-065-0
ISBN-13: 978-1-83674-068-1 (US EBK)
ISBN-13: 978-1-83674-067-4 (UK EBK)

British Library Cataloguing in Publication Data
A catalogue record for this book is available from the British Library

Library of Congress Cataloging-in-Publication Data
A catalog record for this book is available from the Library of Congress

Typeset in Fournier by MJ & N Gavan, Truro, Cornwall
Printed and bound by CPI Group (UK) Ltd, Croydon, CR0 4YY

Contents

'Excuse me,' said he, after a while; 'I am not laughing at anything you could be thinking of, but at that silly nineteenth-century fashion, current amongst rich so-called cultivated people, of ignoring all the steps by which their daily dinner was reached, as matters too low for their lofty intelligence. Useless idiots! Come, now, I am a "literary man", as we queer animals used to be called, yet I am a pretty good cook myself.'

William Morris, *News from Nowhere*, 1890

Preface

In 2013 I was living in a dilapidated, unheated house in South London while working at a respectable gastropub called the Canton Arms. That year, in a newly refurbished and rebranded 'Brixton Village Market', a small restaurant called Champagne and Fromage opened.

The appearance of a wine and cheese bar in a formerly working-class shopping arcade that was home to many Caribbean and African businesses, and in a period of austerity, was controversial.

Activists, including members of a group called Class War, held a protest on the opening night that called for 'Yuppies out!' and advertised an alternative to the French menu in the form of White Ace – the strong, cheap cider – and Dairylea, the tasteless, processed cheese packaged in triangular tinfoil wrappers. Despite the endless rain, I went to the market to see what was happening and found there a small but noisy party getting drunk on cider and waving packets of processed cheese. Later, when I returned home, I spoke to a neighbour who had lived in a council house in the area for decades, who told me she'd love to go to the new wine bar and drink champagne with her friends.

Looking back at it now, I have the feeling that the people at this protest were not only saying that the issue with the wine and cheese was that its price was exclusive, but also that the food itself was 'posh', and posh food is bad.

Would the same people say that a roast dinner or fish and chips is posh, I wonder? Roast beef and Yorkshire pudding eaten in a pub with a pint of beer may be slightly cheaper, in addition to being more filling, than a glass of champagne and a plate of artisanal cheese and ham. But is the high price of a given calorie the only reason we think of food as posh? Fish and chips, for example, has gone from cheap and filling to quite expensive and occasionally dainty (my local chippie offers portions that, compared to what I ate growing up, look miniscule), while a glance at the various recipes available online suggests that it only qualifies as posh when someone has taken time to season the fish, triple cook the chips, make a quality batter and a home-made tartare sauce, and serve the meal with a wedge of lemon (a mistake, in my view, if the citrus replaces malt vinegar). You can buy Camembert in a supermarket today for roughly the same price as cheddar, but it's the French cheese, packaged in a delicate wooden box, that comes with a whiff of poshness.

Thinking about that protest today, I realise that there was something peculiarly English going on here.

This book is the product of leading two lives. On the one hand, I have worked in professional kitchens in one way or another since the age of sixteen. That was when I got a job making sandwiches: foot-long or six-inch, thousand island dressing or honey mustard. At seventeen I got a job in a vegetarian café and the food I made extended to things like soup. With its structured environment and the sense of achievement that came with cooking, the café saved me from a long, confusing post-school depression. At eighteen I was opening oysters and cooking burgers at a restaurant-cum-club in Melbourne, Australia, where I made extra money doing the early cleaning shift, occasionally sweeping the drinkers and drug-takers out the front door at sunrise. I was about twenty when a chef at a fish restaurant in London showed me how to make a lemon tart and I learnt what words like 'sauté' mean, and what a soufflé is and that there is more than one type of salt, and that flaky salt should go on everything, *including salad*.

On the other hand, since coming back from Australia all those years ago, I have studied sociology all the way to a Ph.D. The kind of sociology I've been interested in has tended towards the historical and political, and at one point in my life I thought I'd attempt to carve out a career as an academic. But after the first Covid-19 lockdown, I was desperate to go back to the kitchen.

Some chefs reading this may think that was a stupid

decision. But I'm not the only one who has found their desk job unsatisfying and who has given up the hope of a tenuous middle-class career to pursue a life spent shaking pans in a windowless kitchen. Such people typically do not last very long in professional kitchens. I have seen recently graduated culinary students from Leiths mop the floors and take out the bins at 11 p.m. and watched it dawn on them that cleaning up is a bigger part of the job than they must make it sound in college – and then I have seen them quit. Not all, but some.

Being a chef is hard, and it gets harder as you age. There are almost no full-time cooking jobs I know of that require less than a forty-five-hour week, and that is progress on what the industry was like ten or fifteen years ago. In serious kitchens, being ill is rare while injury can be a standard part of what the job involves. In some places having a break, even ten minutes to eat or smoke a cigarette during the course of a fifteen-hour shift, can feel like a luxury. Cooking at the highest level can involve chefs working upwards of sixty hours a week, every week, as we'll see.

Many of the best chefs I've ever met don't post about food on Instagram, they don't wear branded kitchen workwear and they use a 'disposable' Victorinox bread knife for most of their tasks, including cutting shallots into tiny, perfectly square *brunoise*. This hard-working band of kitchen-lifers seems less charmed by the lure of the stove than myself and others who have previously worked in relatively pleasant desk jobs.

I've had the luxury of a life lived both inside and outside the kitchen. I've spent a lot of time in the library, taught courses in politics and sociology and even worked for a spell in Parliament. But the net result of all of this seems to be that I remain drawn to the kind of careful, physical work that is done with human hands. If there is a single explanation for the abundance of culture that glamourises professional cooking today then perhaps it is that many people like me crave a creative, sensual, authentic life spent working with their hands.

Introduction

There's a lot of reductive thinking when it comes to thinking about what we eat. There exist serious people today who will describe other forms of human culture in complex, historically layered social terms and yet characterise our dietary preferences as a simple matter of biology. Perhaps the only other sphere of life that is so frequently treated as a thing of nature rather than culture is the domain of life that we bracket off and label 'the economy'.

Take the debate about ultra-processed foods, which the British doctor and minor TV celebrity Chris van Tulleken helped to initiate with his bestselling book *Ultra-processed People*. Van Tulleken's book describes his adoption of a diet consisting of 80 per cent ultra-processed foods (since this is what one in five of the British population eats) and finds after a month that he's 6.5 kg heavier and that his brain is showing signs of addiction. The book's subtitle is *Why Do We All Eat Stuff That Isn't Food ... and Why Can't We Stop?* In an apparent effort to answer the former, historical question, the book provides a geological sweep of life on earth: from the earliest life forms which consumed minerals in the planet's oceans to more advanced plants and animals that consume other plants and animals. Any detailed discussion of the history of human societies is left out.

That seems to be what often happens when so-called 'hard' scientists talk about why we eat the things we do. An article in the prestigious medical journal the *Lancet* is one example among many.[1] The article by Barry Popkin and colleagues offers a table with human biological traits on one side – these being an innate preference for sweet and fatty foods, an innate tendency to snack and a biological desire to eliminate exertion – and the modern technology that has taken advantage of these traits on the other, namely forms of ultra-processed foods and their marketing. Scientists like these imagine that when you strip away the thin shell of human culture you will find in each of us a naked, evolutionary desire to eat Doritos.

One final example. In 2019, Henry Dimbleby, founder of the food chain Leon, was appointed by UK Prime Minister Boris Johnson to write a national food strategy. The proposal captured a spirit of post-Brexit optimism, the idea that leaving the EU could amount to doing something good for the nation. In the end, little of Dimbleby's recommendations became government policy – framed as they were by the press as nanny-state interventions in poor people's decisions to drink cola and consume cheap ready meals. Partly out of frustration, Dimbleby wrote up his research as a book. In *Ravenous: How to Get Ourselves and Our Planet into Shape* Dimbleby summarises the science by saying that humans are 'biologically programmed' and 'predisposed' to crave diets high in fat and sugar.

He then points out that the British eat more ultra-processed food than any other European country. Fifty-seven per cent of what we eat in Britain comes from ultra-processed foods, compared with 46 per cent in Germany, 14 per cent in France and 13 per cent in Italy. As a result of diets that are high in calories but low in nutrients, Britain has some of the fattest and *shortest* children among rich nations in the world. But how do we explain these national differences? If every human being wants to eat Doritos, why are we British eating so many more of them?

We might imagine an experiment with mice. Offer mice a choice between a plate of grilled anchovies, boiled spinach dressed in grassy olive oil and a thimble of white wine (on the one hand) and a plate of chicken nuggets, curly fries, ketchup and a Diet Coke (on the other) and for all I know the mice might choose the junk food. Perhaps. But offer these two meals to a person from England and a person from Italy and it's not obvious that both humans will choose the curly fries. Our national food culture matters, and so our diets have social histories.

It was the Scottish philosopher Adam Smith who, in the late eighteenth century, argued that human nature contains a certain propensity to barter and exchange. In this way Smith provided a naturalising view of the origins of capitalism as a realisation of our economic destiny. But many social scientists – some of whose work underlies what follows in this book – have seen this view as ahistorical and have pointed to the emergence of capitalist relationships in England, the ways by which they have spread unevenly throughout the globe, and how they continue to be reproduced.

The appearance of diets high in ultra-processed foods is best seen in the same way – that is, not as arising from an innate human tendency to prefer easy-to-consume foods that are high in sugar and fat but as the product of a social history. A history that has made us who we are as a nation and that can be narrated by looking at what we eat and why.

In what follows, I make the case that a common pattern of culinary taste in England has been fundamentally shaped by the experiences of urbanisation, empire, industry and war, or what I refer to as England's peculiar experience of modernity. What we eat today is shaped by modernity, both through these great moulds of modern history and in reaction to their consequences.

I say peculiar experience of modernity because it was only England that, from the middle of the nineteenth century, 'presented a unique and amazing spectacle to the enquiring foreigner: it had no peasants'.[2] By 1851 Britain had become a majority urban country, decades ahead of other industrialising nations. The US only reached this point in the 1920s and France in the 1930s, by which time approximately 80 per cent of people in Britain lived in urban areas. In Southern Europe, including Italy, Spain and Portugal, majority urban status only arrived in the 1960s, more than a century after it did in Britain.

In the majority-urban Britain of the 1850s, a popular diet centred on shop-brought bread had eliminated an older one characterised by home baking and brewing, as well as various country stews known as pottage. At the middling and elite levels, the late nineteenth century saw a gradual decline in the stature of English country cooking – think of roasted meats, pies and puddings – a trend that represented England's native break with medieval cuisine. This century saw the rise of new working-class foods, above all fish and chips, as well as imperial tastes, especially for curry. Ironically, since the English country cooking tradition was initially formed out of a self-conscious contrast with France, it was fine French taste that came to dominate the upper ranks of late-Victorian inequality. Yet it was industrial foods that defined the British diet above all else, since, as was evident by the turn of the 1900s, nowhere in the world ate as much factory-made white bread, sugar and margarine as was being wolfed down in the UK.

Part of the reason Britain industrialised and urbanised so early – part of the reason the country has long lacked a substantial peasantry – is due to what was once Britain's capacity to rule the waves with its navy, to enforce a doctrine of 'free seas' and 'free trade' and so exchange textiles for grain and cattle within the Empire while allowing its fishing smacks and steamers to trawl for cod wherever they so pleased.

Highlighting the imperial aspects of Britain's modern culinary history is not meant to make any British person reading this feel bad the next time they sit down to a Sunday roast. The point is instead to show you just how unique our history has been and so to guard against the idea that every nation's past is simply a matter of following a universal standard of 'development'. What I'm trying to say is that a fried breakfast with a mug of tea is indeed as peculiar to the British palate as red postboxes and grouse moors are to the nation's landscape.

It has been a long time since Britain was referred to as the workshop of the world, yet our history of urbanisation, empire, industry and war leaves edible traces everywhere, as we will see. Besides, in the grand scheme of things, modernity is still quite new in the human history of these isles.

It was during the post-war, post-imperial era in Britain that a suite of foods – above all fish and chips and fried breakfasts – began to serve as unifiers of a newly national taste. Today, that sense of unity, formed in large part through the direct experiences of modernity, has faded. Britain, and England, faces the difficult consequences of contemporary modernity in terms of both the environmental and bodily costs of our modern diets, and also in terms of popular anomie and social alienation, which in turn have given rise to xenophobic forms of nationalism. This is despite the fact that, as we'll see, the imperial experiences of trade and immigration are far more central to our island story than we're usually led to believe.

Several recent food trends have responded to the ways in which England's modern food system has generated discomfort, both physical and spiritual, yet insofar as they appear within a context of growing economic inequality, these trends – such as sourdough, the taste for 'rustic' Italian food, and regenerative farming and 'rewilding' (all discussed in the chapters that follow) – tend only to reinforce cultural divides (other trends, like the taste for Huel, as discussed in chapter six, are at their worst extreme expressions of modern alienation). England is thus in great need of a new, unifying cuisine. Yet in this book I make the case that for self-affirming ways of eating to be truly national they must accompany a broader movement aimed at the enrichment of all.

The focus of this book is England. I am a child of the East Midlands, and my knowledge of Scotland, Wales and Northern Ireland is, typically, quite dim. However, at times what follows is directly relevant to the UK as a whole, and also to elsewhere (there are many overlaps with North America, for example, especially in chapter six).

But there are less personal reasons for this focus too. Contemporary meanings of Englishness have been dominated by an increasingly powerful far right that has used both the British and English flags as its calling cards. Mainstream politicians such as Suella Braverman, who is of Indian descent but who was born and privately educated in Harrow, and who studied English Law at Cambridge, have claimed both that multiculturalism has failed and that to be English one must be white.

Until recently, whiteness was the most common way by which people in England of all backgrounds defined what it meant to be English, including white people themselves: some proudly, others, one senses, with a degree of embarrassment. Plenty of academic research, both qualitative – asking people what they think in detail – and quantitative studies of census reporting, reflects this fact.[3]

And yet, other evidence – such as research conducted by the think tank British Future – points to increasing numbers of all kinds of people defining themselves as English, with decreasing numbers seeing Englishness in terms of race.[4] This data appears to show that what has slowly been taking place in some parts of society over the past three or so decades has been a shift from a racial or ethnic understanding of Englishness to a cultural one. According to this view, if you drink mugs of tea with milk but you see artisanal coffee as a bit posh, then, I'm sorry, but a part of you must be English.

There are of course other contexts for the ongoing interest in Englishness, from the effects of multiculturalism to the campaign for Scottish independence and the consequences of devolution; from the long shadow cast by the break-up of the Empire, the motifs of which were often genuinely popular sites for patriotic investment (think, for example, of the great number of pubs called the Lord Nelson), to more recent efforts to come to terms with our nation's post-imperial identity; from leaving the European Union to football, particularly since Euro '96 when, for the first time, the St George's Cross was waved by England fans in place of the union flag. Then there is the endless flow of globalised culture, be it represented by the ubiquitous Brooklyn-style coffee shop or another trendy, authentic Korean pop-up, all of which can leave us wondering what part in this sprawling cosmopolis is the part that belongs to 'us'?

There are, and will always be, many who think that national identity is a scam, that patriotism is dangerous, or both. My own view is that Englishness is a live cultural idea grounded in the peculiar experiences of this country, an idea that exists whether you like it or not. To borrow the stock phrase from Benedict Anderson and view the nation as an 'imagined community' implies that who does the imagining and what the image portrays matters. At the very least, Englishness is something worth investigating. Yet it is also, in my view, worth investing in as an inclusive, modern identity.

To write this book I have carried out the usual forms of desk-based research while also undertaking over a year's worth of what academics might call ethnography but what in cooking terms might be seen as number of short internships, or *stages* (I'll come back to this French word in chapter two). These include grinding out my craft in two of London's leading restaurants, one inspired by the courtly traditions of France and another by (a largely imagined) Italy, plus stints baking bread, hunting whelks, cooking curry, drinking Huel, exploring an aristocratic estate in Yorkshire and eating a sausage roll with a glass of champagne at a Greggs in Newcastle (where else?).

In what follows, my account of these experiences is interwoven with historical analysis, and together these strands tell us about the ways we eat and why. The overall picture is one of a nation whose food culture is in many ways discernible, but often only in the sense that it reflects the unmooring effects of England's peculiar experience of modernity. This, then, is a story about tradition: old traditions and new contexts, new contexts and invented traditions, and what happens when traditions are warped, eroded and exclusive.

The picture of English food here is an incomplete one. Endless themes, trends, dishes and places have been missed out. Nevertheless, a general sense of English taste – one resting on the claim that ours is a peculiar diet formed by a peculiar experience of modernity – should become quite clear. As should be the call here to invent a prouder way of eating, one that rejects neither modernity nor the careful craft of human hands.

1

Sourdough

Everybody knows that one of the housewife's cares in life is yeast.
Charles Dickens, 'The Miller and His Men', 1853

The night before my first visit to Quince Bakery I went to the pub. My shift at the elegant, modern European restaurant where I had worked for three years had been a particularly long and busy one. The scratchy battery of orders from the printer eventually became an occasional trickle of dessert checks: an ice cream, a choux bun, two almond tarts, one with a candle, the hum of a full restaurant toning down to a moody hush above which you could make out a polite rendition of 'Happy Birthday' from the kitchen. I packed away my section, cleaned the stove, wrote down my orders and called in a cold after-work beer – the best kind of drink you will ever have. I drank one beer while getting changed and another while sat at a table in the dining room with the other chefs.

Our allowance of free lager now exhausted, we transferred to our local: a warm boozer full of drinkers steaming up the windows. Within an hour most of the front-of-house team joined us. The momentum of the busy service was kept up at the bar till closing, when eventually I found my way to home and to bed.

At 4 a.m., as I slept, a baker at Quince clocked on for her shift. 'Early starts are OK,' Anna Higham told me when I met her later that day. 'You get to be alone for a bit,' she said. 'Except you're not alone,' Fiona Fitzpatrick, a baker from Dublin who had been on the early shift, corrected. 'You're here with all the bread.'

With the terrifying bleeping of my alarm at 7.30, I woke up at the same time fresh bread was being peeled out of Quince's deck ovens. It was one of those bright, sunny mornings in October where you do not yet know just how dark and cold it's about to become and instead allow yourself to embrace the change of seasons. Cycling from South to North London in the yellow light of the day, I pulled up to lock my bike to a lamp post near the bakery and, although I had never visited Quince and was yet to set eyes on it, I knew I was in the right place from the smell on that corner of the street: brown butter, sweet and nutty, a signature of Anna's pastry which for several years could be found in the Michelin-starred restaurant Lyle's, where Anna used to be head pastry chef.

October is my favourite time of year to eat. The remnants of summer linger while stone fruit and apples come into season along with pumpkins, mushrooms and game. A crisp chill in the air makes heavier food – pies, roasts, puddings, all things savoury made delicious by the presence of fat – appealing, like putting on a well-loved jacket for the first time in months.

October is also the perfect time to visit Quince because there in the window, in wooden crates by the door and ornamenting the shelves are quinces, 'the most beautiful of fruits', according to Anna. 'There's something feminine about them,' she says. Perhaps it's their soft curves, which resemble those of misshapen pears.

Quince is the perfect – because natural and somewhat rare – culinary symbol for this bakery, which is located in the London borough of Islington, an urban idyll whose many middle-class inhabitants have at times imagined themselves to be living in a village offset from the rest of the capital. It was in fact Islington that prompted the sociologist Ruth Glass to coin the term gentrification.

I feel a little awkward after entering Quince. The storefront is crowded with healthy, tote-bag-wearing shoppers. There are two women in yoga gear, one of whom has a pram with her, and a large man with a neatly trimmed beard, a corduroy jacket and expensive red spectacles. On display is an earthy bounty of pies, cakes and bread, plus shelves lined with homemade jams, organic cold-pressed juices and natural wine. I introduce myself to Anna and right away she welcomes me behind the counter where I take up position next to her, sipping a fruity black coffee and asking questions while she destones a box of plums – skins the colour of burgundy and flesh the texture of waxy honey.

Anna adores fruit. She makes a big deal of it in her bakery. So it's plums to line the base of a crumble tart, then on to a box of overripe quinces. She takes each quince and removes brown patches of fermented flesh with a large, hand-forged Damascus steel bread knife and puts the good bits into a bowl – for 'fruit cheese', she explains as she works. Fruit cheese, I find out, is the term Anna prefers for what others might know as membrillo: fruit, usually quinces but sometimes apples and pears, that is boiled down with sugar and set like jelly by the fruit's pectin.

Anna is a generous, skilful and confident baker. The two words she uses most frequently to describe her approach to cooking are 'tenderness' and 'romance'. She has done her time as a chef: seventy-, ninety-hour weeks, early starts, late finishes, loud, sweary, hot, elite kitchens and all the rest. 'I don't know how I did it,' she says of her time as a young chef, having moved to London from Scotland in 2011. Yet she does not tell these stories in the way other chefs might, with a sense of heroism or machismo. It's all modesty and matter-of-factness with Anna. All part of her subtle outlook and gentle demeanour that, to my mind, makes her one of the best bakers in London.

Quince is special because it's one of the few places in the wave of celebrated artisanal bakeries that shuns croissants (along with the panoply of other things that these bakeries make out of yeasted laminated dough: pain aux raisin, pain Swiss, cheese scrolls, chocolate discs filled with orange meant to resemble an expensive Jaffa Cake, and so on). 'It's not that I don't like croissants. Bakeries like Toad or Eric's, they make fantastic croissants. So I figure, let them get on with that. Plus we don't have the space for it,' Anna explains. But I suspect there are other reasons, too. Anna is intrigued by Britain's peculiar baking traditions, by those parts of our cookery that are not obviously French. I bring this up, and she disappears and comes back moments later with two books she says inspire her baking: *The British Cookbook* by Ben Mervis and *Oats in the North, Wheat from the South* by Regula Ysewijn. From a quick glance I see that both contain several recipes from Hannah Glasse. In a minor key, and in a world of French-inspired patisserie, Quince is animated by a desire to revive some of Britain's native baking traditions.

Revive is the word here, since who has heard of, never mind eaten, drover's loaves and cockle bread? Where did the Bath buns and the Sally Lunns all go? The bannocks, the scufflers, the church and chapel loaves, the pyclets, the wigs and the lady cakes? You're unlikely to come across the Kentish huffkin, an enriched bun once eaten by cherry pickers, even if you're in a bakery in Kent in late summer. Nor are you likely to find rose-scented Wood Street cakes in London, where they were once so famous. No Roehampton rolls, rumpy bread, Hawkshead whigs, Cornish splits, Devonshire Chudleighs, Norfolk rusks or jumbles, either.

Croissants, you might say, have colonised our baking. Then there is sourdough. At Anna's bakery in North London, biscuity-brown loaves of well-sprung sourdough stand upright on unvarnished wooden shelves like proud works of art, ready to be scooped into paper bags and hurried away in off-white shoulder-slung totes. But it's not only in Islington that sourdough is exhibited. In every city between Liverpool and Grimsby you can find an artisan bakery that will sell you bread fermented with wild yeast. From coast to coast further north, sourdough can be found at Lovingly Artisan in Kendal and Bakerman in Darlington. On the south coast at Bread Addiction in Portsmouth and Heyl in Plymouth. In the Midlands – in Nottingham, where I'm from – you can take your pick between Tough Mary's, Small Food, Breadmill, Hambleton and others. That's leaving aside all the sourdough, or bread labelled as such, now sold in most supermarkets across the UK.

Sourdough's platonic ideal is round or oval-shaped, with a hard and jagged crust: dark brown on the outside, sometimes with flecks of char, and soft light brown – the colour of unrefined sugar – on an interior pockmarked with bubbles. This is 'bread with an old soul', to quote a description from Chad Robertson, a charismatic baker in San Francisco who has arguably done more than anyone to promote this style of baking.

It was Chad's book *Tartine Bread* that so many people turned to in lockdown. Its pages are saturated with the loving craft of a true, traditional artisan. Photos of hands dusted in flour alternate with pictures of Chad surfing, of a man liberated in ways that those of us trapped in cramped spaces with eyes burning before blaring screens could only dream of. The key to this bread is its starter, which captures wild yeasts present in the air; sourdough appears to connect us to natural forces we cannot easily observe. A return to our baking heritage and a crust of long-lost freedom in the matrix of modern life.

But while it is true that bread fermented with wild yeast crops up in English culinary history, it is hard to make the case that it is the predominant and preferred form of raising loaves. Where sourdough appears in the historic evidence, it resembles something quite different to the distinctly modern artisanal wheat bread we eat today. Like the national anthem and serving turkey at Christmas, sourdough has the hallmarks of an invented tradition. To understand why, we have to tell the story of bread in England, beginning with barm.

Barmy army

The English language shows us just how important bread has been to the social history of these isles. The words we use for this staple food reflect changes in the social order of things while also hinting at the historical character of English loaves over time.

Etymologically speaking, the word 'bread' is a relatively recent stand-in for the Old English word 'loaf'. And from loaf – or *hlāf* – comes our word 'lord'. *Hlāf-ord* – loaf giver – denotes a feudal landowner in control of bread, a phenomenon also expressed in Old English by *hlāf-weard:* loaf-ward.

The word 'company' derives from the Latin *com*, meaning 'together', and *panis*, meaning 'bread'. Company therefore denotes the sharing of bread; a company, thought of in terms of a group or organisation, is etymologically comprised of those whose bread is held in common.

The phrase 'the greatest thing since sliced bread' took off in the middle of the twentieth century. Its popularity from this point onwards speaks of a ration-weary England that, from the late 1950s, embraced the new industrially produced loaf of soft, white, pillowy sliced bread that was the antithesis to the grey and heavy National Loaf consumed during the war, as we'll see. The various words we have in English for a bread roll – a 'cob', in Nottingham, 'bun' in the North East, 'barm' in Lancashire, bap, batch, muffin and teacake elsewhere – are a hangover from a time in which the country was far less interconnected than it is now.

The root of the word 'fermentation' is *fervere*, an Old French word meaning 'to boil'. The word 'yeast' may derive from the Germanic word *gist*, meaning 'foam' or 'froth', or it may come from the Old English word *derst*, which itself derived from *dros* (meaning 'dregs'), which referred to the sediment of yeast that collected at the bottom of a lightly brewed beer. And that brings us back to 'barm' – the word used in Manchester for a bread roll.

As a child, I often accompanied my dad to see his beloved Sheffield Wednesday Football Club play at Hillsborough. Much to my dad's dismay, I cannot today recall a single kick, goal, sending-off or anything else from any of the many games I saw with him – but I remember the chants. One, which at times felt like it looped and looped for half the game, simply went: 'Atkinson's barmy army', with an emphasis on every syllable of 'At-kin-son', often recited to the 4/4 pounding of a brass band's drum with an occasional trumpet flurry. 'Atkinson' was a Wednesday manager in the 1990s, their last briefly successful era; 'army' referred to us, the fans; and barmy means mad, or excitable. The word 'barm' was first used to describe the bubbling, excitable froth that rose to the surface of fermenting beer.

Beer barm was an important source of yeast used in baking up to the early twentieth century. There is evidence to suggest that Ancient Egyptians may have risen their loaves of bread using this method; there exist, for example, small wooden models recovered from 4,000-year-old tombs that depict baking and brewing occurring in the same rooms in Ancient Egypt, while archaeologists suspect that the frequency of pharaonic brewing would likely have introduced yeast to baking.[1] Etymology again offers a clue, since the barley beer of ancient Egypt was called *zythos* by the Ancient Greeks, which we find connected to the Ancient Greek words for 'leaven' and 'yeast'.

In his *Natural History*, completed in the year 77, Pliny the Elder describes several methods of fermenting dough in Ancient Rome, including with the use of grape must, which, as we now know thanks to the invention of the microscope, contains concentrations of yeast that consume sugars and expire carbon dioxide, giving life to dough. In the same work, Pliny also tells us definitively that the Celts of Central Europe leavened their bread with beer.

One plausible origin for the word 'bread' itself links it with the word 'brewed'.[2] Yet the evident connection between baking and brewing is always overlooked in the many mythical histories of sourdough.

In his book *Sourdough Culture: A History of Bread Making from Ancient to Modern Bakers*, the American academic Eric Pallant is on a quest to trace the origins of a sourdough starter that was handed to him at a party. He is told that the starter came from Cripple Creek, a former gold mining camp in Colorado. Could Pallant's starter, he wonders out loud in the book, be traced back to the American gold rush, to European immigrants, to the Pilgrims or even to the tears of Jesus Christ? The answer, he finds out, is no.

Around halfway through *Sourdough Culture* Pallant is forced to come to terms with the idea that old starters don't necessarily make good bread; in fact some bakers, including Chad Robertson and Anna Higham at Quince, claim old starters tend to be too sour. Pallant also overlooks the fact that making a new sourdough starter (the ingredients for which can be as simple as flour, water and exposure to the air) is a far easier task than carrying old, sour and sometimes needy starters over miles of sea and land. The starters we use in sourdough baking today, when not being used frequently, require half of their contents being thrown away and the addition of new, perfectly edible flour. All of this seems obvious. The question then is why Pallant has this obsession with his bread's lineage?

'Without ancestry and history, who are we?' Pallant muses. 'Feeding your sourdough is a brief reminder of who we are and why.'[3] Sourdough, then, appears to satisfy an existential desire for tradition as much as, or more than, these loaves satisfy a need to eat. No wonder that so much sourdough mysticism comes from Americans who, looking backward at the Old World, may feel themselves adrift.

Whether or not it matters that we cannot meaningfully trace certain sourdough starters back into the recesses of time – there is no forensic way to do this, akin to mapping DNA – there is evidence for the practice of fermenting bread with wild yeasts in England. At the same time, we find evidence that the most desirable bread was raised using beer.

Pallant's narrative is that sourdough was the predominant form of fermenting bread from Ancient Egypt up to the Industrial Revolution which, for reasons I cannot quite discern from his book, gave rise to the demand for brewer's yeast. To support his case, he cites work by Ruth Goodman on the baking habits of the Tudors.[4] Yet here, as elsewhere, we find he has overlooked the obvious links between bread and beer, between baking and brewing.

In fact, in the book cited by Pallant, Goodman tells us that in Tudor England if you wanted to raise *a good quality* loaf of bread 'you would simply pop into the brewhouse alongside the bakehouse and gather up the frothy yeasts that bubbled to the top of your vat of ale as it brewed'.[5] This beer barm was used with the finest sifted flours available to make the best type of bread, known as manchet. As we brew, so we must bake – or so the old proverb goes.

In her book, Goodman points us to what she says is one of the earliest detailed recipes for baking a loaf of bread. It comes from *The English Huswife*, written by Gervase Markham in 1615, in which the instructions call for three pints of the best ale barm to each bushel of 'meale'.

But then, citing Markham still, Goodman points out that there also existed less desirable loaves raised with a leaven – in the form of a portion of yesterday's batch of dough which is mixed with water and left to ferment overnight. Having a look at *English Huswife* myself I see that even in this recipe Markham calls for the addition of barm, which it is safe to assume means yeast as derived from brewing beer. Thereafter follows a recipe for 'brown bread' or 'bread for your hinde-servents'. This requires ground barley, peas, wheat or rye, and malt. The mix is put in a 'sour trough' along with hot water and salt, and again left to ferment overnight. The next day more of the flour mix is added and kneaded before the heavy, dense loaves are shaped and baked.

Markham then offers the following advice: 'Now if your trough be not sowre enough to sowre your Leaven, then you shall either let it be longer in the trough, or else take the help of a sowre Leaven with your boyling water; for you must understand that the hotter your Liquor is, the less will the smell or ranknesse of the Pease be perceived.'[6] This was a method for making what was clearly an unattractive loaf of bread in late Tudor England, made with peas as well as rough flour – a far cry from the modern sourdoughs of Islington.

But the evidence for the use of beer barm in England goes back further still. According to the scholar Ann Hagen, the ties between brewing and baking predate and were present throughout the Anglo-Saxon period.[7] Hagen offers us another Old English term for yeast: *beorma*, etymologically connected to the word *breowan*, meaning to brew.

It is thought that the Anglo-Saxon king Edward the Confessor created one of England's first laws on food regulation: the *Hlafclaenness Dom*, or Bread Purity Law, which in 1047 required bread to be made with nothing but fine flour, water, beer barm, and salt. It appears that around this time the English were peculiar among Europeans for adding concentrated yeast to their ales (which, unlike Continental beer, contained no hops), rather than relying on spontaneous fermentation, i.e. on yeast obtained from the atmosphere.[8] It would plausibly follow that the same was true of English bread. And indeed we find evidence from the fifteenth century of the interwoven nature of brewing and baking in the form of a local law in Norwich that obliged brewsters (female brewers, also known as alewives) to provide their neighbouring bakers with yeast at a regulated price. According to one historian of English drinking habits, 'bakers were entirely dependent upon brewers for their yeast'.[9]

The baker and historian Walter T. Banfield once wrote of an 'age of barms' spanning 2,000 years up to the twentieth century. By 'barm' Banfield here meant not only yeast obtained from brewing but also kinds of sourdough starters (there were many techniques for making a barm, hence the plural). The age of barms was, according to Banfield, an age that lacked modern control over the baking process, most likely producing a sour-tasting bread. Pre-modern methods of fermenting dough involved unpredictable sources of yeasts and enough fermentation time that the development of bacteria – the component that lends a dough its sourness – would have been inevitable. Indeed, the distinction between baking with beer barm and sourdough would have been blurry: bread made with beer contained a diversity of yeasts, and, since the dough made with barm required a long fermentation, the presence of sour-tasting bacteria must have been quite common.

Banfield cites a recipe for barm written in 1858 which offers advice for instances in which the preferred beer froth is unavailable. Its author calls for a barm made of hops (which must be yellow, not green) that are boiled in water, strained and then cooled. Salt and sugar are then added, as well as wholewheat flour. After three days being stood near a fire, mashed potatoes are mixed in, then, as fermentation occurs over time, the baker must stir the mixture at frequent intervals. 'It very soon assumes the appearance of the finest brown-coloured brewer's yeast, rising to a crown.'[10] On the fourth day the starter is mixed and decanted into bottles, with loose corks fitted – exploding glasses of barm being a well-noted hazard of the self-reliant cook.

The date of this recipe also shows us that the commercialisation of yeasts was incomplete even while the Industrial Revolution was already quite far advanced. 'No other branch of industry in England', Karl Marx wrote in *Capital,* 'has preserved up to the present day a method of production as archaic, as pre-Christian … as baking'.[11] It is a testament to the deep significance of bread that, in a Victorian world increasingly dominated by machines and markets, traditional baking methods were among the last production techniques to go.

Before the late-nineteenth-century industrialisation of

milling and baking, bread of any kind was heavier, darker and drier than we know it now.[12] Bread as a whole contained a greater diversity of yeast (there are some 1,500 known varieties) than the commercial yeast (*Saccharomyces cerevisiae*) available today in powered granules or in its waxy fresh form. As a result, most bread likely had a more bitter – at times sour – flavour than the commercial white loaves we are familiar with, including modern sourdough.

Yet before the dominance of wheat that set in from the late eighteenth century onwards, it is impossible to speak of any one type of grain and therefore of any one type of loaf that was eaten by a majority in Britain. Many types of bread, particularly in the North of England and Scotland, were for a long time consumed unleavened – i.e. flat, like the crisp 'clap breads' of Lancashire. Not until the National Loaf appeared in the Second World War (to be followed by the sliced white loaves with which we are still familiar) is it possible to speak of a common type of bread in England at all.

Nevertheless, it is a safe bet that before the industrialisation of baking – and going back as far as Roman Britain, if not further – beer barm was the preferred leaven for rising loaves. And indeed, in a country with a rich tradition of commercial and home brewing, and still today with a strong taste for pubs and beer (as my colleagues and I can testify), it is likely that most leavened bread prior to the late-nineteenth-century commercialisation of concentrated yeast was produced with beer barm, particularly in households and bakeries in which baking did not occur every day (such that yesterday's dough could become today's starter).

Insofar as we can point to a traditional English loaf, this bread would be a far cry from the sourdough that is today ubiquitous in contemporary artisanal bakeries. Despite its rustic appearance, the sourdough we know today is distinctly modern. Like sliced white bread, it is the product of England's peculiar experience of modernity.

Raising bread at night-time

The difference between bakers and chefs is the difference between night and day. Anna accepted my request to spend a week baking bread with her at Quince, and the evening before my first shift I'm going to bed around 12 a.m. with my alarm set for 4.30. This is a later start than usual, I'm told, offered up by Anna 'to ease me in'. It's now January. 'Bring a jumper', she messages me in the morning, 'it can get a bit chilly when the ovens aren't on.' I wake up before my alarm, slide out of my warm bed and stumble into my kitchen to make coffee. A little before five, I push out on my bike and retrace the route I made over the Thames several months ago in autumn.

The shutter on the Quince storefront is half raised, and I check the air for the smell of brown butter. Nothing. It's a prep day, which I'd forgotten. Inside I'm greeted by the team, all friendly and pale. I'm shadowing Anna, who is on bread duty and who arrived at 4 a.m. It feels symbolic that, on a morning when the sun barely appears, one of the first tasks I'm given involves roasting a large cockerel for a pie.

As I season the bird, Anna explains how the baking at Quince works. She makes one large batch of dough, which is used for the standard sourdough and sticks, but then she adds an oat porridge to a portion for a creamy tinned loaf, and rye flour with a purple hue to another portion for her rye bread.

All the mixing is done in a large machine that works a human-like steel arm up and down in the belly of a mechanically spinning bowl. A prover, an upright fridge that can warm as well as chill, is used to ferment the dough or keep it stable overnight. Then there's the two steam-injection deck ovens, which have postbox openings and a flat stone surface inside that stretches back for a metre. Modern machines are even more essential in the production of the British-grown heritage wheats that go into Anna's bread; machines are used to plant and harvest the grain, to dry it and so prevent it rotting, and to stone-mill and sift the wheat into flour. This is artisanal bread but using industrial technology.

Anna has a tactile relationship with her dough like a mother nurturing young. There's the recipe – which is a spreadsheet of ratios, rather than a list of exact amounts – but then she tweaks this with a little water, a little more stretching, then a little more water again, added by hand and judged by touch. A small pinch of a starter kept in a plastic tub is enough to ferment several kilos of dough.

Flour behaves differently day to day, Anna tells me; its dryness is a variable that changes with age and with the seasons. Anna likes to build tension in the dough, she explains with a hand gesture, then to let it relax and avoid building too much tension thereafter (this is radically different to what I'd learnt from Chad Robertson). The balance, Anna tells me, is struck between too much strength (such that the bread is bouncy on the teeth) and too little (such that it fails to hold its proper shape).

Anna encourages me to feel the dough. To stretch it. At one point it feels like wet clay. Later it's gassy and light. Then she says it's become silky, and I feel it to find that it has. Anna teaches me to pull dough by what she calls its skin, by the part of the dough that has been exposed to air. 'It's like human flesh,' she says, pinching her muscular forearm to illustrate her point; the trick is not to grab the 'meat' of the bread but to form a grip at the surface. I learn that dough should never be torn, and how crab hands – forming a pincer between thumb and forefinger – are deployed to cut it into portions.

In the afternoon, once the dough has been mixed, rested, folded and portioned, we bring it to a wooden table to shape, which I find stressful at first. I'm totally focused but also tired. Anna is supportive and uncritical even though I know I'm making a mess. I need to move my hands without thinking, I tell myself, shape the dough without hesitating, but I can't.

I cycle home around 2.30 and eat a Wispa bar before an early dinner. At around ten I put myself to bed. I lie there like a stick of butter between folds of dough as I try to will myself to sleep.

Like the ubiquitous croissant, the sourdough we know today comes from France, although its entry into Britain was by way of California. In her book on British bread and baking written in the mid-1970s, the cookery writer Elizabeth David reports favourably on a loaf of sourdough she was sent via airmail from San Francisco. 'It was very much akin to some of the good *pain de campagne* made on the old leaven system, and still to be found in French country bakeries', she writes. 'Very genuine' – although the idea of making sourdough at home was a process she declared to be a waste of time.[13]

The kind of bread that is described as sourdough in the chef Anthony Bourdain's bestselling *Kitchen Confidential* is made from a starter that contains 'grapes, flour, water, sugar and yeast' and is fed, we're told, by putting this foamy blob into an industrial mixer and adding warm water, fresh flour and more yeast. At times, red pepper and mushrooms are mentioned as possible additions to the mix. I highlight this simply to suggest that, as late as the 1990s, the meaning of what constituted sourdough was far from fixed.

If anyone would know this first-hand, it's Dan Lepard, the friendly Australian baker and author whose cooking career began in 1992 at Alastair Little, a pioneering restaurant in London's Soho that was once located just metres from where we meet for a glass of wine. After this, Dan found a job baking at the iconic restaurant St John in 1995, less than a year after it opened. It was a newspaper editor who convinced Dan that he should be baking the kind of sourdough that was all the rage in America, and happily he had encountered just such a loaf while working in New York.

When I ask Dan if he knows who the first baker to popularise sourdough in London was he says, without flinching, 'Yes: me.' In 1997 Dan was overseeing the bread operation at Baker & Spice, working alongside Yotam Ottolenghi and the restaurant's owner Yael (Gail) Mejia, who later became a founder of Gail's Bakery. Ottolenghi and Mejia were inspired by the sourdough being baked in Israel, which Dan is convinced wasn't a product of Eastern European baking traditions but was instead in the vein of the bread coming from San Francisco.

'It's not like there was much competition in London,' Dan says to give context to his uncharacteristic outburst of pride. 'No one was doing that kind of bread here, no one wanted it in the '90s.' The Baker & Spice cookbook, written by Dan and published in 1999, features the generic loaf of bread we now know as sourdough; under the chapter heading 'Baking with Wild Yeasts' comes a recipe for a 'San Francisco sourdough starter'.

'I'm convinced,' Dan tells me while fidgeting with an empty wine glass, 'that it was San Franciso that made the bread *in France* far better than it was in the '90s.' The history I'm assembling here with the help of Dan's CV underlines the point that sourdough as we know it today is a distinctly modern import. Sourdough is a modern loaf, not a traditional bread of Britain – not in the time-honoured sense, at least – even though its rustic appearance suggests a long lineage. One final point can make this clear.

A Treatise on the Art of Bread-making, written by Abraham Edlin in 1805, gives us an account of the tough, relentless life of a pre-industrial baker. The working day in a bakery with, we are told here, a good reputation spanned from two in the afternoon till seven the following morning. The labour of the baker included upwards of an hour and a half of hand-kneading a beer-yeasted dough.

Commenting on Edlin's description of a bakehouse, the historian Diane Purkiss suggests that all this working of the dough was owing to the fact that pre-industrial British bakers used soft – i.e. low-gluten – flours.[14] The problem with this idea, though, is that by 1805 bakers in England were already importing harder wheats from Eastern Europe, Russia and Canada. The consensus among historians like Purkiss was that traditional low-gluten wheats produced a heavy dough. Yet French bakers have long worked with soft flours, kneading their dough far less than did the British and yet yielding a lighter result. And that chimes with what I observed at Quince, where Anna, mindful of the toothsomeness of her bread yet using low-gluten, heritage wheats, kneaded her dough for less than ten minutes. She then refrained from working it again, instead simply folding the dough in on itself at half-hour intervals.

One reason for this difference between France and Britain, and between the past and the present, may be that even at a bakery in 1805 with a good reputation, flour was adulterated with any number of cheaper but non-glutinous additives, from potato starch to chalk. Another is that gluten is not the only variable in what makes for a good wheat for bread.

But the greater part of our explanation for the fact that bakers in the past worked so hard at the trough may simply be some combination of ignorance and tradition. While British bakers pounded their doughs like boxers at the bag, their counterparts in France were observed to draw up their mixture into long strings, to repeatedly lift and fold 'in order to expose it to the action of the air as much as possible, which tends greatly to improve the bread by rendering it more light and easy of digestion'.[15] Light dough and better bread can be a matter of good technique. And harder work – prolonged kneading of the dough with brute force – does not always mean a good result. The technique used to make artisan bread today, like the machines used to knead dough, is thus distinctly modern.[16]

Nevertheless, in both pre-industrial France and Britain, bread contained far less moisture than our contemporary sourdough (this may have been due to some combination of government regulation and public concern that valuable corn shouldn't be bulked out with too much water). It was baked at lower temperatures for longer (no doubt a product of scarcer fuels and simpler ovens) and inevitably produced a heavier, drier loaf. The sourdough we have today may feel artisan and traditional, but, again, it is distinctly modern.

From a moral economy to the national loaf

As a nation, only a minority of us eat loaves like the ones I helped to produce at Quince.

Market and industry data show that the consumption of factory-produced loaves – the leading brands, aside from supermarket own brands, are Warburton, Hovis and Kingsmill – vastly outweighs that of artisanal baking, which accounts for about 3 per cent of total bread consumption.[17]

This reflects a radical reversal in the way we eat bread in Britain – white bread, once so out of reach for the majority, had by the 1960s become the norm. In her book on English baking, Elizabeth David wrote that 'for centuries the working man envied the white bread of the privileged. Now he may very soon grow to envy them their brown wholewheat.'[18] She may have been right. Today, polling by YouGov shows that white and brown bread are practically neck and neck in terms of preference, while the popularity of sourdough has doubled in the past five years. Fluffy white bread is no longer the aspirational item it once was. Nevertheless, sliced, soft, white and uniform loaves – perfect in size for the toaster – have made up the bulk of the bread we have eaten in Britain for the last sixty-plus years.

The puzzle is how we gained this taste in bread at all. And then, following that, why some among a privileged few have adopted a preference for bread that, in the minds of many bakers and consumers, was eaten by our authentically artisanal ancestors. How did the majority end up eating the fluffy white loaves that were once the preserve of the rich, and how did the rich come to eat loaves that, in the collective imagination at least, were eaten by the humble artisanal poor? The answer lies in the history of England's peculiar modernity.

The enclosure of common land that 'liberated' people from the country and drove them to the cities also withdrew rights of access to forests from which one could obtain bundles of 'snap wood', causing home baking to enter a terminal decline in England. No fuel meant no fire, which in turn meant no home-baked bread – much to the helpless dismay of advocates for popular self-reliance, like the radical MP William Cobbett – and the consequent decline of women's status in the home.

What was true of bread was also true also of beer. In 1819 a farmer in Sussex told a House of Commons committee that, forty years prior, every labourer in his parish had both brewed and baked, yet now they all relied on products obtained through cash exchange.[19] Other reports from some three decades later confirmed that in all but a few Yorkshire strongholds (where coal and wood were still available) home baking had died out. The cash nexus, as historians once referred to this market dependence, had taken its place.

By the late eighteenth century, bread was already the chief food source of the rapidly growing urban working classes. While coal generated the steam that ran the mills, bread powered the human muscle in the workshop of the world. The chief expenditure of workers from 1770 to 1870 was food, and the greatest portion of that – between 40 and 80 per cent – went on bread.[20] White bread specifically.

Historians and contemporaries have debated why workers sought out white loaves that were often more expensive and potentially less nourishing than heavier, darker varieties. Was this a case of simply aping the style of one's betters? The philosopher and MP Edmund Burke certainly thought so.[21] But there are reasons to doubt this – namely that white bread was widely felt to be far more palatable than the darker, drier loaves. It's easy to imagine that a slice of stale bread with no butter, no dripping, no jam and no cheese will be easier to eat if that bread is white than if it is a heavy loaf made out of lots of bran, occasionally peas, tree bark and acorns. With a cup of tea, the unadorned white slice could form the basis of a worker's meal.

For most of its existence, or at least as far back as we can meaningfully go, consumption of bread in England – both in terms of quality and quantity – has been regulated by institutions other than the market. The earliest known regulation we have for bread (putting to one side the order reportedly made by the Saxon King Edward) dates to 1202, and that regulation developed thereafter into the Assize of Bread that lasted in some form for over 600 years. This evolving law effectively made baking a public service, since it set a limit to how much profit could be made in the transformation of grain into edible products.[22] Bakers who failed to sell their bread at the locally regulated price risked being drawn through the streets with the offending loaves hung around their necks, or worse.

The Assize, along with other regulations – including those on the importation of wheat (known as Corn Laws), Poor Laws regulating the state's responsibility to its citizens' welfare, and common and statute laws concerning the hoarding of grain – was the institutional scaffolding that upheld a widely felt *moral* economy of bread. Pre-Victorian society was essentially governed by a Christian sense that the poor were entitled to a fairly priced loaf. And where laws were inadequate or unenforced such that this expectation went unmet, a combination of rioting and local magistrate action could restore the moral code.

Though usually violent, bread riots were typically conducted in a manner that expressed this common sense of fairness: rioters were often known to take loaves by force, but not without offering what the crowd saw as a reasonable price in exchange. Local magistrates, for their part, had powers to override market prices, particularly in the case of dearth and public pressure, thereby restoring a moral order by which the lower classes gave their assent to these ruling elites.

The opening up of a national trade in grain was made possible from the 1760s and '70s onwards thanks to Britain's rapidly growing network of canals and waterways. Nevertheless, bread riots and magistrates would on occasion prevent grain from leaving local areas, particularly at times of famine. But as trade in the market for grain and ground flour expanded, the Assize became harder to measure and harder to enforce. Local magistrates had already mostly opted out of regulation by the time Parliament effectively abolished the Assize in 1822 and declared a new era of benevolent free competition.[23]

As for England's Poor Laws, these had provided some form of relief – funded out of local taxes – to those in need since the Reformation. The Laws were transformed first by the Speenhamland system, which, from the late eighteenth century, attempted to calculate the minimum income a worker needed according to the prevailing price of bread. In effect, however, the system suppressed wages and lowered workers' productivity, thereby increasing the poverty that the Poor Laws were meant to inhibit. The new system of relief that arrived in 1834 made workhouses the only – and a dramatically bleak – alternative to destitution.

By the start of the Victorian era, the institutional scaffold of the old moral economy had gone. The average worker was left naked and exposed in the face of what economists called a free-market price for labour as for everything else, including bread. Trade unions thereafter became workers' primary means of obtaining what had once been a right to a fairly priced loaf.

As we've seen, it was not until late in the nineteenth century that baking underwent its own industrial revolution.[24] Milling led the way, having turned to coal-driven steam power within the first half of the century (flour mills located in areas of cotton manufacturing had before this point competed with the factories for scarce water-power). Stone mills were subsequently replaced by rollers, a technique first developed in Hungary and brought to the UK by German and Austrian immigrants in the 1870s. Roller milling allowed for the efficient separation of wheat into its component parts – germ, bran and endosperm – such that the latter could then be purely ground. While producing the finest white flour with a longer shelf life than had previously been possible, this new method also reduced wheat's nutritional quality. Fortunately, the appearance of rolling milling occurred just as working-class diets were to some extent being diversified away from bread.

Mechanisation was resisted in the bakeries (as in other industries), but machines began to take the place of human skill and muscle, particularly in the kneading process. Few commercial bakers today, I expect, would wish to go back to the hand-pounded trough.

The concurrent urbanisation of England meanwhile created a demand for wheat that far outstripped local supply. Already in 1800, demand in Lancashire was some five times the county's crop, a pattern that became generalised for the UK within the course of the century.[25]

A slump in the price of grain following the ending of the Napoleonic Wars led to Britain's landowners – who at this time formed the bulk of MPs – creating limits to grain imports, thus attempting to restore the price of their products. The repeal of these laws – known as the Corn Laws – in 1846 slowly reversed the increase in prices as wheat entered Britain from abroad, particularly from Canada. The repeal was a testament to the extent to which Britain was being transformed by industry and empire: when the economy was overwhelmingly rural, the lower classes of England had favoured local control over grain, yet by the first quarter of the nineteenth century British workers had allied themselves with industrialists and grain importers against the country's landed elites. This was because cheaper, imported grain was seen as enhancing the spending power of workers, while for employers it reduced the pressure on wages.

It was thanks to the lifting of the Corn Laws that Britain went from producing all the wheat it consumed in 1830 to consuming a great deal more wheat by the advent of the First World War and yet producing only a fifth of what it consumed.[26] Britain so thoroughly dominated the grain trade that the importers of London and Liverpool effectively set the global price for wheat, while British demand had the power to radically transform landscapes and cultures abroad, particularly in North America, the location of its largest suppliers.[27]

From mid-century, wheat became one of Britain's largest

imports, second only in value to raw cotton.[28] A prevailing theory of the era, that of comparative advantage, argued that countries should specialise in products for export and then trade to secure everything else. This theory, in addition to ignoring the structural inequalities of the global system (a system that Britain, above all others, had shaped), was used to justify the romantic transformation of land in Britain from wheat fields into pasture. It was thus that two-thirds of former cropland went to grass between 1875 and 1895.[29] By 1913, more than half of Britain's total arable land was left fallow or else used for grouse moors and grazing cattle.[30] It was this trend of outsourcing production to the Empire that enabled England to maintain the idea of possessing a green and pleasant land even as it urbanised.

When it came in 1914, war raised the issue of Britain's import dependence, particularly as German U-boats began sinking merchant ships making their way across the Atlantic to Liverpool. It was not exactly the first time, nor would it be the last, that the concerns of political and economic elites turned to the malnourished diets of their domestic working classes. Yet in the context of war, state intervention in popular diets was a matter of public necessity.

Although it made a slow start, the government of Britain ended up mandating that land be put back in the service of bread and briefly returned to regulated prices and weights of loaves reminiscent of the old moral order.[31] It experimented with workplace and public canteens that served millions of meals a day and launched campaigns aimed at reducing and redirecting consumption (one advert instructed the population to 'eat slowly [then] you will need less food'; another attempted to rebrand leftover porridge as 'Scotch Trifle'). In 1917, the state requisitioned all the flour mills in Britain, thereby taking control of the price of flour and enforcing a national standard, one that mandated that less of the bran be discarded, plus a mix of up to a third in cereals other than wheat (mainly oats, rye and barley). Nationalisation lasted only briefly, and the dark, dense and damp loaves it produced were widely despised.

While the stage had been set by this experience for continued intervention in the British economy and the nation's diet – leading in the direction of the welfare state – import dependence resumed between the two world wars. By 1930, Britain, a country with less than 3 per cent of the world's population, took nearly all of the world's exports in bacon and ham, some 96 per cent of all the eggs, 59 per cent of all the beef, 46 per cent of all the cheese, 32 per cent of all the wool and almost a third of all the world's traded wheat.[32]

It was in this era too that canned food, pioneered as soldiers' rations, gained popularity among Britons of all classes. Well-known brands such as Cadbury, Rowntree, and Tate & Lyle established lasting reputations in the interwar period. With the denationalisation of milling, three private firms now controlled the flour industry. At the same time, large grocers such as Sainsbury's first appeared, later growing into Britain's gigantic supermarkets. It was thus that national brands and urban shops definitively replaced any lasting notions in Britain that the nation's fields and farms were the direct source of its food.

The advent of war with Nazi Germany saw the re-emergence of debates over public nutrition and self-reliance. Bread was not initially included when rations came into effect in 1940. However, a group of scientists made the case to government that it should be and pushed again for a mandate that white flour go back to brown. The decision to require that calcium be added to refined white flour was taken as a compromise (although, as a result, some consumers suspected the government was poisoning them). Yet as imports were once again undermined by attacks on merchant ships in the Atlantic, a mandate against white flour was eventually imposed. A standardised wartime loaf returned in 1942 as the government embarked upon a campaign to teach bakers everywhere how to bake the unvarying, state-mandated bread. And once again the results were widely disliked, with housewives reporting they found it 'mushy,' 'grey' and indigestible.[33]

By 1956, when the National Loaf finally disappeared, people in Britain had almost forgotten what bread was like before central government intervention. For so long bread had come to mean dark, standardised loaves – a universal source of calories, but one without pleasure. Wheat extraction rates (the technical term for how much bran ends up flour) had become a hot topic in post-war politics and their adjustment towards or away from white was read as a sign of progress or decline. Millers were allowed to reintroduce white flours in 1953, but only if, as per the latest science, they added the new range of recently discovered vitamins and minerals in addition to the already mandated calcium.

In this context, the Rank Hovis McDougall group set about popularising their perfectly white fluffy loaves – Mother's Pride – fortified according to government mandate and advertised under the slogan 'we know what you really want'. Want it many people probably did, but its high price put it out of reach and the National Loaf remained a common, because far cheaper, option.

The Chorleywood process, appearing in 1961, combined with growing post-war affluence, finally put the light white loaf within reach of the majority, even as bread, also for the first time in its history, played a less central role in popular diets. By means of high-speed mixing, vacuum conditions and fast-acting yeasts and additives, the publicly funded research lab at Chorleywood produced a highly automated baking process that could work with low-protein flours and produce fluffy uniform loaves without the need for long periods of fermentation. It was adopted across the board in large factory bakeries and still produces most of the bread the nation eats today.

In Chorleywood Lodge, an elegant white building nestled among pine trees in London's commuter belt, the sciences of engineering and chemistry combined with the state's commitment to public nutrition to give the world an affordable white loaf that older generations could barely have dreamt of. The traditional baking of England had almost completely disappeared. Certainly, the historic link between beer and bread, brewing and baking, was now gone. And this was the world in which the sourdough loaves we know today would eventually take hold.

Inventing tradition

For the rest of my week at Quince I got out of bed at 2:30 a.m., put on thick woollen gloves, left the house at three and started my shift at four – although we got there a little earlier on Saturday. I struggled to go to bed much before ten and, despite feeling increasingly tired as the week went on, I found it hard to fall asleep, probably because I was overcompensating with enormous amounts of coffee. Every evening I took a bath and watched long slow videos of bakers from a new generation of neo-artisans who hand chop wood for their ancient, unpredictable ovens and who drive to natural springs to fill containers with sacred water to make their dough.

Fiona was right: it really isn't lonely being in the bakery surrounded by a large family of portioned dough gently rising in straw baskets. Each day after the first began with baking. Yesterday's shaped and proven loaves were tipped onto a sheet, and these were loaded into the oven with the help of a wooden board. Each day I watched as the loaves sprang and were transformed by heat and steam, emerging out of the oven grown whole, ready to leave the nest.

From the first round of baking on Tuesday Anna selected a loaf and tore it apart, handing me a chunk. We quietly chewed; the flavour of the wheat was complex and nutty and the warm bread had a glossy crust and a tender crumb. After swallowing a mouthful, Anna broke the silence to say: 'See, it's not so bad being awake this early.' And in that moment I thought she was right.

With Anna's help I eventually got the knack for shaping bread, which was a daily highlight. I began to toss the dough into a bowl of bran that stopped it sticking, then on into its basket with the satisfying flick of a bench scraper. I threw flour onto the work surface with a snap of the wrist, creating a fine cloud. I gained a sense of the addictive flow that comes with doing jobs like baking quickly and methodically – like learning to speak in a new language or practising a martial art.

By the end of the week, delirious yet euphoric, I began to realise that while the craft of sourdough baking at Quince may be distinctly modern, it is nonetheless a refuge from automation, a potential balm for our alienated lives spent sat before the screen (as much of a problem today as it was during lockdown). Sourdough baking is a case of 'invented tradition' and yet, to my mind, a positive one.

The two historians who coined this phrase – Eric Hobsbawm and Terence Ranger – suggest that habits that claim an old lineage but are in fact novel are likely to appear 'when a rapid transformation of society weakens or destroys the social patterns for which "old" traditions had been designed'.[34] The rapid transformations we have encountered in this chapter are those of urbanisation and industrialisation – a great transition that was spurred on by imported wheat from Britain's Empire – plus the consequences of two world wars.

Signs in the subconsciousness of the nation that something had been lost amid this transition to modernity are detectable in Hovis's well-loved advert of 1973. Directed by Ridley Scott, the ad is memorable for its soundtrack: Dvořák's Symphony No. 9 – 'From the New World' – played by the Ashington Colliery brass band. We see in the ad a young boy wearing a flap cap, pushing a bike up a cobbled hill in the quintessentially English village where he is delivering a basket of bread. The final scene takes us inside a small village bakery for a close-up of a factory-made loaf of Hovis bread, whose claim to tradition rests on the statement that the roller-milled Chorleywood bread contains a portion of wheatgerm.

Around the same time, a wholefood movement in England was producing loaves of bread that really did contain all that wholewheat had to offer. These loaves were a staple of my childhood, and while I daresay they were nourishing, they were also, on the whole, crumbly, dry yet somehow also damp, wholemeal yet somehow also flavourless – quite likely reminiscent of the National Loaf of wartime. It would take several decades before a new band of artisanal bakers appeared, wielding sourdough as their triumphant Californian invention.

'Sourdough bread is a fascinating blend of tradition, science, and health', writes Vanessa Kimbell, who, like Pallant, is a big name in the world of sourdough myth-making.[35] 'Sourdough is the way we always made bread, until the industrial revolution', she writes. Except that, elsewhere, Kimbell has written an article that references the centuries-long tradition of using beer to raise bread. Bread and beer. Brewing and baking. These are the couplets that resound in the history of bread in

England, and yet you won't hear of them in today's modern, artisanal, rustic bakeries specialising in French pâtisserie and an American-inflected *pain de campagne*, otherwise known as sourdough.

But does recent import and invention mean that sourdough isn't an English food, or that it cannot be celebrated as such? I don't think so. Its Englishness consists in the fact that it satisfies a set of very domestic needs: for bread and for sustenance, certainly, but also for pleasure, craft and (invented) tradition. Contemporary sourdough baking offers a sense of a life less alienated than the one we have inherited from our peculiar modernity. Artisan sourdough – healthy for our guts and typically made with nutrient-dense flours, often locally sourced – could be a proud part of the national diet. The generation of artisanal bakers that the popularity of this loaf has led to could also be nurtured and nourished. Moreover, bakeries like Quince offer a key to a brilliant universe of the now-lost world of traditional British baking.

If that's true, then why is sourdough often also a source of ridicule? Why do we find that the loaf is, often along with avocado and artisanal coffee, a signifier of objectionable taste? On occasion, the loaf's rustic posture can become an excuse for sloppy baking. Remember the care that Anna puts into the balance between her bread's bounce and its shape, the fact that she keeps her starter from making her bread too sour and that she works with wheats that are full of flavour. Not every sourdough baker does this.

At other times, the pushback against sourdough has to do with its high price relative to supermarket loaves, and with the post-class posture of the tote-bag shoppers in Islington who champion it. There is evidence that sales in sourdough have stalled as the cost-of-living crisis bites. 'White sliced bread comes to the fore when people are short of money,' Jonathan Warburton told *The Times* in 2023. This is a theme we will come back to.

But the ridicule of sourdough is also bound up with the extent to which the English see artful food as 'posh'. In 2012, for example, an article for the BBC declared sourdough to be a marker of a new era, that of the 'posh loaf'. This discourse carries with it a historical tradition of its own – a subject among others to which we now turn.

2

Les Rosbifs

With lantern jaws and croaking gut,
See how the half-starved Frenchmen strut
And call us English dogs.
But soon we'll teach these bragging foes
That beef and beer give heavier blows
Than soup and roasted frogs.

David Garrick, from the poem accompanying William Hogarth's engraving *The Gate of Calais* or *O, the Roast Beef of Old England*, 1748

Sourdough as we know it today came to England from France by way of California. But what about those croissants? Indeed, what about the vast number of dishes served in high-end restaurants in England that are French in origin? From bisque (a soup made with the shells of lobsters or crabs) to beurre blanc (a butter and white wine sauce that is often served with fish); beef consommé to beef tartare; tarte tatin to crème caramel, chocolate mousse and soufflé.

There is a general notion in England that French food equals good food – or, if not good, then at least 'posh' food. This idea is so pervasive that almost every serious chef who grew up speaking English appears obliged to tell you that their love of food was realised on holidays to France, whether it's Anthony Bourdain eating oysters in Normandy or Fergus Henderson, the chef behind the restaurant St John, dining at grand hotels with his food-loving father in Paris. In various interviews, Adam Byatt, chef-patron of the Michelin-starred restaurant Trinity in London, has fondly recounted the time he ate artichokes during a school exchange in France, while also remarking that the day-to-day food of his childhood was a mixture of his mum's humble home cooking and shop-bought ready meals.

Why? Why do high-end English chefs look to France for their inspiration? What are the origins of the refinement that characterises elite French cuisine and why can English food feel so crude and slapdash by comparison? And has it always been this way, or did elite French cookery replace a native English tradition? If so, is that another reason why the English are so prone to relishing junk foods – from sliced white bread to sausage rolls – while also denouncing fine dining as 'posh' or else adopting invented traditions from elsewhere?

As winter hesitantly approached spring, I spent a week in the vast basement kitchens of a prestigious restaurant in London, which for various reasons I will refer to here as Restaurant X. This was the first time I have ever been required to appear clean-shaven for work. To me and those who know me, the appearance of my hairless chin came as a shock.

I say work, but in fact I was there, as at Quince, as a *stagiaire* – meaning I was there for unpaid work experience, a common practice among professional cooks. Like much of the kitchen lexicon *stagiaire* is a French word, meaning 'intern'.

And so it was that on day two of this *stage* I had a minor breakthrough with carrots. With my long back bent over a metal bench in a prep kitchen – severely lit and with tiles across the walls and floors, like everywhere else in the restaurant's underground maze – I learnt that I could cut perfect one-centimetre cubes of carrot much faster if I handled several pieces at once. Prior to this realisation, I had on my first day started the same task by cutting every carrot into one-centimetre-thick slices, using a ruler to obtain the first slice and then using that slice as a guide for the rest. Then, as instructed, I cut each plank of carrot into one-centimetre batons and individually cut those batons into one-centimetre cubes.

This had been the first job assigned to me on Monday and I was anxious to make a good impression. I reasoned with myself that it was better to do the job slowly but correctly – to obtain clear and true one-centimetre cubes of carrot – than to do it quickly but risk having my work thrown in the bin, being told to go home, or worse. You always have the sense in kitchens like this that there are far crueller fates available than merely being sacked. Not that I was being paid.

I laboured over those cubes of carrot to the extent that after half an hour of precise chopping, my hands hot and a little unsteady, I felt exhausted. Not even an hour into my first day and my body felt as stiff as my restaurant-issue chef whites.

By day two I was a little more relaxed, and so I allowed myself to cut several slices of carrot into batons at once: first two, then four and eventually eight. I lined up the batons and watched newly formed cubes fall away from the blade as I cut in batches. With this huge leap in productivity, I could now turn several kilos of carrots into a small plastic bag full of perfectly square cubes in a matter of minutes.

Into the bag, as instructed, I added salt and a pat of butter. I vacuum-sealed the bag, delivered it to the *chef de partie* on the larder section and moved onto another task. Having spent too long with the carrots on Monday I did not get the chance to cut radishes into tiny red-tipped matchsticks, no larger than the minute hand of a watch.

The jobs I carried out during my week at Restaurant X included cubing, balling and turning various root vegetables (baby carrots, for example, were sculpted to look like even smaller, bevelled baby carrots); using a stamp to create petal-shaped beetroot tuiles (which are kind of like crackers made from a batter); preparing and serving rolled-up sheets of pickled apple; using tweezers to pick various micro herbs and cresses (this I did several times a day); making a parrot-green pistachio frangipane (the secret here is Sicilian pistachios and a splash of food dye); cooking and picking crab (once a day); peeling and sorting over ten kilograms of grade-A black Périgord truffles that smelled faintly of fresh tarmac (if fresh tarmac could be said to have an appealing smell, which to me these did); perfectly segmenting blood oranges and cutting the segments into tiny triangles; quenelle-ing chutney (that is, shaping a sharp, spicy chutney into pointed ovals with two teaspoons – to go alongside a foie gras dish); forming small domes of wildly expensive caviar using a mould; cooking mounds of wobbly crab custard in a steamer; garnishing cakes with various gels, creams, embossed chocolate discs and gold leaf; forming tart shells (called croustades) with a hot brass rod that is dipped into batter then into boiling oil; and cooking perfectly weighed out choux buns in an oven so large you could stand in it. There was also lots of straining of sauces, vac-packing various things, plating a number of cold dishes for service, and cleaning. I was not allowed to cook anything to order, nor, given the immense pressure in the kitchen, did I really want to. It was enough to be able to do all the small, highly specialised and repetitive tasks with the requisite levels of skill, precision and speed.

Obtaining white crab meat, for instance, was a seven-step process: the live crustaceans were killed, steamed, chilled, broken down (the legs were thrown away), the claws and body were cleanly cracked and picked (most of the brown meat in the shell was discarded), then the white meat was placed on metal trays that were sat on top of ice and picked through to remove any fragments of shell. After this, the crab was picked through again in the darkness of the walk-in fridge using tweezers and a UV torch that would illuminate any shell you had failed to find previously with your latex-gloved fingers. Allowing crab shell to appear on the plate at a Michelin-starred restaurant such as this is a sin worthy of who knows what punishment.

Or take the rolls of pickled apple. These were paper-thin sheets of tart green apples that were obtained by careful use of a Japanese mandolin, which works a bit like a pencil sharpener. The long sheets were submerged in water with the right amount of ascorbic acid to prevent the apple oxidising (and going brown – too much acid would make it overly sour). The sheets were then cut into ten-by-two-centimetre strips and placed in vacuum-sealed bags with a pickling solution of green apple vinegar and sugar. After a day the bags were emptied into plastic tubs (called deli containers) and were ready for service.

When required – when an order came in for a certain dish, in this case a dish involving turbot – the chef responsible for garnish on the fish section had to pluck a strip of apple with tweezers and coil it around the tweezers to obtain a neat spiral. The fastest way to do this was by spinning the strip with a flick of the wrist, which after a couple of goes I found I could do while keeping the roll of apple mostly straight. The difficulty was in removing the tweezers' grip from the centre of the roll: pinch the apple too tight and you'd pull away the centre so that the roll was coned and wouldn't sit flat on the plate, but pinch too little and you risk a loose and floppy roll of pickled apple, or even dropping the strip and needing to start again.

There were at least five similarly intricate garnishes on the turbot dish alongside this roll of apple, each as taxing and exact as the next. Simply adding dots of gel or purée to plates required the right amount of pressure on the plastic bottle and a gradual upward movement to obtain a glossy, evenly rounded ball. Garnishes that didn't look perfect never made it to the dining room.

Under the harsh fluorescent lights of the Restaurant X kitchen, every member of the brigade cooked as if the inspectors of the Michelin Guide were watching. Some twenty-four elite chefs, commis chefs and apprentices spend the majority of their waking hours in that basement, clocking an average of sixty hours per week, although many of the sous-chefs work around seventy. Sixteen chefs are needed at any one time for a restaurant that sits no more than sixty people. There is also a team of porters, steaming away in the far corners of the kitchen, and what seemed like a small army of identically suited waiters, most of whom, for some reason, were Italian.

The kitchen brigade is organised in a strict hierarchy, with clear divisions of labour and exacting requirements for each dish. The kitchen's unrelentingly high standards depend upon thousands of small tasks being done right every single day, an approach that the British chef Marco Pierre White once said defined perfection. The executive chef, whom I never saw cook, wore the tallest hat, even as it impractically skimmed the hoods of the extraction. He worked a regular nine-to-five, Monday to Friday, played golf at the weekend and only occasionally graced the kitchen to poke spoons into sauces and direct his large discerning snout at golden beef Wellingtons as they emerged from an expensive upright oven.

Nouvelle cuisine and English country cooking

In most elite kitchens of this type a towel will be referred to as a *torchon*, as in 'chef, you dropped your torchon!' A chef's cylindrical pleated hat is called a *toque*. To enrich a sauce with fat, usually butter, is to *monter* ('mount') a sauce. Vegetables are cut into sizes that vary from *brunoise*, a very fine dice, to *chiffonade*, meaning a cut of thin strips.

The head chef is simply called the chef – *chef* being the French word for 'chief', or 'boss'. The next in command is the sous, meaning 'under'. A chef de partie is a chef in charge of a section – the sections of a kitchen typically being larder, fish, meat (sometimes called the sauce section) and pastry, although subdivisions exist in large kitchens. A commis is a junior chef, usually at the start of their career. The noun that describes the prepared food you have made ready for service is *mise en place*. Chefs, including those who speak only English, will often instruct you to 'get *en place*!' or say, 'Make sure you're *en place* by twelve or you'll be in the shit' – meaning 'Get ready!'

In the moments before lunch service began at Restaurant X you felt the frantic, intensely focused rush of the brigade as they finished their *mise*. Chefs on every section of the kitchen had their heads down, completely absorbed by their final tasks: reducing sauces, picking herbs and flowers, portioning a fillet of beef. Then at midday the chefs stood to attention at their spotlessly clean sections, their tubular hats like paper chimneys, one or two making final arrangements to the deli containers lined up on their benches. Then the orders come in.

The ticket machine buzzes and scrapes and a sous-chef reads out the check: 'Two covers, two tasting, one duck medium-well.' And the entire kitchen of sixteen chefs responds: 'Oui!' The kitchen jumps into gear.

In a corner where I end up spending most of my time during service, the boys on larder clink clink as ring moulds are placed onto ornate plates and a crab filling is spooned in. To my left, a plancha – a flat metal grill – sizzles as two fillets of turbot meet hot oil, while on the other side of the stove two seasoned duck breasts begin to gently render in a cast-iron pan.

In less than a minute the machine buzzes again. The sous-chef: 'Three covers, à la carte, two foie gras, one crab, two turbot, one Wellington. Gluten-free on the crab and gluten-free on the turbot.' The brigade responds in unison: 'Oui!' At the other side of the pass a row of waiters stands to attention, readied with silver trays. My eyes wide open, I am poised in the corner mostly watching, feeling as though I have found myself caught in the gilded cogs of a great machine.

To understand fully the lasting influence of France on English food culture we have to go all the way back to the 1600s. It was then that European elites, including in England, began to drift away from a distinctly medieval style of cookery, one defined by the intense contrasts of sourness (often in the form of verjuice – that is, unripe fruit, usually grapes), sweetness (with the use of dried fruit and imported sugar) and savoury (roasted and boiled game in particular), all accompanied by heavy clouds of spice. So it was that in the court of Elizabeth I veal could be served with candied plums and pomegranate, the fillings for enormous pies were flavoured with cloves and nutmeg, and sturgeon and herrings might be stewed in vinegar before being dusted with powdered ginger and mace. Sugar was so popular among the Elizabethans that it was fashionable to have rotten teeth, so much so that those unable to regularly consume the expensive 'spice' might resort to blackening their teeth with paint.

In *The Forme of Cury*, a royal cookbook composed in fourteenth-century England, we find such dishes as 'Mortrews of Fyssh', which can be translated into modern English as grounded (as in mortared) fish. The recipe calls for boiled cod mashed with bread, almonds, ginger and sugar. Or take the recipe for 'Egredouce', a medieval sweet and sour dish made of boiled and ground meat, this time fried in lard and mixed with ginger, cinnamon, currants, vinegar and honey. 'Cast the flessh in a pot and cast the syrup therto', the book's anonymous authors say, which to me sounds wonderfully dramatic.

Skip now to the brief reign of Queen Anne (1702–14) and to the cookbook *The Queen's Royal Cookery* to find that much of the spice and the sharp contrasting flavours have gone. Here instead are more earthy flavours – such as mutton shoulder stuffed with a mixture bound together by the beast's own blood – accompanied by fresh local herbs.

Similar changes in elite diets had been taking place across Europe and Russia in the seventeenth century. Yet while it is generally accepted among historians that this shift emanated from France, the reasons why have been the subject of much debate and persistent mythology.

One common myth suggests that the emergence of modern French cuisine came by way of Catherine de' Medici, who, in 1533, brought cooks from her native Florence across the Alps when she married the French king Henri II.[1] Yet while Renaissance Italy certainly exerted a powerful influence on important aspects of European culture, there is little to indicate that it promoted a change in diet.

The cookbook of Bartolomeo Scappi, the personal chef to several cardinals and no fewer than two popes, provides evidence that Italian Renaissance cookery was perhaps more elaborate and artful than anything available elsewhere. Published in 1570, *Opera* provides the first known picture of a fork (English eaters, when they encountered the new-fangled device, saw it as unmanly). However, the 1,000 or so recipes in the book largely stick to the medieval repertoire. In one, a kind of omelette, Scappi calls for a mixture of pig's blood, goat's cheese, spring onion, cinnamon, cloves and nutmeg. In fact, sugar features in nearly all the recipes, including as a pizza topping with pine nuts and rose water. *Opera* shows that the shift away from the medieval palate was far more gradual, and somewhat later, than the myth of Medici allows for.

There are historians – the argument to follow is borrowed from Stephen Mennell – who claim that the transition from medieval to early-modern elite cooking is best seen by looking at important changes occurring *within* France, which by the middle of the seventeenth century was the most powerful, populous and centrally organised state in Europe.[2] Predating *The Queen's Royal Cookery* by half a century, *Le Cuisinier françois* (1651) by François Pierre La Varenne was a manual for cooks who served the French nobility and, thanks to early translations into English, Swedish and German, was also a guide for elites elsewhere. La Varenne's book is an important marker of the change in taste that was underway at this time: medieval spices are toned down though not entirely absent, and fresh local herbs are elevated. The book opens with a recipe for stock, a fundamental component of French cuisine to this day, and explains how egg whites can be used to clarify a broth, a technique still employed by chefs at Restaurant X. La Varenne's cookbook provides hard evidence that it was French chefs who were the first to become interested in 'delicate' flavours, rather than the harsh contrasts that characterised the old cuisine.

According to Mennell, the French court in the seventeenth century, above all that of Louis XIV, played a far greater role in the invention of France's modern food traditions than did Medici. From a young age, Louis XIV concentrated political life in France around his personal rule, gaining absolute power in 1661 and promoting his image as the centre of the universe by referring to himself as the Sun King.[3] At his new palace in Versailles, French nobles gathered to observe the great Louis being served by an army of some 500 cooks and to seek the King's favour, from which the majority of power and privilege in his realm flowed. In this context, strict codes of polite behaviour and excessive displays of opulence governed the boundaries of the King's inner circle, and, in a highly symbolic world, eating and feasting were an essential theatre of politics.

Thus was the flame lit for a new tradition of refined court cookery, as reflected in the book composed by La Varenne. In an atmosphere of competitive consumption, every great French chef of the era denounced his predecessors and his competitors. Yet, taken together, each new cookbook of this period reveals a continual refinement and codification of what became known as the nouvelle cuisine.

In *Le Cuisinier roïal et bourgeois*, first published in 1691, the court cook François Massialot provides some of the earliest known recipes for what were later called the mother sauces, including a recognisable sauce espagnole – a dark meat stock thickened with a roux – and béchamel. (Note here that the word 'bourgeois' refers to country and townsfolk in France of a high status that was usually granted by the state. The term here has a sense distinct from the modern meaning of 'bourgeois' as 'capitalist' or 'industrialist'. The country gentry, an English term with some equivalence, were by contrast relatively independent of the sovereign's power, since their incomes derived from private land ownership and investments – a detail that matters in what follows.)

Jospeh Menon – chef to the Queen of France in the 1730s – gives us *La Cuisinière bourgeoise*, in which we find dishes that are lightened and simplified, and where butter replaces what was once the more familiar lard. Key hallmarks of the nouvelle cuisine included the many complete dishes that began to take the place of what had been the more typical buffet style of service, plus an emphasis on rich sauces, particularly those made from meat stock, a tradition that is still artfully expressed in places like Restaurant X today.

The new style that was emerging anticipates what the food historian Barbara Wheaton calls France's modular cuisine, whereby chefs – then as now – depend less on a given mix of ingredients or precise amounts and more on adaptable techniques.[4] It was here, then, that menu writing started to become the kind of equation that is still used (somewhat unconsciously) in many restaurants now: protein (such as fish or meat) + sauce (such as a beurre blanc or sauce espagnole) + a vegetable (such as blanched spinach or mashed potatoes) + fresh herbs = complete menu item. Watch an episode of *MasterChef* and you will see this formula repeated endlessly.

By the time restaurants appeared in Paris in the 1760s, the foundations of modern French food had been established. These new kinds of eating places – modelled to some extent on the English tavern – offered a commercial setting in which the customer could choose a complete meal à la carte.[5] The invention of the restaurant occurred alongside the growth of a new and hungry public, one that lived beyond the walls of France's chateaus and palaces – outside of all those places that, as it turned out, would soon come under threat as a result of the French Revolution.[6]

Across the Channel, the spread of France's emerging post-medieval cuisine appears to have been uneven. In Shakespeare's *Henry IV, Part 2*, first performed in 1597, we hear of a menu which includes 'some pigeons, a couple of short-legged hens, a joint of mutton, and any pretty little tiny kickshaws'. 'Kickshaws' is an anglicisation of the French *quelque chose*, and the passage suggests a contrast between a list of simply prepared proteins and something French and more refined.

In 1615, John Murrell gives us *A New Booke of Cookerie*, whose long subtitle advertises it as being in the 'English and French fashion', although Murrell's recipes, such as one for capon boiled in the French way, include the use of spices and dried fruit and as such are still distinctly medieval.

Robert May's *The Accomplish't Cook, or the Art and Mystery of Cookery*, published in 1660, both praises the courtly tradition of France and criticises it for being obsessed with sauces to the detriment of ancient, humoral ideas about diet. The book contains recipes both English and French, although their character is again largely medieval.

In 1660s London, the diary of Samuel Pepys reveals the civil servant enjoying 'a fine French dinner' and 'a pleasant French fricassee'. Pepys's cosmopolitan embrace of French culinary fashions reflected the preferences of the restored Stuart monarch, Charles II, who had solidified his taste while hiding from Cromwell in French palaces. Such preferences continued among some members of the upper rank of the aristocracy, which in turn fed the anxieties of English Protestants who wished to maintain the power of Parliament as against the centralising kind of power held by the court in France. The subsequent Georgian monarchs of Britain likewise carried a love of French cooking over from the courts of Hanover, which had long taken its culinary cues from Paris. Surviving menus from George II and III's long reigns are replete with French, or at least French-sounding, dishes, but then so too appear any number of pies, roasts and plainer English fare.

It is quite possible that, as in many other matters, this ambiguity reflected the extent to which the German-speaking kings and their closest supporters were out of step with the rest of the emerging British nation. Indeed, George III's apparent fondness for plainer English fare was a sign that he was seeking to redress this imbalance.[7] Beyond courtly and cosmopolitan society in London a modern, if distinctly rural, style of cookery was taking shape, particularly among the middling ranks of England's landed elites (among whom were many who had recently acquired lands that they intended to 'improve' by using modern farming methods and capitalist incentives). In fact, it was this country, rather than courtly, style that was to form Britain's first *native* break with the medieval traditions of elite European cuisine. And yet this was a native style formed in large part by way of contrasting the apparent plainness and honesty of Britain with the perceived opulence and elitism of France.

In elite English housekeeping guides from the early 1600s (where recipes feature alongside tips on brewing, baking, cheesemaking and medicine) we already find a distrust of the wastefulness of French cooking and a promotion instead of plain and economical English fare. Gervase Markham's *The English Huswife* (published in 1615, and which we encountered in the previous chapter) is one such work. Markham describes the ideal housewife as clean, neat, homely, economical and plain. 'Let [her diet] be rather esteemed for the familiar acquaintance she hath with it, than for the strangeness and rarity it bringeth from other countries', he declares.[8]

Judging by its appearance alongside his other books on husbandry and farming, the audience for Markham's guide is clearly the housekeeper or housewife of a landowner – that is, a member of England's seventeenth-century elite (though not necessarily a noble one). There are no traces in Markham's book of the courtly tradition gradually developing in France; rather, the recipes largely reflect a simplification of the old medieval repertoire.

Later in the century, we find several poems that indicate the emergence of a growing culture war between French refinement and relatively unadorned plain eating in England. In one, the Earl of Rochester praises the belly-filling properties of beef. 'As for French kickshaws, sillery and champaigne, ragouts and fricassees,' the satirist and courtier of King Charles II wrote, 'in throth, w'have none.'[9]

And so it is in the eighteenth century, just as the nouvelle cuisine was hurtling along in France, that Britain enters an age of native country cooking at its most vital. The key cookbooks reflecting the new ethos are Eliza Smith's *The Compleat Housewife* (1727), Hannah Glasse's *The Art of Cookery Made Plain and Easy* (1747), Elizabeth Moxon's *English Housewifery* (1749) and Elizabeth Raffald's *The Experienced English Housekeeper* (1769). These books, all of them authored by women, share themes of domestic economy and plainness, which are often explicitly contrasted with the courtly trends emanating from France and the imitators of French cooking in London.

The books all contain dishes with French names, although Raffald translates some into English, rendering 'crème brûlée' as 'Burnt Cream', for example. A successful housekeeper and entrepreneur in the North West, Raffald is at pains to explain to her readers that while some dishes may sound French she has made every effort to ensure that the recipe is both economical and simple. In place of any elaborate meat sauces, for example, she substitutes a 'gravy' made of caramelised sugar and lemon pickle that, she says, 'answers both for beauty and taste (at a trifling expense)'. Far better than the French 'coulis', she writes, 'which is extravagant'.[10]

Glasse's Francophobia is far more explicit. 'If Gentlemen will have French Cooks,' she is well known for having written, 'they must pay for French tricks.'

> I have heard of a Cook that used six Pounds of Butter to fry twelve Eggs, when every Body knows, that understands Cooking, that Half a Pound is full enough, or more than need be used: But then it would not be French. So much is the blind Folly of this Age, that they would rather be imposed on by a French Booby, than give Encouragement to a good English Cook![11]

Glasse offers several recipes for gravy, most of which are less complicated than fine French sauces, although many of her recipes make liberal use of butter, wild mushrooms, veal and truffles, and some are likely unwitting copies from elite French chefs. The use of these ingredients and her explicit address to servants in the book's introduction show that the audiences for this food were, despite all the denunciations of opulence, still the well off, if not quite the highest classes.

The cookbooks of this high age of country cooking together express a broader sentiment of the time, one that pitted the beef-eating British against the frog-eating French. Indeed, it was in the eighteenth century and up to the end of the Napoleonic Wars that roast beef became a political symbol of an 'imagined community' in England, a community that had a class of self-reliant landowners at its core. Yeomen, small land-holding farmers, had in this respect long occupied a particular place in England's self-mythologising, having apparently supplied the bowmen that defeated the much larger French forces in the fifteenth-century Battle of Agincourt. The royal guard, once derived from this class of yeomen, are still today known as Beefeaters because, in the eighteenth century, that is exactly what they were: soldiers who received generous rations of beef alongside large quantities of mutton and beer.[12]

It was also during this age that the English acquired the nickname *les rosbifs*, a phrase that could also describe in French the cooking of animals whole upon a spit, as with *mutton rosbif*. The reputation the British had for greater consumption of beef infused national comparisons that were later deployed to explain Britain's economic superiority. Commentary from the 1840s, for example, favourably compared the bodies of British railway workers, who were supposed to have been fed on beef, with the inefficient labour of their soup- and vegetable-eating French counterparts.[13]

Some foreign observers of early-modern England, including French ones, perceived there to be a native vigour that resulted from the country's carnivorousness (some saw the population's ruddy skin as a sign of this, although more likely the cause here was excessive drinking). So it was that John Churchill, the 1st Duke of Marlborough, Winston Churchill's great-great-great-grandfather, claimed that 'no soldier can fight unless he is properly fed on beef and beer'. This was a widespread sentiment that persisted into the Napoleonic Wars, where doomed bands of cattle could be seen following in the wake of marching British soldiers.

In *The Grub-Street Opera,* written in 1731, playwright Henry Fielding deploys commonplace xenophobia to satirise members of the aristocracy and the apparently corrupt court to which they belong, in part by contrasting their preference for French fashion with 'old English hospitality'. The play includes a sentimental song about roast beef, a dish which apparently, back when it was the food of the nation, 'ennobled our hearts, and enriched our blood', producing brave soldiers and a virtuous ruling class. That is, the song claims, until England's political leaders adopted the effeminate tastes of the French. The tune was a favourite in British music halls for over two centuries, as evidenced by reports of women celebrating the end of rationing in 1954 by singing it in Trafalgar Square. Here, and also in the modern Sunday roast, we find a tradition that was more or less invented in the eighteenth century – that of beef-eating being quintessentially English – becoming something of a tradition proper.

The culture war against members of the English aristocracy

who remained wedded to French fashion (and, it was supposed, popish tyranny) was expressed in the remarkable prevalence of beefsteak (or 'beefsteake') clubs, which began life in the eighteenth century and persisted in popularity late into the nineteenth. In these clubs, patriots gathered to sing, joke, network and, of course, eat beef, which was served with either mustard or horseradish alongside simple accompaniments such as boiled potatoes. The patriotic artist William Hogarth was a founding member of the ironically named Sublime Society of Beefsteaks, established in London in 1736 (apparently still active today). Members of this club produced a range of merchandise such as medals on which were engraved the club's motto: 'beef and liberty'.

Such clubs functioned in the way historians have often viewed coffee houses – that is, as signs of an emerging public sphere, albeit a more chauvinistic one and one connected to the arts rather than to trade. The fact that members of beefsteak clubs went on to include earls, barons, princes, King George IV and the Prime Minister William Gladstone is testament to how extensive the country-cooking-as-national-identity trend became, encompassing every level of the ruling class and not just its middling ranks.

At the height of England's competition with France for colonial supremacy in the Americas, Hogarth produced a series of drawings with xenophobic culinary themes. One, titled *The Gates of Calais* or *O the Roast Beef of Old England*, was intended to provoke fear of a French invasion while at the same time depicting a scrawny and degenerate rival: the foreground of the picture shows a monk sadistically testing the sharpness of his axe, and on the edge of the frame a French soldier can be seen barbecuing frogs.

The contrast with France lent England's native cuisine its independence and underlay the production and celebration of plain, economical dishes, many of which – such as pork pies and steak and kidney pudding – persist along with a more general attitude towards food into our present, a point to which I will return below.

According to Mennel, the two distinct elite traditions – courtly in France and county in England – reflect differences between the organisation of power in the respective countries. Where France was centralised around the monarch, landed elites in post-Restoration Britain (many of whom could acquire their land through purchases rather than titles) had a degree of political influence and financial independence that did not require them to loiter like peacocks in the palace. The pressure for conspicuous consumption (that is, showing off with displays of opulent eating) was therefore relatively slight in England. Britain's country cooking – roast beef above all – could thus become a symbol of English liberty, understood by its proponents in terms of their 'self-dependence' and most forcefully expressed in moments of opposition to the popish power of France.

It is only in the nineteenth century, in the decades after the Battle of Waterloo triumphantly concluded Britain's wars with its imperial rival and neighbour, and with the urbanisation of England now well advanced, that the balance in elite English taste finally began a near-conclusive shift towards the repertoire of French nouvelle cuisine, a modern culinary tradition that had by then accrued some 200 years in experience. In the immediate aftermath of the war, the celebrity chef Marie-Antoine Carême, who had done more than most to codify the new French cuisine, briefly became the personal cook of beefsteak club-member King George IV, while the French-born chef Alexis Soyer furnished the spectacular modern kitchens of the private members' Reform Club, a home from home for many of Britain's most powerful MPs. However, Carême was dissatisfied with his reception in England and with the English palate, which, like his employer, continued to champion the likes of roast beef; he left this post within nine months. Likewise, a glance at Soyer's menus shows the prevalence of the English country style – for example in the form of Soyer's famous dish of breaded mutton served with chopped egg and ham.

The crowning of France as the origin of good taste among Britain's elite was only fully established towards the end of the nineteenth century, since it was only at this point when the very nature of that elite had changed. Those who demanded a fine meal in late-Victorian London – by then the most populous and wealthy city in the world by far – increasingly belonged to a class whose power derived neither from land nor from title. Members of this group – merchants, industrialists, financiers and representatives of their associated trades, a bourgeoisie in the modern sense of this word – had benefitted from the economic boom in the middle of the century and had little idea of what was to come in 1914. So it was that in the handful of decades before the First World War, referred to, in French, as the belle époque, a short moustached chef named Auguste Escoffier would achieve great acclaim and come to symbolise a new era for French fine dining in Britain, an era that would see the native elite tradition of English country cooking pushed aside by the tastes of the new, urban, moneyed classes.

Auguste Escoffier

On day four of my *stage* I arrived early, a little before 8 a.m., and was sent by a senior chef to have a look at the pastry kitchen. This kitchen – a small room set back from the main area that had its own ovens, chillers and a Bluetooth speaker playing Kiss FM – was crowded, and so the head pastry chef sent me off to look at the bakery operation. Restaurant X has a line in fine French pâtisserie, bread and cakes, serving these to some 200 people each day.

I found my way down to a lower floor, into the basement's basement, where I was surprised to find another labyrinth of kitchens inhabited, it seemed, solely by women. Here, in one room, three chefs in hairnets assembled hundreds of triangular, crustless sandwiches. Next door, in a room in which the surfaces were all marble rather than the usual stainless steel, I found four pastry chefs busy decorating rows of cakes.

This cool room was a welcome break from the intensity of the restaurant kitchen upstairs, yet here too the work was relentless, repetitive and exacting. In eight hours I learnt that the best way to make 200 perfectly round choux buns is to pipe the pastry into moulds and freeze it; I found out how absurdly difficult it is to quickly decorate hundreds of tiny carrot cakes with a small frill of gold leaf; and I was tasked with piping three dots – small, medium and large – of bergamot caramel onto 150 banoffee pies. I completed maybe twenty of these pies with varying success before one of the pastry chefs stepped in, told me I was painful to watch, and then piped over a hundred cakes in the time it took me to complete another twenty.

Down, down, downstairs, the women working here appeared to have an easier life. They did a mere nine or ten hours a day, with a healthy thirty-minute break, usually spent in the equally windowless staff room, and they rarely did overtime. Best of all, they talked. Nowhere during my week spent at Restaurant X did I experience more banter than I did with the four chefs working in the bakery. Jokes were made about the size of the birthday cakes (who could tell the difference between four inches and six), about a particularly steamy oven, and other innuendos of the kind that are never as funny written down as they appear to be when uttered in the midst of hard work.

I quickly became the subject of their jokes, especially after I wiped the sleeve of my chef jacket through some icing, complained that my hands were cold after unmoulding 200 frozen chocolate mousses and struggled hopelessly with transferring flecks of gold leaf onto bite-sized cakes using a metal pin. Although I laughed along, I felt a little lost and out of place in this subterranean matriarchy. My fingers were all thumbs. My long limbs flopped into tiny puddings. I couldn't keep up.

My skin itched, I had gold leaf in my fingernails, and I had started to wonder to myself who or what this was all for. Was all this hard, precise work really worth it, whatever 'it' was?

Taking tea with fancy cakes has been an elite pastime in England since the 1840s, but it was transformed by César Ritz during his management of the Savoy Hotel several decades later. In the middle of the nineteenth century, taking afternoon tea was a private and distinctly aristocratic affair. But at the end of the Victorian era, afternoon tea, or 'Le Five O'Clock' as it was called in France, was calculated by the famous hotelier to be a way to bring women into the Savoy's pioneering restaurant (still today the afternoon tea menu at the Savoy is decorated with watercolour paintings of roses, hinting at the same purpose).

Opening its doors in 1889, the Savoy was the first hotel in Britain to have electric lights, electric lifts (which, when the hotel first opened, guests would often ride for sheer enjoyment), hot and cold running water and bathrooms in every room. Lavish parties were held at the hotel, particularly after performances of the latest Gilbert and Sullivan opera, the events of which – who was there, what was eaten, who wore what – could be marvelled at by readers of *The Times*.

In the 1890s, seeing elite women eat in public was practically unheard of, and reports of any member of the upper classes eating out publicly would have been a novelty. Until Ritz appeared, members of London society dined in private houses or at their numerous members' clubs. Ritz saw it as his mission to change that, and the theatrical display of women formed an important part of his plan. At his hotel the Ritz Carlton he went to great expense to have the ground floors raised so that women could dramatically sweep out of the restaurant and into waiting cabs, descending the stairs in their fashionable dresses.

To Auguste Escoffier, the French chef charged with making Ritz's culinary enterprises a success, Le Five O'Clock with all that tea, cake and jam simply undermined dinner, 'the king of meals'.[14] Escoffier would probably have approved of all those gilded cakes, though. One of his innovations was putting a decadent twist on classic country dishes, for instance by adding truffles and butter to an otherwise simple meal of potatoes and artichokes, as the cookery writer Elizabeth David pointed out.[15]

Escoffier is often credited with refining the tradition that flowed from the opulent court of Versailles, but a great deal of nouvelle cuisine's codification – its modular organisation into 'mother sauces', for example – had already occurred by the time he wrote his famous *Guide culinaire*. Yet his influence is still everywhere evident in elite kitchens today. The orderly call and response of the head chef and the brigade: that was Escoffier. The division of the kitchen into sections: that was him too. He changed the name of the person whose job it was to read out the orders from 'barker' to 'announcer'. He banned, or attempted to ban, drinking at work and he outlawed swearing. Although some decades behind the rest of the economy, which had already seen self-directed artisans become slaves of the machine and the factory clock, Escoffier set out to professionalise the restaurant kitchen, making chefs part of his grand artistic and distinctly modern vision.

Several dishes at Restaurant X were Escoffier-inspired. I know that because there was a framed poster on the wall saying so. The poster was a blow-up of a menu the executive chef had prepared in honour of Escoffier, from which a handful of dishes are still prepared today. Escoffier claimed to have simplified the courtly tradition of French cookery – dispensing with elaborate inedible garnishes, for example – although a sauce accompanying one of his dishes served at Restaurant X nonetheless took four days to make and involved a vast number of expensive ingredients, from truffles to foie gras.

Escoffier and Ritz's real innovation was their ability to manifest the desires of a new elite that had taken shape in London from the middle of the nineteenth century. The chef and the hotelier were talented, creative workers, sure, but they also found themselves in the right place at the right time. Whatever the anxieties of the age (and there were many, from the growing power of trade unions to the threat of a global downturn), the final decade of the nineteenth century was a time in which the rising urban middle classes could be said to have truly risen – risen enough that they were able to enjoy the fruits of their investments and use their money to access the grand feasts that had once been the exclusive pastime of Britain's landed elites.[16]

Indeed, it was the self-reliant country gentleman who at times found himself turned away from Ritz's dining rooms, especially when he failed to adhere to the strict formal dress code and expected to be served meals while wearing his country tweed. Complaints about the door policy and objections to the distasteful opulence of the hotel's prosperous guests were published in local newspapers and serve as evidence of the social transition underway.[17]

It was during the belle époque that the economic and political power of Britain's landlords finally fell behind that of industry, retail and finance; between 1858 and1879, the majority of the British millionaires who died were landowners, yet by the end of the century they had been definitively overtaken by capitalists. Similarly, for most of the century, the nobility formed a majority in British governments, yet after 1895 they would never do so again.[18] The rise in elite taste for all things French reflected these trends.

The three or so decades before the First World War were characterised by a form of bourgeois festivity that the previous generation had been unable or unwilling to enjoy. The truffles, the caviar, the rivers of champagne, the mountains of butter, the professional discipline and the immense hard work in the kitchen – who it was all for back then was quite clear: the new urban elite.

This was a transformation and democratisation of upper-class consumption patterns, albeit along the lines of a strictly market-based democracy, one where money meant power and privilege. Opposition to French food had softened in a late-Victorian world in which Britain dominated its old European rival. And although for some the appeal might have been enhanced by the knowledge that their taste for French culinary fashions had long been shared by some of England's aristocratic cosmopolitans, in the belle époque such food now carried a distinctly urban note. Whereas the country cooking whose great age was in the eighteenth century had reflected the patriotism of the Georgian middling ranks, it was fine French food that became a means by which the late Victorian elite could express its capacity for opulence. On top of this change in power, the country tradition would be all but buried as a result of the two world wars that followed (as was also the case for beer-yeasted bread).

For evidence of this history you can search the number of restaurants at the high end of the dining scene that today serve food belonging to the courtly French tradition, as represented by Escoffier, and compare this number to the places serving the kind of food that was proudly eaten by most of the English elite in the eighteenth century. I can count on one hand the number of restaurants in London that belong in the latter camp (Rules in Covent Garden is perhaps the best example), while French-style restaurants are not only more numerous but also seem to draw far greater admiration on the part of chefs, critics and passionate eaters with sizeable budgets.

And why would this not be the case, when the very point of English country cooking was to oppose food's refinement? Leaving aside the effects of industry and war on the raw materials of what was once simple, patriotic food, one might ask why any restaurant working in a competitive economy would opt today for plain old English fare when the French courtly tradition has artful eating and conspicuous consumption at its core.

That is not to say that the country tradition has been eliminated entirely. The Victorian Mrs Beaton continued to produce cookbooks full of such dishes, although these were largely for the lower-middle ranks. Important remnants of the country cooking trend survive, transformed by the Victorian era and appearing now, for example, in the well-loved Sunday lunch of roast beef and Yorkshire pudding. Yet they are just that, remnants, since there is a vastness to the number of dishes – from pigeon pie to black cap pudding – that are far less familiar to most people today than soufflé and beef bourguignon. As the new Victorian elites pulled away towards France and the landed gentry in England lost its relevance, the plainness of eighteenth-century English dishes was passed on to the lower orders, which explains why meals like steak and kidney pudding now have a plebian, mostly northern vibe.

Posh

All of this history is reflected in the way English people use the word 'posh', especially when we talk about food. It is widely believed that this word was an acronym for 'port outward, starboard home', which was the most expensive ticket that one could buy when sailing to India. Being port side when leaving Britain and starboard side when returning kept one's cabin out of the sun, or so the story goes. Unfortunately there's no evidence that this is true: the oldest written account of the word 'posh' actually comes from a transcript of a court session held at the Old Bailey in 1830, and here the word has to do with money. 'He had not got the posh yet,' a defendant tells the judge.[19] Scholars speculate that 'posh' may originally have been Romany in origin, where the word means half, as in half a crown.

Now jump ahead to evidence from 1914, where we find the word 'posh' referring to a 'cavalryman, far more than the infantryman, [who] makes a point of wearing "posh" clothing on every possible occasion'. The author of this passage explains that 'posh' is 'a term used to designate superior clothing, or articles of attire other than those issued by and strictly conforming to the regulations'.[20]

Indeed, we find that the word 'posh' was often used to describe dandies, that new breed of nineteenth-century men who were concerned (or, we might say, overly concerned) with their appearance.[21] Urban men like Oscar Wilde, for example, who was a regular at the hotels of César Ritz and admired the elegance of Escoffier's culinary compositions, and who in his novel *The Picture of Dorian Gray* captured a world of elite decadence – one in which traditional morality was being eroded by the vanities of the modern age.

The word 'posh' can be seen as a critique of this new form of urban, moneyed culture, this new market-based relation wherein power is no longer tied to land or titles but only to cash. The critique becomes particularly acute when the cash in question is used to opulent effect. Posh, as a result, is not the roast dinner with two veg and gravy, which is to say that it is not the roast beef of old England (no matter how expensive roast beef may in fact be). Posh is the delicately poached fish with white wine and butter sauce, neatly presented on a warm plate and finished with finely cut chives and paper-thin shavings of truffle.

The word 'posh' carries an anti-French, anti-effeminate, anti-refinement lineage; it reflects a world not quite at peace with a new bourgeois age of modern, urban tastes. It is a throwback to an England of beer-swilling, beef-eating John Bulls. 'Posh' is the anti-artful cry of nostalgic English nationalism, a cry that echoes into the present. It is an expression of a deep sense, grounded in the history I have been describing, that we are a nation that eats to live, not the other way around. Good food – 'posh food' – is thought to be a privilege, not a right, in England, and as such the desire for it should be regarded with suspicion.

Service please!

Saturday was my last day at Restaurant X and we were fully booked. There was an issue with the fish delivery. There were VIPs expected. The ice machine had suddenly stopped working. That morning, the entire brigade seemed on edge. The radio was turned off in the pastry kitchen. I tried to be helpful, chopping vegetables and picking herbs, but also generally keeping out of the way.

Lunch service passed without much drama. A large delivery of ice arrived just as the final tables were receiving their mains, and a senior chef raged when he saw a puddle emerge under the delivery trolly.

In between dinner and lunch, the chefs cleaned down, reset their stations and furiously got to work. At 5:30 p.m., when the cleaning routine marking the last half hour before service began, the chefs formed a line outside the laundry room to collect fresh aprons and then danced around the porters pushing their great scrubbing machine as the chefs set up their sections. Around 6:15 it started.

The ticket machine begins its electronic scratching, but instead of one ticket, it spits out three. A senior sous-chef calls them out: 'Right, listen up. Two covers, two tasting. Three covers, three tasting with one duck medium well. Got that? Harry?' Harry, who is cooking the duck, doesn't appear to be listening. He looks up. The sous repeats: 'Five tasting, one duck medium well. New order, two covers à la carte. We're going two crab, one beef Wellington, one pigeon.'

The brigade: 'Oui!'

One of the boys on larder, a young man called Umar, has a tendency to shout his responses so that his voice bounces off the tiled corner we're working in, ringing in my ears. When at the start of the week he asked me why I came here I told him it was to see what a busy service at a restaurant like this one looks like. And so, finally, here we are.

Plates leave the kitchen on silver trays. Dirty crockery comes back in exchange. More orders are scratched out. I stop mentally noting the dishes we need to make on my section and instead work according to the plates I see in front of me. When Umar begins plating scallops I attend to each one with a sufficient quantity of fennel pollen. When he arranges the fresh langoustines, I fill up the correct number of pots with an orange sauce. I slide small domes of caviar onto the circular piles of picked crab and I add quenelles of chutney to the ballotines of foie gras. At a certain point, as the service reaches its peak, I begin recording the audio on my phone.

'Check on. Four covers. À la carte. We're going one crab, two foie gras, one brioche. Then two turbot, one duck, medium, one hake.'

'Oui!'

'Have you got the soufflé in? That needs to be in right now, Liz!'

'Two lamb coming on the pass.'

The oven: ring-ring, ring-ring.

The ticket machine: buzz, scrape-scrape-scrape. 'Check on. Two covers. À la carte. One dairy free. Both crab to start. Wellington. Langoustine as a main course. Dairy free on the langoustine.'

'Oui!'

The recording picks up the constant high-pitched suck of the extractors, the sizzle of skin meeting hot oil. Pans are being placed down on hobs, plates are being lined up on metal surfaces. Chefs on the hot sections all have rows of timers and one or other seems to be beep-beeping every minute.

The ticket machine buzzes and scrapes: 'Mains away, that's two turbot. How long please?'

'Two minutes.'

'Two minutes I want two turbot and two pommes soufflés.'

'Oui!'

'Service, please.'

The ticket machine makes a terrifyingly long scraping sound.

'Check on, listen up, six covers, à la carte.' Umar, whose chin is within kissing distance of mine as we operate with tweezers on a plate of beetroot, moans. 'We're going two crumpet, two artichoke, one langoustine, one crab. To follow, one sole, one turbot, three lamb, one lamb medium-well, one Wellington. We've got a sesame allergy on this table.'

'Oui!'

'Chris!' The sous-chef reading the orders calls over to the pastry team: 'Sesame allergy!'

'Seen it, yeah, OK.'

'Service please!'

'This is all green sorrel but it needs a mix.' Umar is addressing me now. 'Find some red sorrel and replace it on the plate, OK?'

'Umar, how long on three crab, one liver?'

Umar, booming in return, 'One minute, chef.'

'You said one minute three minutes ago!'

The phone recording catches a snippet of a conversation between a pair of waiters, primed at my shoulder with trays: 'I only love two things, sleep and money,' one of them says.

'I've got four lamb in front of me but I need some sauce. Right now, Harry. Harry. Sauce. Now!'

Beep-beep-beep-beep. The oven: ring-ring-ring.

'Mains away, two turbot. Umar, how fucking long?!'

'Service, please!'

At 11 p.m. the scraping of the ticket machine was solely confined to the pastry section. Those of us on larder had already cleaned down. The chefs on mains had started to do the same, and so I rolled up my knives and made moves to go home. Umar looked exhausted. He took off his paper hat, threw it in a bin meant for food waste and gave me a look that said, 'Well, now you know.'

I shook his hand when I said goodbye, leaving him to complete the ordering and think about tomorrow. Umar is not the kind of chef you will ever see amassing likes on Instagram, but he is the only chef I have ever seen who can cleanly pick a crab, without any mess or broken shell, in less than a minute. The boy could cook.

As I got changed in the locker room I came upon a young Eastern European waiter sat on a bench almost in tears. Alongside him was a colleague attempting to calm him down with a sandwich from the canteen. I headed home, planning to eat something, go to bed and sleep in. The kitchen brigade had less than nine hours to go until a new working day began. Thinking of this, I left wondering again what it was all for.

Dinner

On Sunday I woke up late and shaved for the final time before going to Restaurant X for dinner. The fact that we can eat a meal at a restaurant on a Sunday is a privilege that we happen to owe to César Ritz, who successfully campaigned to change licensing laws so that public dining would be permissible at the Savoy on what had traditionally been a day of rest and prayer.

I put on my only suit, complete with a borrowed tie, and arrived at the restaurant at 7 p.m., this time entering through a front door held open for me by a smartly dressed waiter whom I recognised as the man I had seen almost crying the night before.

Inside, I took my first glance at the grand dining room, the always-out-of-reach place where everything I had been making this past week had been served. There was the polished marble, the details in gold leaf, the light a shade of peach and the thick, thick, thick carpets.

I was shown to my table by a waiter as another pulled back my chair. Lifting my smart woollen trousers slightly, I sat down. The chair was soft, the tablecloth was a rich cotton. I ordered the seven-course tasting menu, the wine pairing (a different glass of wine with each course) and a bottle of fizzy water, the price of the latter, assuming it had one, being left unclear. While I waited, I adopted a pose I had learnt in the kitchen downstairs and placed my arms before me, one hand on top of the other.

The first things to arrive were the petits fours: two small parcels, one nail-gloss red, the other white and lime green. I popped the red one into my mouth. This was one of the few times in my life that I have dined alone, and so I focused intensely on what was happening on my tongue, sensing the richness of duck liver, the crispness and sweetness of the ginger cracker and the tart blot of cherry jam.

Soon after arrived a tartlet of freshly picked crab with caviar and the house-made fluffy white sourdough served with a pat of salted butter. While these were being laid before me, the sommelier poured my first glass of wine. This, he explained, was a Riesling from Germany, and could I taste the flinty minerality of the soil? I could! The wine tasted of sharp, crisp green apples. These grapes were grown on some rare south-facing slopes, the waiter added, mentioning something else about its balanced sweetness and acidity as I nodded along and the candle on my table gently flickered.

By the time Escoffier had cemented the tradition of fine dining in England that I was now enjoying, British food had been decapitated from above while it was being hollowed out from below: elite French cuisine had pushed aside the taste for country cooking, while the combination of urbanisation, empire, industry and war inhibited its rural return.

To modern Britons living through the belle époque, the renaissance in French fashion was not perceived in terms of a loss of national culture. One view of the elite embrace of French food in late Victorian England is to see it as an acceptance of the limits of Britain's power: while Britannia might rule the waves, culture, from music to food, could be the domain of others.[22] Yet the exact opposite was more likely the case, since to accept the cultural exports of what had once been England's greatest rival was to be deeply at ease with Britain's global power. Just as imperialism in Britain assumed that the curry invented in India could be 'ours', to some extent the same eclectic attitude was being applied by English elites to food that came from France.

Protests against French 'kickshaws' receded after the Battle of Waterloo brought centuries of conflict between Britain and its neighbour to a close; by 1904 and the Entente Cordiale between the two nations, the contrast that had once given English food its vitality hardly made sense. To drink champagne and eat Escoffier was à la mode. It was British. And most important of all, it was a form of cookery that the new urban elites could embrace.

With the arrival of the next course my focus shifted back to the meal and to the new wine before me, which, according to my notes, was a white that came from Burgundy and had the distinct taste of vanilla. With each new glass poured, the waiter offered a backstory of a timeless craft being perfected by artisans in some idyllic valley.

On the table behind me an older couple were debating where to spend the following weekend. Would it be their country retreat, which I gathered was somewhere near Norfolk and provided access to a private boat, or should they stay put in Richmond. There were the grandchildren to consider, and a daughter returning home from a trip to Dubai. In front of me were two women from China who were also being treated to the seven-course menu but who as far as I can tell touched almost none of it, and yet nonetheless gave a broadcast of each course for their followers online. At a respectable distance to my left were sat a father and son. It was the son's birthday, and the father used the occasion to give him an expensive-looking watch.

Another course appeared: lobster, poached in an aromatic butter and served with a light, herby, foamy sauce that brought together the taste of the sea with the creamy freshness of pasture. As it was served, I observed the diners around me and thought about the small encampment of homeless people that I had passed on my way to the restaurant.

Are we living in a new belle époque, where a market in luxury goods is booming alongside food banks and poverty? Who is this all for? Is eating at Restaurant X simply a form of conspicuous consumption? Is luxury simply a matter of price? Is it the case that chefs, especially high-end ones, are simply slaves to posh, upper-class tastes? Perhaps we suffer from a version of Stockholm syndrome, whereby we learn to love our affluent captors. We love them so much that we'll break our backs for them, we'll accept terrifying treatment from our peers and give over our one shot at life to spend most of it tweezering thin strips of apple in a windowless basement. Worst of all, we'll hand over our wages to our captors in order to eat the expensive food they make us produce and then praise them for the experience.

For the next act came a wobbly savoury custard served with a dark and glossy sauce and a shaving of the truffles that I had cleaned earlier that week. And now to red wines. The first, from Italy, was matured without oak, the second, French and served with the pigeon, with oak. Did I notice the difference, the waiter asked. I did! Oaked. Unoaked. I enjoyed them both. The pigeon was iron-y and the sauce deep, rich and spiked with pepper.

What if we saw chefs and their work in the same admiring way as sometimes we see artists and their art? As a child, Escoffier dreamed of being a sculptor. In his free time, at the start of his career, he carved intricate flowers out of wax.

Progressives have tended to view culture in two ways. There is Culture, with a capital C, that belongs to the elites in the form of painting, poetry, theatre, architecture, music, opera and sometimes fine food and drink. And then there is the culture of everyone else and of the everyday: pop culture, domestic culture, cultures of work, sport, and so on. Since the 1960s the left has promoted the idea of democratising the *meaning* of culture so as to include the field of human relations outside of that which had, up to then, been deemed worthy of serious attention – to include oral history alongside the study of kings and queens, for example. This was to see the world 'from the bottom up', from the perspective of the 'lower orders', whose nonetheless rich lives were left out of standard narratives. We have come a long way in that regard. Today you are more likely to find serious criticism of a popular rapper than a write-up of an opera performed at Glyndebourne.

But what of democratising Culture with a capital C? Here too we find that access to these once-elite domains has been broadened in Britain, be that through state- and corporate-sponsored art galleries, theatres and concert halls, or via institutions like the Arts Council and the BBC, or, more recently, through the use of National Lottery funding. Food has generally fallen outside the remit of these programmes, however.

Why is it still so hard to accept that fine food is worthy of democratisation? When we follow the progressive logic and we shift the meaning of good taste to include what everyday people eat every day, in England we find ourselves confronted with the beige legacies of modernity and so at times end up celebrating sausage rolls. But surely there can be more to our eating habits than this?

Limiting our progress on this front is an idea that has its origins in the anti-French nationalism of the eighteenth century: that opulent food and connoisseurship – what today we often denounce as posh – are somehow suspect. We can savour a pork pie just as much as we might savour a good quality wine, yet to savour at all – at least publicly – cuts against the original intention of post-medieval English cuisine. To praise refinement in our food was in the eighteenth century un-English; connoisseurship, especially in the domains of eating and drinking was, and remains, something dismayingly foreign.

Like painters in the days before publicly funded arts, the best chefs today enjoy the patronage of the uber-rich. But is it so hard to imagine a world in which public bodies could sponsor fine food? Could this, what I had before me now, this immense skill, these exquisite ingredients, this artistry with grapes, soil and oak barrels, the profoundly material experience in which time slowed while I took account of my senses, could all this be democratised? What if money wasn't the only means by which you could gain entitlement to a meal such as this one? What if, as in other forms of high culture, we believed that everyone had a moral right to such an experience?

That few can likely imagine a world in which food receives public funding just as other forms of Culture do is testament to a persistent attitude in England that sees fine food – even more so than music, painting or literature – as posh.

By now it was safe to say I was drunk. Fortunately, the last of the main courses had been and gone and so I sat there in my padded seat as a man in a tuxedo flambéed my dessert while another waiter poured a sweet wine the colour of polished brass (I lost track of the details). Full and drunk, I devoured it still.

After sweet petits fours and a coffee, the bill was a sobering kick. Including the fizzy water (£9), the likewise ambiguously offered espresso (£9.50) and the 12.5 per cent service charge, the total came to £369.56. It is the most I have ever spent on a meal. There was to be no discount or special treatment in repayment for my week of anxious carrot-cubing toil.

This was a decadence that everyone in England is, in theory, equally free to obtain – working or not, powerful or meek, titled or commoner, well connected or lonely. It is available to all those, at least, who can don smart clothes and pay the high price. Such a liberty was the product of Escoffier's generation.

I handed the waiter my credit card, expressed my thanks to the sommelier and wobbled away to the Tube.

3

Whelks

England! 'twas where this promontory rears
Its rugged brow above the channel wave,
Parting the hostile nations, that thy fame,
Thy naval fame was tarnish'd ...

Charlotte Smith,
'Beachy Head', 1807

It's 2:30 a.m. by the time I arrive at Sovereign Harbour in Eastbourne. I finished my shift at the restaurant some four hours earlier, cleaning down my section, filling out my prep list and placing orders for the following day. When I got home, I boiled a couple of eggs, made a flask of coffee and headed out. The boat I'm spending the day on, named, appropriately enough, the *St George*, is due to leave at 3 a.m. But the harbour is empty. I place my bag on some pallets and loiter in the beam of a street lamp, eating the eggs. It's now late spring and the night air is salty and cool.

There is an intense smell that reminds me of the colourful flakes that I fed to my pet goldfish as a child, and I see on the ground my first whelks, the carnivorous sea snails that the crew of the *St George* hunts for in the English Channel. These ones are dead escapees, some of them crushed. Eventually, the boat's skipper, Scott Possnicker, arrives with Keir Spreckley, a muscular lad in his late twenties who joined Scott's crew after leaving a badly paid job in farming. Without much of an introduction, Keir has gone again. Scott explains they're a man down (a regular member of the crew was last seen spending his wages in one of Eastbourne's pubs) and Keir has gone to search for a replacement. In the boats in the harbour, I'm told, a crew of lads are sleeping in bunks and one of them has been chosen to join us.

'Where are they from?' I ask Scott, aware that some boats employ crew from the Philippines whose visas dictate notoriously bad conditions, low pay and a miserable existence.

'I dunno, but not local,' Scott replies.

Keir comes back alone, having struggled to find the stand-in. 'I dunno which one he is,' he says. 'They all look the same.' Now Scott hops over the side of the *St George* and heads off into the darkness to see if he can find the guy while I anxiously type out a few notes. Moments later Scott remerges with Sonny Brewitt, a slim young man with a build like a lightweight boxer. Hood up with the drawstring tied in a bow, a lit cigarette in his mouth, he mumbles hello in a broad Yorkshire accent. Sonny grew up in Hull.

On the boat, I discover that the smell I noticed on the harbour comes from a neat stack of plastic crates containing the rotting crab and frozen dogfish that whelk hunters use for bait. Sonny, Keir and I silently sway in the *St George*'s dimly lit wheelhouse as Scott sets the boat on its course into the Channel. Keir tells Sonny there are bunks below deck where they can sleep, and the two lads wobble away. I'm left with Scott, who is forty but looks much younger, almost boyish.

Sometime after 4:30 a.m. I begin worrying that I'll be sick, and I regret eating the boiled eggs. Not long after that I fall asleep on a bench. At about 6 a.m., work starts.

The common whelk – *Buccinum undatum* – is a creature that, however much I try, and however much I understand is important to our sea's ecosystems, I struggle to find endearing, or even edible. The carnivorous gastropod spends its ten to fifteen years of life shuffling around on the seabed hunting other crustaceans and eating carrion, which it does by expressing stomach acid through its mouth, like a fly. Whelks lay up to 2,700 eggs in one go, but only 1 per cent ever hatch because the first to do so eat their unborn siblings. Dried clumps of empty egg sacs are easy to find on the shoreline and, I'm told, have been used by fishermen in the past as sponges.

I'm not alone in not eating whelks. Almost no one in Britain does or does so regularly. And yet from 2013 to 2018, the number of vessels targeting sea snails in England doubled with the total catch rising from 4,000 tons to more than 30,000 in a fishery worth some £20 million each year (the figure has since plateaued). Cod, by contrast, is worth three times that amount to English fishermen, but not to fishers like Scott, as we'll see.

The market in East Asia for canned and frozen whelks explains why tens of small fishing boats, like the *St George*, spend the period extending from late spring into autumn hunting sea snails in what for over half a century has been one of the busiest shipping lanes on the planet. And yet this foreign demand for the seafood available and caught in British waters doesn't explain why England, one part of an island nation, consumes so little of it, and why the fish we eat in the largest quantities is almost all imported.

To tell the story of seafood and fishing in modern England is to tell a story about Britain's unprecedented maritime dominance and its subsequent decline. It is a story that tracks the rise of Britain as a mercantile empire, home to the most urbanised and industrialised people on the planet, followed by the rise of newly *national* powers (including Britain itself), which appeared in an era of American hegemony, leading us into our present globalised world.

Woven within this story is a dynamic of competition and advances in human technology which chase a declining natural stock of fish. As the sea shanties of fishermen often recall, fish is a resource given freely by the sea, while grain and land cost a farmer money.[1] Unlike the modern use of the land, however, the sea's supply of food is largely immune to 'improvement', meaning that its bounty can be finite.

Black gold

I was put in touch with Scott by a man named Graham Doswell, whom I met in Eastbourne about a month before setting sail on the *St George*. I'm waiting for Graham at the train station when he messages to say he's outside in a white pickup. This, as it turns out, is not the statement vehicle it is in London but a practical truck with room for a pallet of fish in the back. When I hop in, Graham, who is wearing a thickly woven brown woollen jumper, gives me a friendly greeting. He is seventy-one but he looks ten years younger (perhaps it's the sea air?).

He drives us up to the cliffs of Beachy Head, today blanketed by a thick grey mist that resembles a salty smog. Tourists, many of them appearing to be from East Asia, are drifting around looking a little disappointed apart from at the brief moments when they flash smiles for photos. 'I brought you here so you could see the view,' Graham apologises. But there are also big chunks of carrot cake to be had in a visitors café, over which he tells me about a long career spent at sea.

Fishing is a seasonal business, especially in small boats like Graham's. Not only is it dependent upon the weather and the tides, it also necessitates following various animals' life cycles and migratory patterns, if they have them (whelks do not). When Graham started fishing, in the late 1960s, in the winter he would take his open-decked wooden boat into the Channel to target cod, herring and sometimes mackerel using long lines with multiple hooks (called, literally, long lines). In the spring he caught codling – small cod – and trawled close to the ocean floor where flatfish like plaice and sole can be found. In summer, he might do some potting, meaning catching crabs and lobster in mesh traps. Then back to long-lining again. In this way Graham followed a proud family tradition of small-scale artisanal fishing that goes back three generations of Doswells.

When Graham was a young fisherman, cuttlefish often got caught in his nets. But like other fishers of the time, Graham had no use for them. The crew would untangle the fish from the trawls, or cut the nets to release them, and then unceremoniously throw the cuttle overboard, dead or alive, mostly dead. As the boat moved on it left a trail of cuttlefish floating upside down like flabby buoys on the sea's surface. 'It was a sin really,' Graham repents, with a mouth full of cake.

Then, in the early 1980s, a man named Duncan turned up at the harbours of the South East in a white van, offering fishers ten pence a kilo for cuttle. Graham had no idea where the fish were being taken, but he was happy to get money for nothing, as he saw it then. Within a few years Duncan was pushed aside by larger merchants who were offering better prices, and it suddenly became worthwhile to target cuttle intentionally.

Towards the end of the summer of 1986, Graham was on the phone to a friend who lived on Alderney, one of the Channel Islands. Graham's friend was a fisherman who caught lobsters off the coast of France. Catching up on news and gossip, Graham's friend reported that some of the French boats were targeting cuttlefish in pots, just like lobsters. 'I thought "that's funny",' Graham says, 'because sometimes we were working our pots, especially in certain areas, and you'd find one coming up with three, or four, or five cuttlefish in it. So I knew there was a bit of a potential.'

Graham gave it more thought. The following summer he sketched the outlines of a cuttlefish trap on a cupboard door in his garage (the rough drawing is still there) and built a prototype: a square box, made from a steel frame with panels of chicken wire, that had a tapering hole through which, it was hoped, the fish would be able to enter but not return. Inside, Graham placed a CD, the shiny underside of which he thought might attract a curious cuttle.

At this point, Graham and his crew were already targeting cuttle in the Channel using nets anchored to the seabed. On one trip, with the chalk cliffs of the Sussex coastline behind them, Graham threw his chicken wire trap into the sea along with the usual net and came back the following day to find out if it had worked. 'We went to haul it and we were all sort of laughing, going, "Oh, yeah, I wonder if we'll catch one." But we haul it up, and in there there was, I don't know, about five or six of them.' Graham and his crew put the result down to luck. They removed the fish, placing them in plastic crates, left the shiny CD in the trap and threw it back into the water. The next day when they hauled it again the trap had a dozen cuttlefish inside.

'The old brain started ticking,' Graham told me, leaning over the table slightly so that his jumper hung away from his broad chest. 'If you could times that by, you know, a hundred, you'd be laughing.' And so, he did. Over the winter of 1988–9, Graham got to work in his garage making a hundred chicken wire traps. He hid his project from other fishers in the area until, at the beginning of May, it was time to start taking them down to his boat. People asked Graham what he was up to and so he explained: 'Well, it's a cuttlefish trap.' None of the other fishers in Eastbourne's Sovereign Harbour thought that could work, and Graham did not try to change their minds. 'Yeah, it probably won't,' he told them.

But out on the salt water, Graham and his crew could not believe their luck. 'On our first day's hauling we giggled from start to finish. You just couldn't go wrong. There was so many cuttle there. There wasn't an inch of space left in the traps, they'd filled up.'

Landing back in Eastbourne each evening, covered in ink, it was as if Graham and his crew had found oil. The only limit to how much the boat could catch was the number and size of his traps. The next year Graham made 300 new traps, each twice the size of the previous ones. 'That year we made our money in about two and a half months. It was fantastic. It meant that we didn't need to care about what happened for the rest of the year, whether we had good catches or bad ones, because we'd already earned our keep.' Out on the English Channel, surrounded by plastic crates of spluttering cuttlefish, their faces smeared with ink, Graham and his crew kept laughing.

As the season went on, friends demanded to know what Graham was up to, why he was happier and richer. One of Graham's friends begged him to reveal how the traps – which by now, the early 1990s, he was producing with nylon netting rather than wire – were made. Despite protests from his crew, he gave in. It was not too bad at first. Graham's friend was down the road in Hastings, and the fishery was easily big enough to support two crews fishing with pots. But Graham's friend must have been even less tight-lipped, since other boats in Hastings soon joined in. Graham knew the secret was well and truly out when cuttlefish-trapping featured on an episode of *River Cottage*, the popular TV show where the Eton-educated Hugh Fearnley-Whittingstall goes to live in a smallholding idyll. In fact, the traps that Graham had helped his friend construct in Hastings were the very same ones that appeared on an episode of the programme, after Graham's friend had sold his boat, gear and all, to a fisherman in Dorset.

'So instead of there being 300 pots in the water, there were thousands,' Graham said. Fishermen soon found themselves attempting to shoot their long daisy-chained lines of traps in the same spots on an already crowded shipping lane. People working the fishery at this time tell stories of tangled traps and crews hauling pots that belonged to other boats, and then dumping their competitors' gear out at sea.

Despite the increase in landings, the value of cuttlefish was going up, from around 20p per kilo in the early 1990s to £1.50 by 2009, reaching a peak of almost £4 a kilo in 2018. Over the same period, annual landings of cuttlefish soared, from less than 500 tons to over 7,000. In 2018, cuttlefish was the fifth most valuable fishery in England.

By the turn of the millennium, around the same time that Fearnley-Whittingstall was encouraging us to eat the mysterious cephalopod, the beam trawlers of England's South West had started targeting them as well. Beam trawlers, so called because of the beam that sticks off the side of the boat to which the gear is fixed by ropes, drag a long, weighted, tapering net that scrapes across the seabed.

Putting to one side the negative impacts of churning up the ocean floor, the problem with this method of targeting cuttlefish was it caught them before they had had a chance to migrate up the Channel to reproduce, which they do only once in their two-year lifespan. As the amount of cuttle caught in the South West shot up – 94 per cent of all the cuttlefish landed in England today is from beam trawlers – the amount available to catch in traps during the spawning season in the shallower waters of the eastern Channel fell. For Graham, as for other fishers on the Sussex coast, cuttlefishing went from boom to bust in little more than a decade. The rush for black gold came to a sudden stop.

From salted fish to fried

Unlike the whelk, the cuttlefish is a species that I find both interesting *and* delicious. The one that appeared in Graham's traps is called the common or European cuttlefish, although its name sounds suitably more impressive in Latin: *Sepia officinalis*. The species boasts a range of characteristics, some of which are hard for humans to observe. They shimmer and hover in the water, changing colour, pattern and texture in order to camouflage, communicate and reflect their complex moods. They have three hearts and mysterious W-shaped eyes. Then there's the cuttle's ink, which it ejects like a cloud of black smoke – to potential predators it looks like the silhouette of a cuttle – behind which it jets itself away.

My preferred method for cooking cuttle is to chop the cleaned flesh into thumb-sized pieces and stew it, low and slow, in passata with a little wine and water, along with small cubes of potato, garlic and whatever aromatics you like (lemon rind and hard herbs work well, as does some paprika and olives). Cooked like this, for at least an hour, the dish benefits from a good glug of olive oil, maybe some parsley and a little more garlic, and some good bread to serve. I also adore the meat when it is baked within a black and glossy risotto made with the cuttlefish's ink.

More traditionally English recipes for cooking cuttlefish are hard to find, although there are a handful that go back to the sixteenth century. In *The Good Huswifes Jewell*, published in 1585, Thomas Dawson offers instructions on how to 'stewe Calamarye' (there isn't always a distinction between squid and cuttle in English cookbooks, even now). While in her *Book of Household Management* the Victorian Mrs Beeton offers readers a recipe for 'Calamars à la Française'. Indeed, despite the fact that cuttlefish thrive in the salt water around these isles, it is in France, Spain, Italy, Portugal and Greece that we find the greatest number of recipes. Some dishes, like Portugal's 'choco frito' – not chocolate but fried cuttlefish – were the inventions of fishing communities that have become part of a national tradition. Food historians, cooks and celebrity chefs have all at times wondered why there is no English equivalent to such dishes.

If it's true that we don't eat much fish, then the British are not alone in this. Many countries, even coastal ones like ours, prefer terrestrial proteins. The food historian Rachel Laudan offers several plausible reasons why: fish are difficult to eat, difficult to preserve, dangerous to acquire and not available all year round. They are sometimes seen as a low-status food and, essentially, as animals without arms and legs that can breathe underwater, we tend to find fish a bit weird.[2] To describe something as 'beefy', Laudan points out, tends to imply a virtue, but to call something 'fishy' suggests that it isn't quite right.

In French, Spanish, German and Italian, bulls and oxen can figuratively denote something powerful and large, as in 'as strong as an ox'.[3] But it's only in English that the meat – beef – as well as the beast is implied to be a source of strength. The English language has a peculiar, playful capacity to morph nouns into adjectives along the lines of 'beefy' and 'fishy', although it is still curious to note that there appears to be no other language in which the smell of fish is associated with suspicion. (In several East Asian languages, I'm told, the smell of fish can symbolise something indecently sexual.)

It is tempting to view this peculiar connection between suspicion and fish as a legacy of English anti-Catholicism, based upon the fact that Catholics maintained the Christian tradition of eating fish on fast days even as Protestants and non-believers gave it up. However, evidence of the metaphor only appears in the first half of the nineteenth century – that is, around the point at which Catholics were being officially accepted into public life in England.

Salted fish, above all herring (which when also smoked is known as red herring), and to a lesser extent the more expensive and harder to prepare salted cod, formed an important part of English diets for several hundred years, gradually falling out of fashion in the eighteenth century. Efforts were made by monarchs to uphold the religious consumption of such fish, although largely for the secular purpose of protecting the domestic fishing fleet (which in turn helped supply the manpower of an expanding English navy).

Under Elizabeth I, three fast days were enforced in each week, non-observance of which was punishable by a fine or imprisonment. And in 1619 James I, the first unified king of both England and Scotland, ordered stricter observance of 'fish days' in Lent, deploying magistrates to ensure that inns and taverns complied and that butchers shut up shop for the period. Oliver Cromwell paid little attention to fast days, however, and the restored monarch Charles II was the last to enforce them.

In the time of Elizabeth and the Stuart monarchs, salted herrings are found in the purchasing records of almshouses, hospitals and England's navy. Yet by the eighteenth century, the same sources show that fish consumption had declined in the navy, where too much salted fish was thought to cause scurvy, and that it had all but disappeared elsewhere. Instead we find a distinct preference for flesh with hooves and fur.

Part of the trouble was the quality of salt in England, which, combined with the wet air and a reckless approach to preparation (there are reports that the English preferred using their thumbs for gutting fish, rather than knives), produced a poor-quality product – one that most Europeans rejected when it was exported, and that hence found its way onto naval boats and slave plantations, as well as the tables of the domestic poor.

As the English diet gradually became secular so it became terrestrial, and salted herring – a totem of religious fasting – maintained only the smallest foothold.

If we revisit the eighteenth-century cookbooks that in the previous chapter I said reflected England's first native example of a modern national cuisine – the books by Eliza Smith, Hannah Glasse, Elizabeth Moxon and Elizabeth Raffald – we find fish of any kind to be a minor feature.

There is a little of the pike and carp that were favourites of the medieval elites, and which, I suspect, were eaten mainly to show off one's fish pond. Then there are a few preparations for turbot, lobsters, cod and haddock. There are recipes for eels and oysters, which were widely popular in London, where they could be lifted from the Thames (although many found eel, another wonderfully mysterious fish, far too weird to eat). Pollution and overconsumption saw the quantities of these latter species collapse, with oysters and lobsters going from being a popular food to a preserve of the very rich in the course of the 1860s – just in time for Escoffier's entry into the capital, in fact.

The central problem with seafood is that it does not travel well unless it is preserved using salt. Unlike earthbound proteins, fish contain microbes and enzymes that can thrive in cold temperatures, meaning that even when we put them in the fridge they continue to do the work of decaying the body. It takes a very low temperature to slow this process down. Even at optimal conditions, white fish only last around eight days from the point of catch. Oily fish, such as mackerel and herring, even fewer.

For the very rich in pre-refrigeration England, cool cellars, wet larders and tanks were available. For those inland, fresh fish was transported on packhorses at great expense, either from the coasts or from London's Billingsgate, a market whose size ensured that it sucked in a large proportion of the catches made in English waters.

In pre-industrial coastal communities, scarcity could occasionally be interrupted by glut. Pilchards – an English term for sardines – were a favourite in Cornwall, where they acquired the nickname 'fair maids', apparently owing to the species' sensitivity to noise, and where they were baked into stargazy pies.[4] 'When the fish came,' the historian Diane Purkiss writes, 'they were like a great red stain spreading over the sea – fish by the millions.'[5] Entire communities were put to work preparing the pilchard catch for salting and export as villages were engulfed by the smell. In Whitby, the hunting of whales and the rendering of their blubber likewise produced a stench that hung over the town, while whalebone was used for scrimshaw and incorporated into buildings' walls, with fishermen's sheds being constructed out of whale ribs and jaws.

But it was in London, thanks to Billingsgate, that we see fish being served as a popular street food, battered and fried in oil in what was known at the time to be the 'Jewish fashion'. We hear of 'fried-fish warehouses' in *Oliver Twist*, written by Dickens in the late 1830s, and reports of Alexis Soyer, chef at the Reform, travelling to London's slums to buy himself the snack.[6]

It is at this moment too that we first come across the term 'fishy' being used to mean 'suspicious'. The idiom probably reflects the way in which some vendors acquired the least fresh fish on offer at Billingsgate for the lowest price. At this point, frying flatfish such as plaice was more common than cooking cod, and this new method of serving fish allowed any rankness of the product to be masked by a jacket of batter. Was it fresh, hungry consumers might wonder as a street vendor offered them the meal served cold, or was it fishy?

It was from the 1840s onwards that fresh and lightly cured fish became available in other urban areas of England, thanks to an expanding rail network and, from the 1870s, the industrial production of ice. By the middle of the nineteenth century, herring makes a reappearance in the form of kippers – split herring, lightly salted and smoked – and bloaters: ungutted and whole herring salted and smoked, which apparently have a faint taste of game. Victorian workers used the fish much like bacon, as a strong-tasting protein that could add a little 'relish' to an otherwise plain meal of bread or boiled potatoes.

Yet it was the taste for fried fish that spread most extensively across the iron rails of a newly connected nation. By 1860, battered and fried fish, now mostly married to chipped potatoes (whose origins are assumed to be from Belgium), became an established part of life in working-class areas of Britain. By 1888, estimates suggest that some 10,000 chippies were in existence, rising to 25,000 by the outbreak of the First World War, when 500 fried fish and chip shops existed in Oldham alone. By 1936, the great vats of oil that provided warm, comforting meals to Britain's working class were swallowing up more than half of all the white fish caught by British boats (prior to that, most fish was exported), as well as a similar fraction of all the potatoes grown in British soil. At this inter-war peak, an army of fish friers served 30 million meals to hungry Britons each week.[7]

Fish consumption continued to rise during the Second World War, when it fell outside of rationing, although the reputation of any fish that wasn't entombed in batter and bathed in hot fat was, again, somewhat 'fishy'. When wrapped up in newspaper and gently steaming in a pile of hot chips, fried fish was a comforting boost. But in other forms fish was seen by many as a temporary and unfortunate stand-in, forced upon the population by the necessities of war.

While fish and chips remained popular after rationing ended, overall demand for seafood began to fall. Post-war affluence, such as it was, came with a greater desire for red meat, poultry, eggs, dairy and, of course, soft white bread. Yet as workers with a greater capacity for leisure took to seaside resorts like Blackpool and Brighton, so there they expected to find their beloved fish and chips.

When the chippie first appeared in urban slums, England's middle and upper classes were likely to complain (often with good reason) about the smell and poor hygiene standards. From the same sources came complaints that workers and the poor spent too much money on what was seen as an under-nourishing food (prompting George Orwell to defend the desire for something cheap and tasty in a well-known riposte).[8] Yet the dish had become a great unifier during the Second World War, when MPs in Parliament called for the state to ensure that it reached those relocated from urban areas, and trawlermen – over 1,000 of whom lost their lives fishing, mine-sweeping and (with a great deal of symbolic potency) transporting home British troops left stranded in Dunkirk – were hailed as national heroes. So much so that in the 1951 Festival of Britain, the takeaway meal was celebrated as a national treasure.

It was during this era that the symbolism of fish and chips, like Britain itself, became fully national. As the UK lost its Empire, as new Indian and Chinese restaurants started to appear in British cities, and as nations globally sought to embed themselves within the prevailing current of nationalism, fish and chips was refitted in a strip of red, white and blue. No longer solely the looked-down-upon food of the urban poor, it is a testament to the numerical and cultural strength of Britain's working class that, by 1960, when one thought of British food one no longer thought of roast beef but, instead, of fish and chips.

A meal that almost no one makes at home, but almost everyone at that time desired and, most importantly, could afford. Fish and chips was, for a spell, among Britain's first truly national meals.

From closed seas to free seas

Most narratives on our relationship to eating fish tend to emphasise the role of urbanisation in creating demand for cheap takeaway meals – particularly where cramped terrace housing afforded limited scope for cooking – along with the steam power that drove both trains and trawlers. Historians sometimes also take account of the industrial manufacture of ice, the engineering of which preceded the science of refrigeration much as the development of steam engines preceded the knowledge of thermodynamics. Without these developments, fresh fish, fried or otherwise, would have remained the preserve of a fortunate few.

Yet to leave things here is to miss the definitive role played by the once-vast power of the British Empire in shaping not only a persistent English taste in fish but also aspects of working-class culture more generally. It is to miss the rise and fall of a Pax Britannica that, along with our taste for fish and chips, has left a lasting perception of Britain as an independent coastal state with a right to a borderless and increasingly scarce supply of seafood.

It was the Dutch who, before the British, saw themselves as possessing a divine dominion over all the fish of the sea. Their expertise in sailing and salting, together with their ready deployment of capital enabled by a pioneering use of the joint-stock company, helped give rise to the world's first ever factory ships. From the middle of the sixteenth century, these large boats, known as herring busses, on which fish could be caught, gutted, salted and barrelled all at once, dominated the once-rich waters of the North Sea.

A fleet of some 2,000 such boats was fishing off the coast of Britain around 1620, when the industry supported the livelihoods of some 450,000 people in Holland.[9] It is no wonder that the kings of England and Scotland had long been upset by the extraction of all this wealth.

In the reign of James I, and in a context of competitive European naval powers, the Dutch commissioned the 'father of international law' Hugo Grotius to write a legal treatise as part of their case against the Portuguese monopoly on trade with China.[10] Grotius's complete work, *De Jure Praedae* or *Commentary on the Law on Prize and Booty*, remained unpublished until the nineteenth century. However, in 1609, one chapter appeared anonymously as *Mare Liberum* or *The Free Sea*. This tract conveniently argued that everyone had 'the right of navigation and the liberty of traffic'.

In England, Grotius's treaty was seen by the court of James I as a justification for the Dutch herring busses. In response appeared a 'Proclamation Touching Fishing', which, in 1609, asserted England's sovereignty over its local waters. In 1617 James I employed the highly praised legal scholar John Selden to further his case. While Grotius had argued that 'all men are permitted to sail in the sea though leave be obtained of no prince', Seldon claimed that 'the Sea, by the Law of Nature or Nations is not common to all men, but capable of private Dominion'. Seldon's conception of England's maritime territory was vast, stretching as far south as the Bay of Biscay, and encompassed the North Sea plus the entire Northern Atlantic. Seldon's rebuttal was left unpublished until 1635 (when it was written the English feared offending the king of Denmark, whose fishermen also frequented British waters), by which point, under Charles I, England was determined to build its own naval force capable of rivalling those of the Dutch, French, Portuguese and Spanish.

After false starts, in 1653, during England's brief republican interlude, Dutch ships left British waters and for the rest of the century their naval and fishing fleet was bogged down by wars with Spain. In 1651 Parliament issued the Navigation Acts, an important marker on the way to Pax Britannica that effectively made England's trading networks a closed shop, requiring all goods entering or leaving English territories to do so on English boats.[11]

By the 1730s England had emerged as Great Britain, a naval superpower with extensive global colonies and a foreign policy that centred on the maintenance of vast networks of trade over which it had exclusive control. After the Battle of Waterloo concluded the Second Hundred Years' War with France, Britain was left to rule the waves without any major rival for a century. Britain now mobilised the concept of free trade and Grotius's idea of the freedom of the seas, an ideal that concealed the fact that this was, in effect, the freedom of the victor, who could act as it wished within its global Empire.

With this imperial supremacy was combined Britain's urbanisation and its Industrial Revolution, which gave rise to demand for fish as well as the trains that brought it into the cities and the steam trawlers that made up Britain's distant water fleet. These factors enabled Billingsgate to become, by the mid-Victorian era, the largest market of its kind in the world – home to a unique working-class culture, language and set of rituals. In the fishing ports of Grimsby and Hull, then also the largest in the world, there likewise developed a life centred on seasonal cycles of hard work followed by bouts of leisure. The maritime community on the banks of the Humber included merchant boats' crews as well as fishers; it was interlaced by solidarity, religion, occasional heavy drinking, and heroic tales that recalled storms, foreign lands and bountiful catches of cod.

This was the social infrastructure that gave the world fish and chips – a structure that by the mid-1970s had gone.

Cod wars

In the nineteenth century, a nation's territorial waters were considered by the British to extend just three miles – judged to be the distance that could be covered by a cannonball fired from the shore. The rest was meant to be the free sea. But even this small national boundary failed to stop British vessels exploiting fisheries in the bays and fjords of Iceland, as well as other abundant fisheries in the North Sea around that small and then-impoverished country. Yet gradually, over almost a hundred years, the small Nordic island fought back.

1894 was the first time Iceland passed its own laws regarding foreign fishing in its territorial waters, failing to consult Denmark (which traditionally oversaw such matters for the island) before doing so. When British trawlers objected, some crews were arrested, fined, or had their nets confiscated by the emerging nation state. To quell the potential for a conflict over cod, the British government sought an agreement, not with Iceland but with the Danes, who were keen to export butter and bacon to the vast British market. Resentment towards this deal helped to spur on calls for Icelandic independence (which the island eventually gained in 1945).

As the twentieth century began, and as stocks of cod in the North Sea became depleted, Britain's reliance on its distant water fleet increased. The amount of fish caught in the sea around Iceland between 1934 and 1937 was more than double that landed from the North Sea closer to our shores, and it was some twenty-seven times the total netted in the English Channel. After the Second World War, as diesel engines replaced coal and steam, and on-board freezers allowed for even larger ships and longer outings, Britain's exploitation of the stocks off Iceland intensified, and the size of the fishery again declined.[12]

From 1952 to 1973, Britain and Iceland engaged in four conflicts over what the newly independent state saw as its exclusive right to fish in the sea close to its shore, which taken together are known as the Cod Wars. Each dispute had a similar pattern. Iceland, whose economy depended on fish, would begin by extending its territorial waters: from three miles to four, four miles to twelve, twelve to fifty and eventually 200 miles out to sea. Each time British trawlers, the UK government and the Royal Navy refused to accept the change. Yet, on every occasion, the small, newly independent state won.

The Cod Wars, remarkably, only claimed one man's life, and mainly consisted of games of cat and mouse between the Icelandic coastguard and British trawlers with, at times and at great cost, support from the British navy. The use of live ammunition was rare, but ramming, net cutting and the wielding of improvised weapons were common. British crews disguised their ships and pelted the Icelandic coastguard with salted cod, potatoes and coal. When the latter persistently harassed the former over the radio, trawler captains were known to drown out the noise by blasting 'Rule Britannia' in return.

The conclusion to each episode in the Cod Wars was ultimately underpinned by an overriding greater concern with maintaining the global order that had emerged as Britain's Empire crumbled after the Second World War. Iceland was a founding member of NATO and had accepted an American military base on the island that, owing to its position in the Atlantic, was considered by American and British generals alike to be invaluable. When Iceland extended its territorial waters and Britain initially resisted, Icelandic voters – unified in their opposition to Britain – would threaten to leave NATO and kick out the American military. In each episode of this war, Britain was consequently convinced to give in by its now far more powerful ally, the USA.

Alongside these battles over cod, a new legal framework was also taking shape – again instigated by America, when, in 1945, President Truman extended US territorial waters to 200 miles (this was partly with a view to extracting oil from the seafloor, but also to securing exclusive US access to fish). The coastal states of Latin American soon followed suit as, eventually, the UN instigated a process that helped to justify the thrust of Iceland's territorial extension and which eventually resulted in every coastal state (or group of states, including what would become EU) possessing an exclusive economic zone that extends 200 miles from the shore.

With Britain entering the European Economic Community (EEC) in 1973, the same year the Cod Wars were declared over, and with the conclusion of the UN process on maritime law in 1982, Britain's freedom of the seas was well and truly over. At the same time, the UK was left to face the fact that it was one country among many in the shared territory of what would become the European Union. Its surrounding seas were now shared, and this time Britain wouldn't determine the rules alone, a fact that many in England have more recently struggled to accept.

This fallout from the Cod Wars brought to an end the distant water fleet upon which the working-class communities of Hull and Grimsby had depended, and which once gave the world fish and chips. These industrial fishing communities have since disappeared, leaving behind piles of handwritten ship's logs, a quiet maritime museum, occasional remembrance events and a handful of plaques and statues. Without the distant water fleet and the trade unions that went with it, wages in the fishing industry have fallen almost as fast as the decline in the catch.[13]

From sea bass to whelks

'Do you know much about bass?' Graham enquires after finishing his carrot cake. I feel a little unprepared because I don't know anything about bass, other than that every celebrity chef seems to have a recipe for baking it with lemon and herbs nested in the cavity where the fish's guts used to be. 'Well, there was a bass bonanza at Eastbourne,' Graham explains patiently. 'Actually, it went all the way along the south coast, but it sort of kicked off here.'

European sea bass – *Dicentrarchus labrax* – the species Graham is talking about and which I later go away and research, is a shimmering, elegant creature beloved of anglers as well as cooks. A beautiful fish with skin like 'worked stainless steel', according to the chef Rick Stein.[14] Bass grow slowly, only maturing between four and seven years of age, and can live well over twenty years if they're lucky. After spending their infancy in estuaries, mature European bass migrate from colder, coastal waters in the North Sea to deeper waters in the western Channel, where they spawn. Their relatively predictable migratory patterns make them easy targets, while their slow growth makes the beady-eyed bass vulnerable to overfishing.

Under the system that emerged after Britain entered the EEC, small fishers like Graham generally lacked adequate fishing quotas for species like cod and skate, whose numbers had in any case radically declined. Around 2008, the small vessels of Eastbourne's Sovereign Harbour moved into targeting bass, which at the time was an unregulated species, like cuttle.

'The lads were bass drifting,' Graham recounts. 'And you'd see them shooting their nets as close as they could get to the beach, then straight out to sea, a quarter of a mile long.' Drifting involves leaving a curtain of fine net in the water to float with the tide, then coming back to retrieve it and any fish that have been unlucky enough to become ensnared.

Graham noticed that the bass the boats were catching were small, and he asked a crew down at the harbour if they'd thought about leaving their nets further out, where the herring and mackerel that the bass fed upon are found. And so, they did. 'In the end there was probably forty to fifty boats along this part of the coast doing it. And they were going right out, getting into all sorts of tangles with ships going through their gear. But it was successful. They were making bloody fortunes.'

While bass was being targeted by boats the length of the Channel, Eastbourne became the port with the highest number of vessels fishing for the species with drift nets, earning the fleet over £2.7 million a year. The south coast fishery was so successful that in less than a decade the numbers of bass began to plummet. Falls in total landings were being seen across the EU, causing scientists and eventually politicians to raise the alarm.

In 2015, the UK government sought emergency measures from the EU to stop the targeting of bass. Catch limits were then enforced in 2016, and pair trawling (where two boats drag one net) was banned for catching bass the year after. In 2018, all targeting of bass was ruled out of bounds. Research has since shown that the fish has been making a gradual recovery, although it remains vulnerable.

The problem that fishers on the south coast faced after the ban was that loans had been taken out for new boats and gear during the peak of the bass bonanza, as Graham calls it. Skippers and investors were heavily leveraged, but now they had lost their anticipated source of income. Fortunately for them an answer was found in the form of a rather less elegant and far more sedentary species: whelks.

These days Graham won't touch whelks. He likens the work of hauling up pots of sea snails to harvesting potatoes (which, funnily enough, is what many seasonal fishermen did in the pre-industrial past when there was no fishing to be done). For other fishers in Eastbourne, especially ones with loans for their boats to pay, lacking quotas for species like cod, with bass off limits and with a lot less cuttle around, whelks are pretty much all they have left. And so it is that at 6 a.m. I wake up on a hard bench in the wheelhouse of the *St George*. I put on an old pair of yellow oilskin overalls and go out on the deck with Keir to cut up the crates of dogfish.

Tipping side to side as the sun comes up behind grey clouds, I try not to think about boiled eggs. Then, as I throw a severed piece of frozen dogfish into a crate, I look down and notice that there's a large gash in the toe of my plastic boot; instantly I realise my foot is wet.

It turns out that catching whelks is a bit more complicated than digging up potatoes. Whelking pots – typically large plastic kegs with concrete bottoms, sides with holes and a drawstring entrance – are attached by rope to a much longer rope, or string. At either end of the string are crude weather-beaten floats and sometimes a small flag to make them easier to find. A carefully stacked string of pots is baited before being very strategically shot out the open-ended back of the boat. When this happens, each pot is followed by the whish of ropes that, were they to catch your boot, would drag you out to sea and quite possibly down to the ocean floor to meet the carnivorous snails.

As we arrive at the first string of the day, Scott reaches over the side, hooks it and tucks the rope into a mechanical wheel which hauls the first pot up the side of the boat. From there, Scott pulls it on board and passes it to Sonny, the boy from Hull, who while barely large enough to lean over the bench he's working on opens the drawstring and shakes out the whelks. A metal grid, or riddle, allows smaller whelks to fall into a discard crate. The rest, minus any leftover bait, seaweed and starfish, Sonny pushes into an open sack. Keir then baits the pots and neatly stacks them, ready for shooting again. The idea is to haul, bait and shoot twenty strings in a trip – each string having a hundred pots – six days a week during the season.

My job, insofar as I had one, was simply to stand behind Sonny and remove each filled sack, hand him a new bag and tie and stack the full one. Between each full sack I mostly watched and focused on not vomiting. While my task sounds straightforward, each sack weighs forty kilos. I think of myself as reasonably strong, but try moving a sodden, bulging sack of whelks – their shells are tough and sharp – on a boat tipping from side to side, with a wet floor and a hole in your boot, without falling off the open back end of the boat as it steams along in one of the busiest shipping lanes on the planet. No wonder fishing remains one of the most hazardous jobs in our economy.

In the morning, as we first started to haul, Sonny was slow and quiet. I watched as towards the end of one string he was distracted by a whelk that had a pink spot on it. Over his shoulder I saw as he brought the whelk closer to his face to inspect it. At that moment, while Scott and Keir were focused on their work, the spot squirted something in Sonny's eye. He jumped back, shocked and upset. Scott had just dumped another pot on the bench and the whelks were piling up. Sonny groaned, but nothing he said was audible over the rough sound of the motor.

At the next string, Sonny was even quieter and slower. He complained that his eye was stinging from the whelk squirt. Not understanding exactly what Sonny had said, Scott suggested he must have been caught by a jellyfish sting. The work continued at the pace of the hauling engine, and so I reached over and helped bait the pots to keep things moving.

After a cigarette in between hauls and as the day went on, Sonny began to wake up, becoming alert and cheerful. He told me about his home town of Hull, about a great uncle, also a fisherman, who was lost at sea, about his daughter and the months Sonny spent in prison. At one point Sonny showed me some cuttlefish eggs that were attached to a pot. On his bench, he used the sharp edge of a whelk to cut the black sac open to reveal the cuttle embryo inside and then, as the hauling continued, slammed the concrete-bottomed pots down on top of it without a thought. On our final haul, Sonny even started singing. Everyone on the boat had warmed to him. 'Bag?', I offered, holding out an empty whelk sack. 'No, I'm trying to quit,' he chuckled. Sonny reminded me of a young chef.

At around 6 p.m. we arrived back into Sovereign Harbour. The final job was to move more than eighty dripping sacks of whelks into the back of Scott's pickup. This I found by far the hardest task of the day, and by the end of it I was covered in sweat, whelk juice, crab and dogfish slime. I left the *St George* feeling exhausted. The crew – who made around £4,000 for the trip – were due back at the boat to do it all again in ten hours. The next day the entire upper half of my body ached, and, despite a hot wash, the clothes I hung up to dry still smelled intensely of bait.

Fishing for Leave

On the eve of the 2016 referendum on leaving the EU, a poll found that 92.8 per cent of fishers believed that Brexit would improve their industry.[15] EU fishing quotas had sat alongside immigration as a key issue for the Leave campaign; the two concerns underlay a hazy desire to reclaim Britain's sovereignty, harking back to the days when Britannia ruled the waves. As with the appeal to voters who remembered Britain's industrial heyday, Brexit offered fishers a chance to register resentment at the changes that had befallen their industry since the conclusion of the Cod Wars and the entry into the EU's Common Fisheries Policy by placing blame squarely on the latter.

Leave campaigners circulated secret government memos from the 1970s which showed that ministers and civil servants suspected that joining the European market would have negative consequences for the fishing industry, particularly for smaller boats. Since the EU's allocation of fishing quotas among its member states was determined by each state's historic catch, fishers felt that European boats had inflated their figures (even where there was no evidence that they had done so). The fact that two thirds of the fish caught in British waters were taken by European fleets seemed unjust.

For many, all of the problems with British fishing became reducible to EU membership. Campaigners argued that everything about the industry, 'from its foundation right up to the day-to-day laws', was decided and controlled by Brussels.[16] When interviewed during the campaign, Graham told journalists that this was our last chance to save the industry for future generations. He believed that Britain had given away control when it entered the EEC and that Brexit was a once-in-a-lifetime opportunity to take it back.

With their iconic boats and their salt-of-the-earth demeanours, fishers like Graham lent a vital symbolic component to the Leave campaign. A week before the referendum took place, Nigel Farage, dressed in a brass-buttoned navy blazer, commanded a flotilla of Leave-supporting fishers up the Thames. The trawlers lined up against a Remain-supporting passenger ferry commanded by the one-time musician and campaigner Bob Geldof. The ageing rocker broadcast his rants over a huge stack of speakers – bizarrely Geldof claimed that Farage didn't represent fishermen, despite the leader of UKIP clearly siding with the fleet in attendance – while at one point a trawler came alongside and sprayed the Remain boat with its hose.

Ultimately Geldof was no match for the promises made by the Leave campaign. According to Boris Johnson, Brexit would 'release our fishermen from the tangled driftnets of arcane quota systems'.[17] Fishers were explicitly promised hundreds of thousands of tonnes of extra fish if we left the

EU, while the issue of exclusive access to fishing grounds within 200 miles of the coast became totemic for Vote Leave more broadly.

Yet lost in this thrill of populist belligerence was the fact that Britain already had a substantial degree of control over the way its fishing quota was distributed within the national fleet. While the EU set the total catch for each member state, how each nation's share was distributed was up to them.

Starting in the late 1990s, Britain handed out fixed amounts of fishing quota to the large (ten-metre-plus) boats, or groups of boats, that could demonstrate a strong track record. Not only were these large boats gifted a right to fish a fixed proportion of Britain's total catch in perpetuity, but soon enough, after the handout had been enshrined in law, these boats' quotas became tradeable assets. Fishing rights were effectively commodified.

Representatives from smaller boats weren't in the room when the privatisation of fishing quotas took place, but initially small boats like Graham's were left to do their own thing. Meanwhile, new, much more efficient small boats entered the unregulated world of the under-ten-metres, which came to be known by fishers as 'rule beaters'. So much so that finally, in 2005, the government decided to see how much these small boats were catching. The answer – a far larger amount than the government had anticipated – led to a ban on small boats fishing without any allocated or purchased quota.

To make things worse, privatised UK quota made its way to large ships that were registered abroad. Today around half of England's quota is held by ships sailing for Dutch, Spanish or Icelandic owners. In 2015, Greenpeace revealed that one boat alone – the Dutch-owned *Cornelis Vrolijk Fzn*, then the largest fishing trawler in UK waters – held 23 per cent of England's total quota. Foreign owners were profiting from a resource swimming in British seas – and this was a domestic policy, not a European one.

The Leave campaign had furthermore lost sight of an even more fundamental issue: Britain imports 80 per cent of the fish we eat here, and it exports a similar percentage of the fish that we catch. And the majority – by a long way – of what we land and sell goes to Europe.[18] At the same time, in 2017, fishing accounted for just 0.4 per cent of Britain's GDP. This was less than the contribution made to GDP by sales of sit-down lawnmowers or Peppa Pig merchandise. Fishing generates less in terms of tax revenue than is made via the UK market for OnlyFans. While fishing may have been a symbolically resonant part of Britain's self-image, the industry was far from being as important to the economy as finance or manufacturing. The likelihood that fishing interests would ever be prioritised was therefore low.

On Christmas Eve in 2020, Graham's phone rang. It was his friend from the Channel Islands. 'Have you seen it?' the friend asked. Graham knew exactly what he was talking about. After being slowed down by negotiations over fishing rights, the UK–EU trade deal had finally been released. 'It's out. They stuffed us,' his friend said. To make matters worse, newspapers revealed that when the final wording of the deal was being written, Victoria Prentis, the fisheries minister, had been too busy organising her daughter's nativity play to even read it. Graham's friend had, and he thought they'd been betrayed yet again.

The end result – the Trade and Cooperation Agreement – has required Britain to accept the EU's definition of the total allowable catch and continue to grant access to European boats within the six- to twelve-mile radius around the UK coastline, despite that having been an apparent red line in the Johnson government's negotiations. Britain gained some 135,000 tonnes in quota of certain – mostly low-value – species, but this was short of the hundreds (plural) of thousands that had been promised. The gain in quota has come coupled with non-tariff barriers (new regulations and paperwork) that have reduced exports to the EU by almost 30 per cent, contributing to an overall decline in the profitability of British fishing.

Graham and his friend were not the only ones who felt let down. All of the organisations representing the fishing industry proclaimed their disappointment. Despite this, when the trade deal was signed two days before a new year began, Boris Johnson declared in his characteristically hubristic fashion: 'For the first time since 1973 we will be an independent coastal state with full control of our waters with the UK's share of fish.' A free-sea British Empire was back, he implied.

Beachy Head

The truth is that the British today eat quite a lot of seafood, as we have done since the late 1800s. We consume, on average, just short of twenty-five kilograms of fish per person, per year. While that's less than half of what the average person in Portugal or Spain consumes, it is only four kilograms less than Italy, twice the amount consumed in Germany and, somewhat surprisingly, seven kilograms more than is consumed in Greece.

What is peculiar about our taste in seafood is the narrow range we eat. People in Britain tend to eat what consumer analysts call the 'big five': cod (unsurprisingly, since it has long been the standard for fish and chips), haddock (which for most of us, if we notice the difference at all, is a kind of cod-light), tuna (canned), salmon (farmed) and prawns (also farmed).[19] In fact, demand for all of these five fish (or four fish and one crustacean) is growing and is expected to have risen by 10 per cent by the end of the decade. Yet aside from most of the farmed salmon we consume, the big five are almost entirely imported. Cod and haddock account for a third of our seafood imports, with China having recently become the biggest supplier.

This means that Britain is a coastal state that does not eat the seafood that comes from around its coast – a state of affairs that by this point should be regarded as a long-standing tradition. The salted cod that supplied the navy and merchant ships at the time of Henry VIII came from as far away as Newfoundland in North America. When John Cabot sailed across the Atlantic from Bristol in 1497, he was looking for the Indies and its spices. Instead, he and his crew found the Grand Banks, a cod fishery that was once so vast that sailors could scoop the fish out the water with weighted baskets. Cabot's voyage helped give rise to a British trade route between the fishing grounds of North America, the wine-producing regions of Southern Europe and markets back in England – a triangle of trade that would eventually expand into a network encompassing sugar, cotton and slaves.

In fact, the English and British eat and catch fish as part of our established identity as a nation of shopkeepers. We relate to seafood not as an islander relates to the sea, but as one relates to goods in a global market. And seafood today, in a post–Cod War era, is an expensive source of perishable protein. Indeed, why eat fish, when chicken is so cheap?

As we leave the café at Beachy Head, Graham tells me about the first time he cooked cuttle. 'The flavour was fine,' he says. 'But the consistency was awful, it was like bloody leather.' Graham subsequently developed a recipe for what he calls 'cuttlefish balls', which involves pulsing the flesh in a blender, adding seasonings, binding it with egg and frying it. (Later, I adapted Graham's recipe, adding lots of minced pork fat, and it tasted pretty good.)

The fog at Beachy Head had lifted slightly, just enough to make out the cliff edge where the lonely and the distraught are known to violently end their lives. We nod to a chaplain who is on hand for anyone considering doing so today. Graham mentions that many of the tourists that come here do so because Beachy Head is the setting of a Taiwanese pop music video. Two fans fell from the cliffs after posing for selfies in fog just like this, he says. 'Tragic, really,' he muses to himself.

Now, as I think back to the end of our meeting, I'm struck

by the symmetry between this scene and everything I have learnt about England's relationship to seafood. Taiwan, along with South Korea, is one of the main destinations for the whelks caught in Eastbourne. What in the seventeenth century was a dark alleyway of Empire, the Channel below Beachy Head is now a physical frontier with Europe as well as a logistical passage for giant container ships and a hunting ground for foreign-owned factory fishing fleets, huge vessels which make Graham and Scott's boats look like toys.

While fish may not respect national borders, they have played an important part in making them. Yet our desire to capture, kill and eat the living things of the sea shows us that sovereignty today must in many ways be relative. While sole – *Solea solea* – are spawned near the shores of Belgium and France, these flatfish grow and mature in the western English Channel and in the Celtic Sea. As we've seen with cuttlefish, targeting sole before they've had a chance to grow and reproduce can devastate the species. That makes international regulation necessary.

Unlike in the past, when Britain could determine international law to suit itself, the UK today must negotiate and share its authority with others, especially the EU – Brexit or no Brexit. France's treatment of the fish that spawn off its coast affects our ability to hunt them when they swim over here, and vice versa. The same need to share sovereignty is a feature of many of the key issues of our time, from immigration to the climate.

Britain needs a new relationship to the sea and to the seafood of our coastlines. Not all 'progress' has been progressive.

The giant ships that today catch most of the fish caught in British waters and bring it to market speak of a tradition of technological advances chasing a declining stock. At least as far back as the 1890s, fishermen in Britain have experienced booms in stocks followed by decline. This was evident in 2010, when a groundbreaking study published in *Nature* examined landings of fish in the UK going back to 1889, which just so happens to be when fish and chips was starting to take off. The study showed that, when you adjusted for the rewards of greater effort being put into fishing, the amount being caught has undergone an extraordinary decline.[20] Large, precision-engineered vessels can be better at sticking to internationally agreed quotas (though it is also important of course that those quotas should be set correctly and cooperatively), but small boats like Graham and Scott's may also provide us with a neo-artisanal model of sustainable fishing, one that may in fact be capable of regenerating deprived coastlines – making them destinations for gastronomic delight and sources of the best quality of English seafood.

It isn't Brussels that's standing in our way, nor has it ever been. The problem instead is that successive British governments have sold off access to our oceans and underwritten a system that has only benefitted the largest boats. The owners of these boats, many of whom are from outside the UK, have effectively bought up a privatised right to fish.

As our day together reached its end, Graham dropped me off in town and bade me farewell from his pickup. I decided to get something to eat before taking the train home. Unsurprisingly, there isn't a single restaurant in Eastbourne that specialises in seafood, so I headed to a fish and chip shop that had some decent reviews.

I chose to eat in, sitting down before a linoleum tablecloth and placing my order for chips, peas and battered cod, with the presumably frozen fish no doubt having been imported from Iceland, Norway or China. There were only seven other people in for dinner that evening. Sat to my right were a smartly dressed older couple each of whom had before them a plate of chips and curry sauce.

4

Curry

And what should they know of England who only England know?

Rudyard Kipling, 'The English Flag', 1891

The trick to cooking a naan bread is to slap the rolled-out dough on the side of a roaring hot tandoor oven using a pillow. I find it odd seeing the small pillow on the kitchen bench next to the stainless-steel tandoor, waiting there alongside a bucket of fermenting dough, a box of flour and a rolling pin. But it's a good way of getting the dough from the work surface to the oven wall. You can't peel a naan, like you do a loaf of sourdough, because the tandoor oven is a vertical cylinder. Instead, you stretch the dough over the pillow and then slap, on it goes, close the lid behind you. Ninety seconds later, the side facing the flame is cratered and blistered like a bready moon. Out of the oven, the naan takes a generous lick of ghee, and it's done.

It's the middle of summer and I'm getting a lesson in curry house cooking from Zaf Hussein at his restaurant Shababs in Birmingham's Balti Triangle. Dressed in a standard-issue Shababs embroidered shirt and with smartly combed hair, Zaf begins by showing me how he makes a balti. The definitive elements of a balti are intense heat, vegetable oil (never ghee), a rapid cooking time and a small steel balti bowl in which the dish is both cooked and served and which lends the balti a pleasant metallic note. When cooked correctly, the bowl enables a deep caramelisation of the sauce, which is cooked almost to a crust at the curry's outer rim.

And so Zaf turns up the heat to full and into the hot black bowl goes a squirt of oil, then a mix of roughly chopped onions, green peppers, tomatoes and garlic, which throws up flames; then in goes the protein, in this case chicken, followed by big pinches of paprika, turmeric and chilli powder. As he stirs, Zaf steadies the bowl by using a blunt knife placed in the corner of one of the balti bowl's two signature handles – a peculiar technique that betrays a life spent cooking in a single kitchen.

I ask Zaf why he doesn't just use a wok with a long wooden handle that he can hold. He laughs. 'That's the way it is,' he says in a soft Brummie accent. Now into the balti bowl goes a ladleful of base sauce – the versatile master stock of the curry house kitchen – in this case made of onions, green peppers, garlic, ginger and spices, cooked for five hours. As the balti rapidly reduces, Zaf adds dried fenugreek, ground cumin, garam masala and ground coriander. During a busy service, this is the point you would move the dish to a backburner and work on the next round. Zaf and his team of chefs can cook up to nine baltis in this way at once. The dish is ready in around five minutes, a sprinkle of chopped coriander the sign that it can leave the kitchen, flanked by a fresh naan.

Shababs is hardly serving an authentic South Asian cuisine. Everyone knows the 'Indian' food you get in the UK is a far cry from what you get on the subcontinent. 'We do enjoy foreign dishes,' writes Dorothy Hartley at the outset of her book *Food in England*. 'But when we cook foreign dishes, the dishes, like the foreigners, become "naturalised English".'[1] These are sentiments commonly applied to what we call Indian food in England, but in this context the statement is in an important sense false. It's false because the idea that curry was ever 'outside' of Englishness, and therefore in need of naturalisation, is a myth. Curry is an imperial cuisine, and England is a post-imperial place.

Baltistan

'The beauty of Balti', writes Pat Chapman, 'is that you can combine any ingredient with any other, if you wish.' From the 1980s up to 2013, Chapman, a man who appears from my research to have been of perpetual middle age, ran the Curry Club. This subscriber organisation of thousands of 'curry addicts' provided restaurant reviews, opportunities for Cobra Beer–sponsored meetups, and cooking tips via an in-house magazine and mail-order DVDs.

Chapman spells balti with a capital B. That's because, as he makes clear in the introduction to his bestselling *Balti Curry Cookbook*, the general idea was that the dish originally came from Baltistan. 'Once it was a kingdom complete with its own royals,' Chapman writes of the region. 'Now it is the northernmost part of Pakistan. It is located on the roof of the world and though few places are as remote and inhospitable, few people are more friendly and few have such a colourful history. Their food has evolved over centuries into pan-cooked stir-fries and slow-cooked dryish stews.'[2] Chapman admits that 'many of the balti house owners and workers have probably been no nearer to Baltistan than their customers', but he nevertheless provides a grand Kiplingesque sweep of Baltistan history, replete with fair-skinned nomadic tribes, mighty rivers, fertile valleys and the ebb and flow of great religions. The 'primitive, fierce and aggressive' Balti people who live in Baltistan today, Chapman says, stir-fry their meals with a transportable wok, an item that eventually evolved into the balti pan. Although stir-frying must have been quite difficult since, according to Chapman, the traditional source of fuel for this cuisine is dried dung, which doesn't get very hot.

None of this is true, of course. Rather as in the case of sourdough, the dubious backstory eases the balti-eater into an enduring history – an oriental escape from the rootless, grey lives of industrial cosmopolitans. In fact, the balti most likely made its first appearance in mid-1970s Birmingham, probably at a restaurant called Adil's. The owner of Adil's, Mohammed Arif, a veteran restaurant entrepreneur, appears to have had the idea of soliciting a new type of pan from Birmingham's once-vibrant metal-bashing industry. His vision was roughly based on a cast-iron, wok-like karahi (a pan commonly used throughout northern Pakistan), but his new pan was made of the milder steel used in the local trade.[3] Arif then instructed his chefs to take meat off the bone and cook with vegetable oil instead of ghee. This allowed Adil's to cook curries rapidly and so keep prices low by quickly turning the tables. Careful marketing, clean, simple surroundings (usually with menus on the table under a pain of glass), no service charge and a BYOB policy expanded restaurants that had once exclusively served Birmingham's community of hard-working Pakistani immigrants into a celebrated part of city life.

I eat my first ever balti with Andy Munro, who, as a fellow diner sat at the table next to us at Shababs points out, is 'balti royalty'. Indeed, Pat Chapman called Andy the king of balti (he also described his Birmingham accent as 'rich and fruity'). Andy tells me he's eaten some 2,000 baltis since his first, which he remembers was in 1985 at a place called Azim's. He went there with a group of other men after drinking and dancing at a nearby club. He was hooked, he says, and thereafter made the rounds of Birmingham's balti houses with other members of his 'balti club' (the group of men had their own regalia: cheap synthetic ties featuring a balti pan logo) and even went on to produce several popular balti guides.

'Baltis are good for you,' Andy tells me energetically as we both scoop up curries with naan. He's had research carried out by a local university that shows that one balti is equivalent in iron to about seventy pints of Guinness and contains far less fat than a slow-cooked curry made with ghee. Part man, part balti. This lifestyle seems to have done wonders for Andy, who has nothing but enthusiasm when he recounts how eating curry in his twenties was like seeing in colour for the first time. Andy grew up only minutes away from Shababs, but in his family home, he says, even salt was an exotic ingredient.

The history of balti in Birmingham shares a pattern with the history of curry house cuisine in England more broadly. It is a story of immigrant communities establishing restaurants that proved palatable to English eaters, especially men, and especially men who find themselves hungry after the pubs kicked out. These diners embraced a type of food that packed a punch, marking a direct contrast to the usual plate of boiled beige with no salt. Balti, just like chicken tikka masala, belongs to the annals of British curry lore.

The imperial invention of curry

When in 2001 the Labour MP and former Foreign Secretary Robin Cook declared in a speech that chicken tikka masala was 'now a true British national dish', he was repeating a commonsensical view expressed fifty years earlier by Dorothy Hartley. The curry had this status, according to Cook, 'not only because it is the most popular [dish], but because it is a perfect illustration of the way Britain absorbs and adapts external influences'.[4] But chicken tikka masala, like balti, was never external to the British experience. As the cultural theorist Stuart Hall once remarked of tea and sugar, what is widely seen as an external influence is in fact very much *inside* the imperial history of the English.[5]

To understand this history as it relates to curry, we have to begin by imagining a world in which popular notions of nationhood were only just developing in Europe, a world with weak national alliances, and one in which India itself had yet to be defined politically.

It was spices that drew European merchants eastward, navigating in the tracks of the Portuguese, who by 1530 had established a trading hub in Goa with overseas links to the spice-producing islands of modern-day Indonesia. Granted a royal charter in 1600, the East India Company in England had the Indies as its jurisdiction – a far larger and more vaguely defined area than present-day India (the fuzziness of the idea of India at this time is illustrated by the name Indonesia, a Victorian coinage meaning 'Indian Islands'). Hot, miserable, pestilent conditions killed most seventeenth-century English merchants within two years of their arriving in one of the company's three precarious footholds in what are now modern-day Chennai, Mumbai and Kolkata. Yet company men who survived stood to return home with vast new wealth.

Shifting to textiles and away from spices (recall from the earlier chapter on beef that in the eighteenth century the seasoning of European food was becoming lighter), the East India Company fought off European competition and eventually pursued bloody expansion as it became increasingly involved in the political affairs of the subcontinent. Directing a locally recruited army rendered the private company a de facto state, one capable of collecting taxes and administering a modified version of British law.

Yet to those close to the Mughal court, eighteenth-century

British Calcutta was little more than a 'hell well stocked with bread' (bread, it is worth noting, that was fermented with yeast derived from palm wine, in contrast to sourdough).[6] In the Company's early phases, when it was very much still a paying guest of the Mughal Empire, English merchants adopted local tastes in food and drink (not to mention wearing local dress and seeking out Indian sexual partners, or even referring to themselves as Indians), although perhaps without noticing the celebratory value afforded by local elites to items such as a perfectly ripe melon or an exquisite mango, which were probably wasted on the English palate.

The eating habits of English elites on the subcontinent reflected a peculiar view that saw quantity as food and drink's chief quality. Company merchants gained a reputation for indulging in twice-daily tables of boiled, roasted and pie-encrusted birds – in addition to mutton and beef when it was available – alongside Mughal recipes, which when served in a thick, spiced gravy were captured by the term 'curry' and often eaten as a kind of relish. These merchants were also keen hunters, shooting as many wild birds and other game (sometimes numbering in the thousands) as they could manage in a single hunt, regardless of whether much of their prey could plausibly be eaten. Such were the quantities of food consumed by the British that liver complaints were widespread, while excessive consumption of brandy, arrack, ale and cheap wine (there are reports that English drinkers actively preferred wines of the worst quality) was liable to give rise to food fights: at elite dinners in the Raj 'guests threw chickens across the table', although women, when present, made do with balls of dough.[7] The drunken curry house experience thus first took shape in the Empire.

It has been widely noted that it is a mistake to refer to so diverse a cuisine as that of the Indian subcontinent with the umbrella term 'curry'. And yet that is what the British did. According to the historian Lizzie Collingham, the word derives from three South Indian languages which together were translated into Portuguese then into English as the generic term 'curry'. Not only did this word obscure most of the differences between local foods, it also described the basis of a somewhat mutable yet also distinctive imperial dish in its own right. And it was not only local chefs and domestic servants who adapted what had once been (for the most part elite) Mughal dishes for the English palate, but English cooks, mostly women, who developed the idea of curry as well.[8]

Hannah Glasse, whom we have encountered in previous chapters, gives us the first written recipe for curry in English in her 1747 book *The Art of Cookery Made Plain and Easy*. 'To make a currey the Indian way', we're told, requires frying onions in butter, adding diced chicken, turmeric, ground ginger, salt, and black pepper, stewing in water, then finishing with cream and lemon juice. This recipe, or something quite like it, was still being used as the foundation for the curries that were being enthusiastically consumed by King George V around a century and a half later.

For Eliza Acton, writing in 1897, the correct colour for a 'currie' is dark green; hence her advising against too much turmeric and cayenne (it's not clear, however, where the green is meant to come from). In her book *Modern Cookery for Private Families,* Acton recommends the use of coconut, which she says is particularly good with sweetbreads. 'Spinach, cucumbers, vegetable marrow, tomatoes, acid apples, green gooseberries (seeded), and tamarinds imported in the shell – not preserved – may all, in their season, be added with very good effect to curries of different kinds.'[9] Related entries in the same volume – including recipes for curried macaroni, curried eggs and one which recommends using up 'the remains of yesterday's calf's head' – all include curry powder, the ingredient which might be said to define an authentic imperial curry much as a flat steel pan is definitive of the balti.

Curry powders were most probably invented for export either by or for East India Company employees in the early seventeenth century. The import of turmeric – which increased from four tonnes in 1820 to more than twelve two decades later – is evidence that these powders were mixed and sold in Britain. By the end of the 1800s, most grocers in England stocked curry powders ranging from mild to hot. To the British consumer, this seasoning helped to construct a subcontinent that was as complex and divided as Europe into a singular imagined entity, that of India.

Several historians have pointed out that recipes for spice mixtures were popular in medieval Britain and bear a certain similarity to ancient Indian masalas. We need to tread carefully here: as the academic Susan Zlotnick points out, this reading of curry powder as an enduring British tradition may be a testament only to the extent to which Indian food had been absorbed into British culture by the beginning of the Victorian era – so much so that its presence could be read backward in an almost timeless way.[10] Yet, as other historians have highlighted, at the very moment of England's initial encounter with the subcontinent, there really were similarities between elite European foods and the equally heavily spiced dishes of the latter.[11] The real question, then, might be why Europe moved away from such tastes while India and the rest of the subcontinent did not – and the answer may be that South Asian cuisine was held in place by this very contrast with Britain, much as eighteenth-century English food was formed by way of a self-conscious contrast with France.

So distinct had curry become in England that by the mid-Victorian era travellers to the British Raj found that the version they encountered there turned their stomach. 'I can't touch the Indian fruits or the fish which they say is so delicious,' the wife of an army officer wrote of her first visit. 'And as to the curries it makes me sick to think of them; give me an English one!'[12] Around the same time, the Great Exhibition of 1851, held at the specially made Crystal Palace, celebrated the Empire as a key driver of British industry, displaying both raw imports from India – including the now-ubiquitous tea – and the finished cotton products that were being exported to the subcontinent (which was at that point a key market driving the looms of Lancashire).

While not everyone, particularly many Liberals in Britain, enjoyed the pomp and grandeur that accompanied Queen Victoria's investiture as the Empress of India, this retitling encouraged a celebration and broad acceptance of what by now was seen as Britain's greatest oversea possession, the 'jewel in the crown' of its Empire. Far from being outside the imperial experience, India was at its very centre. For the Tory Party under Disraeli, support from newly enfranchised working-class voters could be won by showing the extent to which the Empire was, like the monarchy, a great British institution. 'It is difficult to describe,' wrote the novelist Paul Scott, 'but I think in a curious way India in those days was every English person's home, even if it had not been visited.'[13]

Curry persisted in England after the high-water mark of Victorian pageantry, particularly in the military, where it has been a constant feature of British rations. Even in the sodden trenches of the First World War curry powder appeared as a welcome relish, while cans of curry were consumed throughout the Empire during the Second World War, just as packeted and fresh versions are a popular component of British army stores today. Curries full of apples, fruit and even jam bumbled along in twentieth-century England, creating a foundation of domestic taste which the curry houses of the 1970s onward built upon through both continuation and contrast. The success of these restaurants was thus far from being a novelty, since the taste for curry had by then become a deeply engrained British tradition – a product not of a world outside of England, but of England itself in the world.

Why 'Indian'?

The postman delivering letters to Pat Chapman must have been busy because, according to his book on balti, the Curry Club founder received 10,000 pieces of fan mail from fellow 'curry-holics' each year. In 2011 there were some 12,000 so-called Indian restaurants in Britain (although most of them were run by Bengalis and Pakistanis), apparently serving 2.5 million customers and employing 80,000 staff.[14] This was the peak for such restaurants, a growth from a base of several hundred in the 1960s, many of which had grown out of chip shops and meat-and-two-veg English cafés. Around the time of Robin Cook's speech, at the turn of the millennium, Brits were consuming 25 million portions of chicken tikka masala a year, nineteen tonnes of which were sold pre-prepared at Marks & Spencer. This was when one could find around thirty balti restaurants in Birmingham's Balti Triangle, and when the anthem of English football fans was a song about vindaloo.

But why India? Why out of the entirety of Empire did the cuisine of the Indian subcontinent, some of it invented by and for the British palate, take root in England whereas the food of Australia, New Zealand, Canada and the substantial British possessions in Africa did not? Some 18 million British people migrated to the New World between 1815 and 1936, an outward imperial flow that despite depending on the sail ship and the steamboat still outweighs the numbers of those who have settled in the UK from the Commonwealth since the end of the Second World War. A large proportion of post-war migrants to the UK, roughly 2.2 million, came from South Asia. In contrast, the British presence in India was always very small, in comparison with both the local population and the numbers of Brits abroad elsewhere. This fact is indicative of the mode of colonial governance of India, which depended upon the lack of any native political and ideological unity (that is to say, before the British, the nations of India and Pakistan didn't exist), and which avoided British settlement (unlike in America and Australasia).

The historically small number of British-born souls in colonial India underlines the puzzle of the latter's culinary influence. India's status as a trading hub, rather than a site of Western settlement, hints at part of the answer, insofar as native exports such as cloth, tea and spices were matched by markets and a general taste for the Orient back in the British Isles. Huge private investments were undertaken by British capitalists in the Americas (including Central America, above all in Argentina), yet here the opportunity for grain production and livestock had been created by the prior killing and dispossession of native populations by settler colonial states. The cash crops of the Americas – as we saw previously – dramatically altered the make-up of Britain, effectively 'liberating' rural populations from the land and channelling them into an urban, industrial tide. But, as cultural objects, wheat and meat from deserted lands could be imported to Britain as the neutral products of whiteness.

In the Caribbean, likewise, slave plantations owned by private investors in Britain produced raw goods, most importantly sugar, which, being white and pure – the platonic ideal of sweetness – entered England unburdened by any pre-existing cultural value, as naked as the calorie itself. The same may be said of some of the chief exports of British-controlled Africa, which, in contrast to the established presence in India, was colonised in the late-nineteenth century 'scramble'. Gold from Ghana and South Africa entered Britain to provide silent heft to the metropol's already opaque financial institutions.

Rubber from Cameroon was, like petrol, stripped of any natural or cultural markers as it became used in tyres and industry. Palm oil, an important export of Nigeria while the latter was under Britain's colonial control, has had a profound impact on our globalised and industrial diet, yet even now the many Nigerian dishes that make artisanal use of it – from efo riro, a savoury spinach stew common in Western Nigeria, to Banga soup (or palm nut soup), which is popular in the South – are practically unheard of in Britain.

Only modern North American food, primarily in the form of soft drinks, snacks and burgers, has reverse-colonised British eating habits to any great extent.[15] And yet the industrious and industrial, carnivorous and calorific qualities of these foods are illustrative of the fact that American culture itself is far from an outsider force when it comes to persistent English tastes.

British investment in the idea of India, as manifest in the invention of curry, in fact expressed a racial-civilisational chain of being in which, for British imperialists, South Asians – particularly when fair-skinned and, ideally, aristocratic – occupied a higher level than black Africans (and sometimes also the white working classes, especially Celts). Indigenous American and Australasian populations were deemed to be on the lowest rungs of the ladder. To an extent, the paternalistic admiration afforded to troops in the East Indian Armies, later the British Indian Army, simply reflected imperial Britain's dependency on a native loyalty that the 'Hindoo and Mahomedan races' were conveniently presumed to have. Yet there was more to it than that: both Christian missionaries and other romantic imperialists at times expressed a respect for a largely imagined idea of Indian religion, culture and language, one that could be simplified like curry and projected back into antiquity. India and Indians could thus be seen as sharing a lineage with Western civilisation, even if this imagined ancient legacy also froze the subcontinent into an idealised form of backwardness.

Such orientalism, however, was at odds with the practicalities and moral justifications of British rule, which, particularly after the Rebellion in 1857, were increasingly conducted in terms of distinct civilisational cleavages. That meant that, just as Victorian Britons were developing a taste for curry, the merchants and officials in colonial India were going to absurd efforts to stand above and aloof from the local culture.[16] As far as food is concerned, several historians have claimed that the British in India were adopting French tastes as early as the 1830s, although the evidence for this centres mostly on their use of jumbled French when writing menus and recipes – the dynamic here is comparable to how Alexis Soyer's presence at the Reform Club in the 1840s was *not* itself evidence that the roast beef of old England had quite disappeared.[17] Far from it. In fact, in the latter half of the nineteenth century groups of Britons in India subscribed to 'mutton clubs', wherein a flock of sheep was held in common, fattened as far as was possible before slaughter and then divided up among members.

Despite the heat and the frequent lack of good pasture, many upper-class Britons in India demanded ruminants, roasted and boiled, as they also did kidney soup, toad-in-the-hole and suet puddings. According to the historian David Gilmore, one

Major Sommerset was typical when he said that he 'liked very simple English cooking and disliked good food being mucked about with fancy sauces so that you could not taste what sort of meat you were eating'.[18] As with the eighteenth-century contrast with French fricassees we observed previously, Indian food served as a foil for British colonials' ideas of civilised taste. Gilmore also unearthed the diet of the artist Edward Lear, who while in India in the 1870s ate only 'wholesome English food': eggs, steaks, stewed rabbit, boiled mutton, boiled potatoes, beer and claret. Beer, it should be noted, was the distinct preference for elite Britons in India, since it travelled and stored better than wine, particularly when it contained extra hops – hence the rise of India Pale Ale.

Meals in the Raj were occasions for contrived displays of social hierarchy. Strict rules organised the entering of the dining room, the position in which each guest was sat, who should talk to whom and how each person should dress. When matters of precedence were unclear, handbooks could be consulted and the views of officials sought back home, with these tending to emphasise aristocratic ties over the more meritocratic status that derived from career advancement. Formality increased as the nineteenth century wore on, with men in the Raj – more English than in England – being required to wear woollen suits to dinner, even as sweat was induced by the hot fog of the climate, the boiling mutton and the steamed suet puddings.

Back in Blighty during the belle époque, the world had changed dramatically, yet in British India the stuffy formality of the Victorians appeared immovable. Indeed, for some the

Raj stood for proper, traditional values in an unnervingly plastic time.[19] Yet the pomp and theatrics performed a function insofar as they underlined the civilisational distinction that the British claimed as a key justification for their continued rule. This, in turn, provided a spur to the broadening of popular liberal democracy back home, since part of the claim to civilisational difference with India rested on a distinction between just government and despotism. Once again, we see that there were no clear borders between the history of England and that of its 'outside' in the Empire.

Despite the violence inherent and explicit in Britain's colonial governance, the British idea of India never lost its romantic, orientalist investments entirely. But there was to be no equivalent fascination with African rituals, despite the governance of much of that continent by the Empire. Nor was there with Māori cosmology, Aboriginal spirituality or Native American philosophy, since white settlement aimed at the erasure of these cultures. There was thus to be no equivalent of curry as the product of these other imperial encounters.

The authentic turn

It was during the balti boom years that Andy Munro, the king of balti, met Madhur Jaffrey, the doyenne of Indian food in the UK and the US. After the unexpected success of his guides to the best balti in Birmingham, Andy had been asked by the ready-made sauce company Sharwood's to do a cooking display at the BBC's *Good Food Show.* Andy says he's more of an eater than a cook, and when he threw frozen prawns into the smoking hot oil of a balti bowl over full gas he almost set his hair on fire. Madhur Jaffrey was looking on. After the show was over, the actor and celebrity chef approached Andy to tell him that balti was – and these are the words that Andy says she used – an invention, and that it lacked authenticity. Andy told her that she was right, but he wanted to know why that was a problem. Every food was an invention by someone at some point, he said.

The reason was that Jaffrey had made a name for herself in part by campaigning against inauthentic curries like Birmingham's balti. There is no chapter on curry in Jaffrey's breakthrough book *An Invitation to Indian Cooking*. Rather, she begins as follows:

> On a recent visit to London, I was astounded to see Indian restaurants flourishing in practically every neighbourhood. Mistakenly, I took this efflorescence to signify an increased supply of good quality, authentic, regional Indian foods ... Upon visiting the restaurants, I found most of them to be second-class establishments that had managed to underplay their own regional uniqueness as well as to underestimate the curiosity and palate of contemporary Britons. Instead of specializing in foods from particular states or districts, they served a generalized Indian food from no area whatsoever.[20]

These 'Indian' restaurants in Britain stuck to the same repertoire, she wrote, because it was already popular and because of the poor 'calibre of the cooks ... often former seamen or untrained villagers'.[21] They produced the same repetitive, mediocre menu, served mild to hot, with the same colour, taste and consistency. In one instance, the use of frozen vegetables was enough for Jaffrey to write off a sincere attempt at authenticity as hapless.

An Invitation is full of advice for the home cook who wants to taste traditional Indian food. Yet it starts with a warning: under no circumstances should you ever use curry powder. 'To me the word "curry" is as degrading to India's great cuisine as the term "chop suey" was to China's,' Jaffrey explains. 'If "curry" is an oversimplified name for an ancient cuisine, then "curry powder" attempts to oversimplify (and destroy) the cuisine itself,' she writes.[22] The campaign against British imperial cooking had thus began.

Jaffrey was not the only South Asian who saw the curry house as backward even when it was first emerging, while the criticism of inauthenticity as it became more general in scope caused many (if not almost all) such places to pepper their menus with claims as to the regionality and traditionality of certain dishes. To some, curry house culture was a symbol of the colonial servitude that independence was meant to have ended. Even as the immigrant cooks, wait staff and entrepreneurs had overcome the overt, and sometimes deadly, racism present in many of the British communities which they served, the submission to the local culture of heavy drinking, the watering down (with cream) or amping up (with chilli) of 'Indian' food and the demand for chips with everything spoke of a persistent colonial ignorance and inequality, as was memorably captured by the comedy sketch show *Goodness Gracious Me*.[23]

Escaping the paradigm of chicken tikka and defying the frequent complaint that South Asian immigrants couldn't be tolerated because of the smell of their cooking, a new wave of restaurants proudly served their own regionally authentic food, while denouncing the flock-wallpapered old guard. At times this trend was backed by a more affluent class of British Indians who, while successfully marketing a new sense of pride, also denounced the inauthenticity of the older Bengali and Pakistani curry houses in terms that betrayed elements of exclusivist Hindu nationalism.[24]

This new wave of restaurants, following Madhur Jaffrey's lead, found a ready and waiting clientele. Jaffrey's hope as expressed in her first book was that 'eating habits are changing, and today's English populace seems to have a great desire to experience the "real" thing, an authentic taste, a different lifestyle'.[25] What Jaffrey appears to have both registered and encouraged here was a new trend towards informality and authenticity within middle-class taste, a topic central to the next chapter. Indeed, Robin Cook's speech was denounced by several broadsheet journalists as being stuck in an inauthentic time warp, with some pointing out that chicken tikka – an 'Indian dish' according to Cook – appeared not to have been the invention of an Indian at all but of a proud Glaswegian born in Pakistan. For the restaurant critic Fay Maschler, London's upmarket Bombay Brasserie was (despite its French name and its Raj-era throwback interior) a welcome break from the otherwise 'terrible parody of Indian food' in which 'a common sauce is slopped on' and 'everything tastes the same'.[26] Authenticity was now a marker of class distinction for British eaters and of ethnic distinction for some South Asians, even as it was also a source of anti-imperial pride for the latter. Even Pat Chapman's Curry Club became liable to mock the standardisation of the Indian restaurant as the 1990s wore on.

As innumerable newspaper features highlight the decline of the curry house in Britain, it is hard, for me at least, not to feel that something will be lost with the disappearance of post-war curry culture, or at least that therein has been something still worth celebrating.

Back in Shababs, I speak to the man at the table opposite who earlier pronounced Andy to be 'balti royalty'. 'I've got an addiction,' Mark from Stafford tells me. 'I drove thirty-five miles to get here.' Mark's wife, elegantly dressed with perfectly styled blonde hair, looks on with a sweet expression at her husband, whose head bobs with excitement. There's a restaurant local to Mark that just doesn't do it for him. 'They do try, but it doesn't really bear any resemblance to what we've just had here,' he says. Mark got his first taste of balti around 1980 when he was an apprentice engineer and the restaurant scene in Birmingham offered a meal out at prices that he and his workmates could afford. It was a break from the blandness of what he was used to, Mark tells me. 'We didn't come here to drink, we came for the balti. Because the taste is different. It's a fresher, cleaner taste. Don't get me wrong, I love Bangladeshi curries, but it's too heavy for me. But with balti, I could eat another one right now.' Zaf, who is stood at my shoulder as I turn to speak to Mark, chips in.

'I'm proud of that,' Zaf says. 'You know balti is a part of British heritage.' I agree, I say. And so does Mark, who is nodding his head with grave conviction.

Despite declaring in 2014 that the craze for balti was over and that curry house food in Britain tastes like mud, Madhur Jaffrey may have joined the trend she couldn't beat, if not quite softened her original line, having since published six cookbooks with the word 'curry' in the title. 'You think of a curry meal and your mouth lights up in anticipation,' she begins in her *Ultimate Curry Bible*. 'Indians', Jaffrey reminds us here, 'tend to call dishes by their individual names ... But the British definition [of curry] seems to have stuck.'[27]

Jaffrey also managed to cash in on the balti craze by lending her name to a 'balti serving set', whose fabrication out of stainless steel and the implication that the bowls are not used for cooking would certainly fail to pass Andy's test of authenticity. For over a decade, Andy has been on a one-man mission to gain some form of protected status for the balti, much as exists for champagne and Melton Mowbray pork pies. He came quite close to EU accreditation when Brexit, ironically, blew his chances. The UK government department that manages the certification of authentic foods has since lost interest. Yet all Andy really wants is a window sticker for certain restaurants that uphold an authentic standard (which according to the Association for the Protection of the Authentic Balti, the one that Andy chairs, is defined mostly by use of a proper balti bowl and a fast cooking time).

And why not? Andy was right when he told Jaffrey that all foods are invented by someone, somewhere at some point. Besides, Jaffrey's books make liberal use of potatoes, cauliflower, tomatoes, garden peas and chillies, all of which were introduced to the Indian subcontinent by Europeans and popularised by the British. Then there's tea, which required an extensive British marketing campaign, plus conditions enabled by the First World War, before it became the popular Indian drink of chai that it is today.[28] There is, in fact, little evidence of a *national* cuisine in India before the second half of the nineteenth century (until then the cuisine of the subcontinent had been, as it remains now, profoundly sophisticated yet infinitely diverse).[29] Then, where some unification of eating habits first occurred, it was as a consequence of the spread of both food and ideas by the British (including the idea of a unified Hindu religion and the idea of a singular Indian nation), plus defiant efforts by the local population to contrast native cuisine with the apparently civilised taste for eating boiled sheep while dressed in woollen suits.

The notion of authenticity is obviously socially constructed, but that doesn't mean that it can't serve as a marker of pride. As such, it can help raise the standard of a nation's culinary culture – something we English could certainly do with. Where claims to authenticity are dangerous, however, is when the nation itself is defined in terms of an exclusivist (for example religious, ethnic or racial) identity, as has in fact been the case in Narendra Modi's India and seems likely to become the case in England today. By contrast, post-imperial identities should be defended, since, like it or not, it is the imperial world that made us who we are and there is no going back from it now. We should of course address the real and lasting hierarchies established between the racialised subjects of East and West, North and South, but one risk of 'decolonising' our culture is that we reinforce the very forms of separation that were reified by the imperial encounter.

England in the mirror of the authentic

The problem with the idea of cosmopolitanism, Stuart Hall once told the anthropologist Pnina Werbner, is that it 'invokes a kind of cultureless, an image of a person who's free-floating, like a global entrepreneur in the first-class waiting room of some airport ... you know they love a bit of Japanese cooking and a bit of Indian cooking, French cuisine. They sample all of them, but none comes from an attachment to a particular way of handling food.'[30] As critics of then prime minister Theresa May pointed out back in 2016, one need not choose between being a citizen of somewhere and a citizen of what May called 'nowhere' – that is, a citizen the world. But in practical terms, for the confused, unconfident, sometimes guilty-minded English, particularly in the domain of food, multiculturalism can feel like a choice between a meal at a great global buffet and eating at nowhere in particular. After all, what is English food today? According to the writer Rose Prince, 'there is now no reason why [English food] could not include the rice noodle dishes of Southeast Asia or the delicious food of the Mediterranean'.[31] No reason, perhaps, beyond our concern with authenticity.

Starting in the 1990s, the turn to authenticity provoked a spate of traditional British and English cookbooks – picture the anodyne James Martin, who, on the cover of his *Great British Dinners*, is photographed alongside a bulldog – as well as a brief fashion in the decade for new British restaurants, the leading lights of which were the chefs Gary Rhodes and Anthony Worrall Thompson. Of this latter crowd, only Fergus Henderson's restaurant St John persists today (although St John arguably sits more comfortably within a modern European current than strictly a British one). Calls made around the turn of the millennium to restore Britain's traditional (read: pre-imperial) foodways overlooked the extent to which food culture is the product of deeper trends in society, including the kind that gave us the iconic, anti-French forms of English taste in the eighteenth century but which no longer have such a firm hold today – as the failure of the British revival restaurants arguably made evident.[32]

The embrace of authentic food from across the globe holds up a broken mirror to Englishness, one in which imperialism does not show. In that glass we see different nations and cultures proudly adopting authentic self-inventions, inventions which most of us in England consume with great pleasure. When we look in this mirror for an authentic Englishness we find the handful of native dishes that frequently appear in the top twenty when polls of the nation's favourite foods are conducted: chips (which usually comes in at number one), fish and chips, the full English breakfast, bangers and mash, roast beef, beans on toast, and toad-in-the-hole. There is no doubt in my mind that any of these meals, including beans on toast, can be wonderfully prepared and perfectly satisfying. But how does our investment in them compare to the vast tapestry of modern Indian food or, for comparison with countries closer in size to England, to the cuisines of Italy, France, Spain, Japan, South Korea or Vietnam?

As we've already seen, fish and chips is a dish that everyone loves in England but almost no one makes at home. The list above contains two dishes featuring sausages, yet beyond tiny pockets of craft production in Cumbria and Lincolnshire our sausage-making culture is thin gruel compared to that found in the rest of Europe. Other than breakfast, which remains a proud artefact of home cooks, especially men, and perhaps roast beef, which is still the preserve of lazy Sunday afternoons for some, when the average Briton encounters the rest of the dishes on this list the food is usually mechanically processed and pre-prepared. The general state of our favourite dishes speaks of our peculiar modernity and our failure to publicly invest in artisanal food culture; it speaks of our lack of pride-worthy meals and prized ingredients that are carefully crafted by human hands. And a lack of pride, particularly in a context where other nations have found good cause for celebration, can breed resentment.

The critical embrace of imperial identities and the tradition of culinary fusion offer an alternative to a grey version of English nationalism. Yet here too the English have more than one reason to feel contrite. As Hall (born in Jamica) tells us, he was never outside of English history. Rather, metaphorically, he was the sugar in the English cup of tea. Yet if the Jamaican Stuart Hall was the sugar in tea, then in the case of chicken tikka masala, the English have contributed the industrially produced, distinctly bland can of tomato soup – is that what English authenticity comes down to? No wonder then that so many in England have pursued the authentic elsewhere, especially, for the new middle class, in a romantic ideal of Italy.

5

Olive Oil

The whole Mediterranean seems to rise in the sour pungent taste of these black olives between the teeth. A taste older than meat, older than wine. A taste as old as cold water.

Lawrence Durrell, *Prospero's Cell*, 1945

As a professional cook, the first thing you realise when you work at the River Café is that it is not like any other restaurant you have ever stepped foot in. Unless of course you have experienced any of the dozen or so restaurants modelled on the Café, most of which were established by some of its influential alumni. In fact, the River Café contrasts so sharply with the subterranean kitchens of Restaurant X that the two restaurants feel as though they belong to entirely different industries, as if one were a coal mine and the other a sunlit amphitheatre specialising in interpretative dance. In every professional kitchen there is the familiar stress of service, the heat, the sweat and the knives, but in their distinguishing features, in their internal organisation and the food that gets presented on the plate, Restaurant X and the River Café are planets orbiting different stars.

The River Café is not actually a café. It is an expensive restaurant serving Italian food in a residential corner of Hammersmith by the Thames. The restaurant was initially set up in 1986 as a workplace canteen to serve the hundred or so members of staff working for the architect Richard Rogers. There is a distinct Rogers imprint in the River Café, manifest in its bold blue carpet, in its open-plan kitchen, in the brightly coloured shirts of the restaurant's service staff, in the long stainless-steel bar counter and the floor-to-ceiling wall of blue-trimmed pane glass windows, which exposes the restaurant to a flood of natural light. Rogers, who died in 2021, was the husband of one of the River Café's founders, Ruth Rogers, a precise, assertive woman in her seventies whose accent betrays her bohemian upbringing in New York.

Ruthie, as she's known, led the River Café from the kitchen with her equally discerning bespectacled partner Rose Gray until Rose died of breast cancer in 2010. Ruthie continues to oversee things in Hammersmith, wandering into the kitchen most days to check on the menu. Each month in the restaurant's private dining room, she records her chart-topping podcast *Ruthie's Table,* a show which has featured A-list actors, pop stars, Hollywood directors, chefs and Tony Blair.

I worked just one week at the River Café in early autumn, another *stage*. One week isn't enough to get to know a place inside and out, although by the end of the *stage* I could quickly find you the right pan when it was called for, sense, by touch, just how high the gas burner knob should be turned, and tell you exactly where to put every item in the walk-in fridge. And one week in the kitchen was enough time to take note of some of the restaurant's characteristic traits.

While heading home from Hammersmith on the Tube after my first day, I tapped out a list of everything I found peculiar about the place. Here is a slightly elaborated version:

—There is no formal hierarchy in the River Café kitchen, beyond head chef, *of which there are several,* with a different head chef per service.

—Every chef does their prep jobs for the kitchen at large, not for 'their' section. That means if you are preparing vegetables to accompany fish, for example, you are not necessarily going to be cooking that fish in service. You might have rolled out fresh pasta as your prep job and then find yourself grilling steaks to order.

—Jobs are distributed by the day's head chef an hour or more into your shift. These are often written on a scrap of paper and posted on the check rail. The chef usually writes a chart with names (Lewis) followed by a list of jobs (season and truss pigeons, make salsa verde, etc.).

—While you're waiting for this prep list you're expected to simply look for things to do. If there are proteins – meat and fish – you might consider butchering or filleting them. If there are, say, four enormous boxes of purple artichokes flown in from the verdant plains of Northern Italy, you may consider putting on some disposable gloves and peeling them. I spent a lot of time peeling artichokes. I'm quite quick at it now.

—What needs to be done in this first hour of prep time is not obvious. That's because the first job the head chef has is writing the menu. She (usually she) apparently does this by seeing what's on hand, by taking a look and seeing what's in the fridges. If sea bass has arrived she will think of a dish to make with it.

—Sea bass always arrives. The possibilities are not endless. There are rules, but these rules are flexible within certain constraints.

—The front-of-house staff are involved in basic food prep, such as peeling garlic, picking herbs and roasting peppers. For the first hour of the day they line up along the stainless-steel bar clucking in front of herbs and vegetables like workers on the production line of a small factory.

—There is no ticket machine in the kitchen. Checks are handwritten. There is only one checkrail, and it is mounted on a surface to the side of the head chef, who stands at a small lectern-like pass, facing the eaters as though delivering a speech to an audience. In a kitchen of ten chefs per service (along with three or four kitchen porters) this system, to me, felt inherently chaotic. Although somehow it works quite well.

—There are no squeezy bottles for things like sauces. In fact, there are barely containers of any type. Everything for service – your *mise en place*, although they don't use the

French terminology here – is laid out in bowls, pots and pans, usually of different sizes.

—The use of instant-read thermometers is frowned upon. Tweezers even more so, although there's practically no use for them. The thought of using a ruler to cut out vegetables – as I did at Restaurant X – would strike every chef in the River Café as absurd.

—Almost everything that is prepared before service (my green sauce, for example) is either used up in service or eaten in the great banquette-like staff meals that follow lunch and dinner.

—Every chef contributes something to the staff meal. The idea is that staff eat what the customers eat, which is broadly what happens in practice.

—Celebrities love the River Café. When Kim Kardashian dined here she arrived in a Range Rover with tinted windows and entered and left via the kitchen door where the bins are. The actor Steve Martin is a fan, as are countless others. Damien Hirst is a regular and enjoys dishes of raw beef for himself and a well-done steak for his dog, a meal that without drinks costs him well over £150.

—More than half of the chefs at the River Café are women.

—The best extra-virgin olive oil goes on *everything*.

Not preparing things for your section was the feature of the River Café I found the strangest. I'd had it drilled into me that 'your section is *your* section', 'you'd better have ordered *your* ingredients', 'you'd better not fuck up *your* prep' and 'you'd better have *your* shit ready by 6 p.m. or else you are going down'.

On my second day at the River Café a new chef with a snotty nose said he was too ill to work, so I took up his position serving cold starters and sides. The first thing demanded of me in service was a basic salad. I put the salad in a mixing bowl and added a small ladleful of dressing from the plastic measuring jug that someone else had prepared it in. But had the chef who'd made the dressing added seasoning? I realised I'd have to taste it. In fact, I realised I'd have to taste everything on my section. Did the picked crab have enough salt and lemon? Were the finely sliced chillies hot or mild? How much seasoning was on the grilled peppers? Did they need more acid?

In each service I required a copy of the menu. Five hours earlier, at lunch, the slices of nutty prosciutto had come with fresh figs and thin shards of parmesan, but now there was ham in a stuffed pasta dish and the figs were going in the salad, which tonight contained rocket but didn't contain purple radicchio, while the dressing was the one with vinegar, not lemon.

When I was cooking steak, I had to touch the meat to tell when it was done rather than probe it with a thermometer, as I would do at my regular job. I had to listen to the polenta bubbling in the frier and watch it go brown, rather than set a timer. I would peer into the stone mouth of the wood oven, its dome painted nail-polish pink, to see if the roast potatoes I was preparing were cooking quickly or slowly – should I edge them deeper towards the flame or drag them back towards a cooler spot near the door? At the River Café there's no way to cook by numbers; the idea is that you feel your way through.

A new middle class

The first dish I cooked during service at the River Café was a lobster risotto. It was a case of simply heating up the nearly cooked rice with a ladleful of lobster stock made from the shells, and then adding to this some seasoning, a knob of butter (which gives the rice its rich glossiness), a squirt of lemon and, at the last moment, small chunks of lobster tail.

Once I had achieved a Goldilocks consistency in the pan that the chef working next to me deemed acceptable – neither too wet nor too dry – I plated the rice and anxiously watched as it cooled on the pass. That day's head chef cast a brief glance at my work before instinctively reaching for a dark green glass bottle of extra-virgin olive oil and adding a rough, fat, drizzle to the dish. Only then did she permit the waiter on standby to whisk the plate off into the dining room. From the open-plan kitchen I watched the lime-green shirt of the waiter reach the table of an elegantly dressed elderly couple; as my risotto landed, the man greedily poised a stainless steel fork in the air. Such is the satisfaction of cooking.

When I made the side salad the following day, having sampled the dressing, added a pinch of flaky sea salt and taken care that each leaf in the mixing bowl was neither naked nor sodden, I again watched for the head chef's reaction as my modest work sat on a pass crowded with other plates and bowls. Again, like almost everything in the River Café, the salad was anointed with a splash of the restaurant's signature olive oil.

According to the River Café website, where you can obtain 750 ml of Estate Bottled Extra Virgin Olive Oil for £65, olive oil is 'the most essential ingredient in The River Café kitchen'. The River Café is among a small clutch of restaurants in London that pioneered a liberal use of olive oil in their dishes, a trend that is now ubiquitous in many Continental-inspired restaurants in England, as it is in many home kitchens. The relative absence of olive oil in post-war Britain only meaningfully changed in the 1990s as tastes and techniques spread from these pioneers to the rest of us, via marketing, supermarkets and, above all, Jamie Oliver, the celebrity chef who honed his craft at the River Café.

There is a widespread idea among a certain demographic of cooks and eaters today that before the '90s olive oil was only available in Britain from chemists. That idea is 'balls' according to the critic Jonathan Meades, who says that olive oil could be bought prior to that in Cypriot and Italian shops across London, notably in Soho.[1] Balls or not – market data shows that very few of us were actually consuming olive oil regularly until well into the 2000s – the *idea* that olive oil was not around until the likes of the River Café appeared is deeply symbolic.

For some consumers in Britain, olive oil is a quintessential taste of the Mediterranean – of authentic *cucina rustica* and piazza communality – as well as a holy grail for long-lasting radiant health. In the 1980s and '90s, the oil was symbolic because of what it was not: neither the heavy French food – mounted in animal fat – that the British bourgeoisie traditionally preferred nor the nouvelle cuisine of the post-war period (new new cuisine, if we take account of the history discussed in chapter two), which tended towards lightness but often favoured formal ornamentation – tiny portions and inedible garnish – at the expense of substance.

Olive oil – verdant, picante, fresh, bronze like tanned white skin – appeared in the '90s to strike a contrast with a drab post-industrial Britain in which, for some, it felt as though colour itself had been rationed.[2] Europe was seen as a medicine for post-Thatcherite Britain, the sick man of the continent, whose rusted industries and ageing pretensions were an awkward fit with the new post-colonial, post-manufacturing world. Olive oil was the cure, a totem for the Mediterranean and of New Labour's updated, cosmopolitan Britain.

Such ideas belonged at root to what the cultural critic Raphael Samuel called the new middle class. This was a group for whom the designer Terence Conran was among the first to provide the trappings of good taste, from duvets (practically unheard of in Britain till Conran sold them at Habitat) to paper lampshades; from the food of Elizabeth David, whose books Conran also sold, to the simple European food served at Conran's restaurants.

Writing sprawling, mostly half-finished essays from his home in a gradually gentrifying East London, Samuel observed a remarkable shift in the middle classes, who, as of the late 1960s, no longer 'aspire upwards, aping the speech of their betters, imitating their furnishings, or reproducing their manners', but instead 'dress down ... in tight trousers rather than dinner jackets, pinafores rather than gowns'. He goes on: 'They go hatless to work and spend long and expensive hours at the hairdressers to cultivate a windswept look. They make a show of peasant pots in their kitchens. Their homes are imitation farmhouses, with stripped pine rather than period furniture, linens rather than chintz, and concealed lighting rather than cut-glass chandeliers.'[3] The world of the new middle class was a mildly rebellious one in which Victorian, bourgeois formality had become distasteful. A world in which, for example, Ruth and Richard Rogers received the latter's contract for the Pompidou Centre 'dressed variously in jeans, T-shirts, sneakers and miniskirts, and hardly speaking any French'.[4] In their knocked-through pair of back-to-back Georgian townhouses in Chelsea, the couple had the building's grand front doors removed – they were deemed to be overly formal, perhaps too posh – and fitted an inconspicuous side entrance instead.

Richard Rogers's rough drawings for the River Café were first sketched on a paper tablecloth. Lights for the restaurant were purchased from the Reject Shop, while ovens were salvaged from a bankrupted business in Coventry. Conran's Habitat supplied the chairs, and the designer produced the sleek clock face that is projected onto the restaurant's back wall (seeing this projected clock during my *stage* made me feel I was a contestant on *Countdown*, or else cooking on the set of a '90s reality TV show). All this anti-pomp and spacious lightness gives the restaurant its 'casually democratic' vibe, to borrow from a glowing review of the River Café published in the *New Yorker*.[5]

Writing in *The Times*, celebrity chef Nigella Lawson declared that 'Rose Gray and Ruth Rogers have changed the way we eat'.

> Before they came on to the scene in 1987, smart food was French and anything Italian was found in greasy spoons masquerading as jolly trats, with waiters winkingly wielding oversized pepperpots and (tinned) pomodori with everything. The River Café changed that entirely. Rogers and Gray came up with a menu that was fresh, simple and bristling with flavour and robust authenticity.[6]

Recipes for the restaurant and its bestselling cookbooks were collected from the pair's experiences in Italy: from a bar near to Rose's home in Tuscany, for example, and from a woman who came to the holiday house to clean and cook. Despite their best efforts at transposing these experiences into their Thameside restaurant, when reading a River Café cookbook you have the sense that the food the pair most enjoy is indivisible from a broader, holistic experience. 'There was a winter's day when we drove for miles up into the mountains of Piedmont' is a typical opening to a culinary travelogue in which Rogers and Gray declare the virtues of frugality, tradition and locality. And here comes our old friend, the sourdough:

> On a trip to Puglia we slept in a bakery just so we could watch the many stages involved in the making of huge four-kilo semolina loaves throughout the night. We were astounded when we found

> out that these loaves used a sourdough 'mother' base that was started in 1945 and was still alive! We felt honoured to be given a piece of this 'mother' to take back to the River Café, and, since that trip, we use Pugliese bread every day.[7]

Theirs is 'honest cooking', as Elizabeth David said of her collection of Mediterranean recipes; it is an approach with 'none of the sham Grande Cuisine of the International Palace Hotel'. Shams like Restaurant X, no doubt. This is a back-to-basics method, as Hugh Fearnley-Whittingstall (another River Café alumnus) would have it. Fearnley-Whittingstall welcomed the figure of the 'Tuscan farmer's wife' who, thanks to the River Café, had taken the place of 'some ladle-wielding maniac in a tall white hat'.[8]

All this was far too déclassé for the area of West London in which the River Café found itself, or so it seemed at first. When it opened, a petition was sent to the council signed by a hundred local residents who felt that the restaurant and its hippyish clientele were 'seriously diminishing the tone of the area'. But complaints like these did not last.

In 1997, Tony Blair reportedly held an election victory party at the River Café. Four years prior, the New Labour leader had contributed a recipe of fettucine with sundried tomatoes, capers and extra-virgin olive oil to a fundraising *Islington Cookbook*. A year later, Rachel Kelly, the privately educated daughter of a steel mill owner (who also happens to be married to a hereditary peer), was cheerfully declaring in a review of the River Café for *The Times* that 'we are all Italian peasants now'.[9] Indeed, with Labour in at Westminster, Richard Rogers found an audience for his piazza-ite vision for the capital, while high-level dealmaking, including a negotiation regarding the use of private hospital beds by the NHS, was conducted at the restaurant over peasant-inspired dishes of Tuscan bean stew.[10] By 1998, the Conservative MP Peter Lilley was bitterly complaining at his party's conference that Britain was 'now all about Britpop and the River Café'. Under New Labour, the new middle class was in the ascendant.

But this vision of rural Tuscany on a modernised bank of the Thames did not start here. It was an idea that took shape after the end of rationing, and the particular form it took was greatly influenced by the food writer Elizabeth David.

Elizabeth David dreams of the Med

In July 1939, just two months before the British Empire declared war on Nazi Germany, Elizabeth David set off on a small sailboat named *Evelyn Hope* in search of the Mediterranean. Aged twenty-six, David embarked on the voyage with her older lover, Charles Gibson Cowan, a left-wing Jewish actor who had lived for a spell in the caves at Hastings and whom David's mother considered a 'pacifist worm'. After navigating the waterways of France, the pair were interned for a month in fascist Italy before they were able to make their way to the Greek island Syros, albeit without their boat or money. David outran the war, as well as her pacifist worm, in Egypt, where she eventually married the boorish military man Anthony David, who at the beginning of 1946 took her to live a regimented life of leisure in the British Raj. There, in New Delhi, David became chronically bored and apparently fell ill, and so finally returned to London.

After six years abroad, the Britain David returned to was in her mind a bleak one. She had experienced none of the solidarity – the Blitz spirit – that the war had induced. Her isolation from popular experience continued as rationing persisted, since David found herself in the privileged position of having occasional access to country living, meaning that she could secure luxuries like butter and cream. Once her husband had returned and set about managing an import business, she was able to obtain items like orange marmalade and sweet biscuits made with fine white flour too.

But David's privilege and wartime adventures also gave her a unique perspective on British food and what it had become: bland, repetitive and stale – in a word, modern. She viewed her first encounter with rationing as a challenge, attempting new dishes such as wild duck – cheap to obtain, although some of the specimens were 'distinctly fishy' – with garlic, onions and stock made from bacon bones. While she did so she worried about how these relatively unknown smells might disturb her uptight neighbours.

While staying with a friend, David attempted to challenge the tradition of a Sunday lunch in which vegetables were peeled and then boiled for hours in separate pans. This, she complained, was a waste of both fuel and effort, all for dubious reward. Yet she was reproached when her friend witnessed how much her children enjoyed her red wine sauce (the plonk came from Albania), rather than the usual 'gravy' produced with the water used to boil the cabbage. 'Back we had to go to that barbarous routine,' she wrote in a letter. 'And so it went on ... I had always thought it impossible not to enjoy cooking, but now it had indeed become that drudgery of which so many English women complain all their lives.'[11]

When, in November 1946, intensely cold weather set in, David fled from London with a former lover to a hotel in Herefordshire that was bathed in the warmth of great coal fires. Here too David complained about the food. While 'shortages did make catering a nightmare', she wrote in the pages of the *Spectator* seventeen years after this staycation, 'there was no excuse, none, for such unspeakably dismal meals as in that dining room were put in front of me. To my agonised homesickness for the sun and southern food was added an embattled rage that we should be asked – and should accept – the endurance of such cooking.'[12] Stuck at the hotel, now alone, David began to dream of the Mediterranean: 'those blessed lands of sun and sea and olive trees'. 'During those icy, hungry, weeks,' she reflected, 'my remote and at the time rather austere Greek island life began to take on the glow of a lost Paradise of plenty and glamour.'[13]

What followed was *A Book of Mediterranean Food*, which at the time would have seemed more like a romantic travelogue than a practical list of recipes. What David describes as the 'ever recurring elements in the food throughout these countries' – olive oil, saffron, garlic, wine, herbs, peppers, aubergines, tomatoes, melons, figs, fresh fish and meat – were sheer exotica to the average ration-weary Briton in 1950, the year the book appeared. 'Looking back to those days ... I see that it was ... largely in a spirit of defiance that I wrote down those Mediterranean recipes,' she reflects in an updated preface. And it was this spirit that attracted a string of good reviews.[14]

Although a child of privilege – the daughter of an industrialist and Tory MP on her father's side and a viscount and mine owner on her mother's – David wrote for a new middle-class generation that was having to make do without full-time help (a consequence of the war and the resulting low level of unemployment in industry).[15] In her *Book of Mediterranean Food* she helpfully offers that her recipes for paella, cassoulet and pilaf are 'fine dishes which are particularly suitable to our servantless lives'.

It was in this context that David helped to rescue cookery from its place within the toil of domestic labour. She encouraged her readers to see that shopping in Soho for olive oil or slowly braising a shin of beef could become a sensual joy quite separate from the tasks of cleaning, rearing children and washing clothes. Help to undertake those lesser tasks could be paid for, where possible, but cooking, in her view, should become a thing of leisure.

Through reference to provincial France and the largely unknown regional cuisine of Italy, David articulated a new way of being middle class, one akin to sleeping under a duvet or buying mid-century modern furniture and watching French cinema. When it came to Italian domestic cookery she admired the daily trips taken to abundant markets, the strict seasonality of the recipes and 'the extreme freshness and lavishness' of the produce.[16] Olive oil, along with wine, lemons and garlic, were for her 'genuine foods' that might make up for the deficiencies of English cuisine. As she saw it, her work spoke for a generation that was interested neither in the factory foods of British modernity, nor in fine dining or imperialist curry, but rather was 'hungry for the luxury of authenticity'.[17] David prised open the histories of pre-modern English foods later in her writing career, but, at the outset, the authenticity that she and her generation sought was firmly located in the land of the grape and the olive.

The River Café follows in this vein. The strict seasonality, the ever-changing menu based upon the contents of a walk-in fridge that stands in for the contents of the market. The sensual method of cooking: smelling, tasting, pressing meat with one's finger. All of it belongs to the outlook of Elizabeth David.

When Ruth Rogers and Rose Gray heard that David, then in her seventies, had a reservation at their restaurant, the pair welcomed her while wearing T-shirts with a recipe for a chocolate tart from her *Book of Mediterranean Food* printed on the back.

Cucina rustica?

For the readers of Elizabeth David's books, as for the chefs and diners at the River Café, the idea of authentic Italian food can summon a sort of pre-industrial idyll in the tradition of British Romanticism. Yet the new middle class that began to take shape in Britain after the war was not alone in harbouring arcadian visions of Europe. Italy itself was in the grip of a great transformation – *il boom economico italiano* – prompting some of the same social dislocations that, as we have already seen in this book, Britain had experienced much earlier. Between 1958 and 1963, Italy saw a huge leap in industrial production, with extensive internal migration from the poorer South to the rapidly urbanising North.

In reaction to this context, the soul of Italian food was often nostalgically portrayed as belonging to a disappearing agricultural past. In his legendary travelogue series *In Search of Genuine Foods: Journey into the Po Valley*, first broadcast in 1957, the urbanite director Mario Soldati – with a charming swagger reminiscent of Anthony Bourdain – comes to terms with the extent of industrial food production in post-war Italy. His series portrays the vast number of thriving artisanal traditions coexisting with the recent emergence of mechanised techniques. It is a snapshot of Italy poised between tradition and modernity in a region which for most Italian viewers at the time – that small proportion of the population affluent enough to afford a television – would have been mildly exotic.

For the historian Massimo Montanari, Soldati's *Journey into the Po Valley* helped inaugurate a new status for the foods and inhabitants of the Italian *campagna*.[18] Adverts for distinctly modern products such as dried pasta and sweet biscuits followed in this vein, tending to depict rural life in Italy as a pre-industrial Eden – a happy and abundant world free of modern alienation. This sentimental idea of (a largely invented) rural culture continued to anchor the self-image of Italy during a turbulent 1960s.[19]

Is it possible that the British reception of Italian food mirrored Italy's own discontents? There are certainly parallels to be drawn. The River Café's first cookbook – published as *Italian Country Cookbook* in America – celebrates what it calls 'rustic European cooking', a term that frequently appeared in reviews of the restaurant. Much as in Italy itself, the English fixation with Italy makes a virtue out of the country's relative 'backwardness' – the idea that Italy has a foot in the premodern past. This idea distinguished Italian cooking from both the grand French tradition and the dull modern English one in which eating could be a mere necessity, speaking instead to the new middle-class taste for down-to-earth informality.

How else to explain the embrace of polenta – once a staple of the Northern Italian rural poor – by well-heeled diners at the River Café? Around 1870, the average agricultural family in Veneto spent some 60 per cent of their income on cornmeal. The boiled porridge they ate was typically served without condiments, except a little salt, and eaten without cutlery, except perhaps a spoon. 'Tradition has it that a smoked herring was hung above the table and the piece of polenta was rubbed with it just to add a little flavour', the historians Alberto Grandi and Daniele Soffiati tell us.[20] The herring itself was reserved for a special occasion. The amount spent on cornmeal in Italy had fallen to less than 5 per cent by 1950; by the 1980s consumption of this old-fashioned staple was relatively rare. 'As soon as economic circumstances allowed, no one remained faithful to the peasant diet of polenta.'[21] Yet the grain came to be celebrated by the new middle class in London.

During my *stage* at the River Café, a dish of fried polenta with sage was on the menu priced at £30. 'This is about dreams', as Rachel Kelly made clear in her review. 'No one thinks it is really poor man's food.'[22] And, so, when we eat at the River Café or cook from one of their books, we enter into this fantasy.

Here I was, during my *stage*, happily working with my hands: chopping fat chunks of juicy tomatoes, peeling new season's artichokes, cutting the crusts off a loaf sourdough for use in *ribollita,* a rustic Tuscan soup (the bread was ordered in for this purpose and left to go stale), and filleting large wild sea bass that were caught on small boats fishing out of Cornwall using only a hook and line.

When it comes to jobs that could be completed much quicker using machines such as a food processor, the preference at the restaurant is always for the use of analogue instruments such as a pestle and mortar. There is no Vitamix, Thermomix or Pacojet, and God forbid a sous vide machine. (Elizabeth David went so far as to outlaw garlic crushers when she ran a shop in London's upmarket Pimlico.)

And yet the big balls of squidgy mozzarella are flown fresh into London from Naples every day. The price of this cheese varies according to an international market for dairy. The buffalo that provide milk live in sheds, they eat mechanically harvested hay and imported grain, they are fed hormones and antibiotics, they are milked by great sucking machines and the milk is processed in sterilised metal tanks in which it is heated to a legal temperature by the burning of imported gas. The bouquets of artichokes are picked by wage labourers, not peasants. These are transported from the fields by tractor, packed into plastic crates and loaded into refrigerated lorries that drive north, transiting through tunnels that have been bored out of mountains.

While simple and strictly seasonal, a single dish at River Café may combine wheat grown in France, tomatoes ripened in Sicily, cheese from the Alps, basil flown in from Florence, oil from olives milled in Tuscany, peppercorns from India, sea salt from Essex and endless clean water from a treatment plant in Beckton.

Is this *country* cooking at all? Pizza and pasta come from Naples, once one of the largest cities in Europe. Ragù, tortellini and mortadella all come from Bologna. The best prosciutto comes from Parma. There is *bistecca fiorentina*, *risotto alla milanese*, pesto from Genoa and *cacio e pepe* from Rome. Carbonara is a product of American military bases and, yes, it was originally made there with cream. A close reading of David's *Italian Food* reflects the urban nature of the cuisine. With guidance from the tourist board in Rome, we can see that the doyenne of provincial cookery conducted the vast majority of her research in cities and towns. It seems David knew that, as the historian John Dickie has put it, 'the real adventure of Italian food is not to be found by trekking off into the Tuscan hills', but rather by those who 'roam the city streets'.[23]

It is Italy's post-war *modernity* that made cooking in the relatively young nation a celebrated matter of leisure and eating something that the majority of people could do for reasons other than sustenance. Around the time of unification in 1861, some 60 per cent of Italians lived rurally and almost never consumed meat, other than pork fat, and typically rarely consumed fish, milk or cheese. The average diet actually became worse as Italy approached the twentieth century, with calorie intake falling below subsistence levels and prompting millions of the country's rural poor to flee to the Americas. It's only after the war that basic nutrition improved. Take, for instance, the fact that Italians are known to be shorter than many of their fellow Europeans: it would be more accurate to say that they have simply been stunted. Over the course of the economic boom, the average height of a man in Italy gained four centimetres, a figure that has continued to increase ever since (while, in contrast, average heights in England are declining).

It is thus that we see the extent of the River Café's dreams. The bucolic image conjured by handmade dishes of bread soup and spikey Tuscan olive oil speaks to a tactile life, a life connected to collective craft and the natural cycle of the seasons, one perhaps less alienated than the average urban experience. Yet, like the architecture of the restaurant itself, it is an artisanal, 'rustic' way of living that remains distinctly modern.

Like Soldati's *Journey into the Po Valley*, the River Café holds together the modern with the invented and the almost-swept-away. When Elizabeth David set out to write about the Mediterranean, the sense among the new middle class was that England had long lost its culinary connection to nature and small-scale artisanal production, whereas Italy, poorer and backward, had not. But it was only in the post-war conditions of Italy's modernity, which combined relative abundance with inventive nostalgia, that the culinary craft economy – the one that eaters in England so admire – had begun to thrive.

Utopia

Already on the first day of my *stage* at the River Café I was struck by the sense of having entered a sort of commune. In the absence of any obvious leadership, I watched as chefs hurried around the kitchen carrying boxes of vegetables and trays of meat and fish. On a bench by the recently lit wood-fired oven, a pair of cooks stood shoulder to shoulder ripping through a sack of purple cannellini beans while chatting about their weekends; another chef was entirely occupied by a leg of lamb, peering over tortoise-rimmed glasses as she directed a sharp knife into meat the colour of an aged red wine. All the while, sat at a dining table drenched in sunlight, the day's head chef sipped a cappuccino as she dreamt up the menu for lunch.

According to Rose Gray and Ruth Rogers, the plan for the River Café was to create 'a kind of utopia on the banks of the Thames'.[24] It's depicted as such by Richard Rogers. 'Outside, on a summer's afternoon,' the architect wrote of the restaurant attached to his former offices, 'the garden feels like London's best secret: hidden away down residential back-streets, with children playing on the lawn while their parents eat under the trees among the planters filled with fresh herbs and vegetables.' Inside, the open-plan kitchen happily blurs the boundaries between cook and customer. 'We wanted the restaurant to be like a big family,' the two chefs reflected, and that to me is more or less how it felt.

The River Café's cookbooks are meant to bring a sense of this utopia into the reader's home. More than recipes, the books provide you with a list of rules. Apricots, for example, 'should be eaten at room temperature, never chilled'. Asparagus may only be appreciated between April and June, 'for when the season ends it should not be bought again until the following year'. Dried porcini are best acquired in person, in Italy, since only then can you discern their value. Quality is paramount: 'the olive oil must be the best extra virgin, the salt must be Maldon sea salt and the parsley must be flat leaf'. Growing your own herbs, we are told, is 'essential for a civilized life'.

The books contain advice, such as what to do if you cannot get hold of fresh Italian vegetables: 'If you have a garden you should experiment with growing your own. If not, try farmers' markets, pick-your-own farms and organic box schemes. But above all develop a relationship with your greengrocer.'[25] And there are simple recipes for times when all you have to hand are organic lemons, parmesan, pasta and that handy bottle of the best olive oil.

The mantras in the River Café cookbooks, like their depictions of artisanal life in Italy, are perfectly pitched for British audiences who feel themselves adrift from earthly culinary traditions. They speak to the same feeling of anomie as self-help manuals. And yet the cookbooks are not for everyone – the price of olive oil alone should make that obvious. Except, at times, it isn't.

Compared with the River Café, Restaurant X is an unashamedly elitist, bourgeois environment. By contrast, one consequence – or indeed the very purpose – of the new middle-class pursuit of down-to-earth, rustic authenticity is the tasteful obscuring of the elite nature of that class's modes of life. The ideological function of middle-class culinary culture is to conceal material realities by proposing that plain, honest, humble living is simply a matter of taste, and therefore a matter of choice. The point can be illustrated in the case of Jamie Oliver.

Jamie (who like other English culinary national treasures is generally known by his first name) is a celebrity chef who has sold more books in Britain than any living author, apart from J. K. Rowling. After playing a small part in a documentary about the River Café, Jamie went on to enjoy success with *The Naked Chef*, a series that embodies the informal values championed by the new middle class, here given a matey twist of authenticity by Jamie's Estuary twang.[26]

In 2005, Jamie began a successful mission to change the food served in school canteens. At Kidbrooke School in South-East London, we follow the chef as he attempts to wean children and dinner ladies off a diet that at that point was almost exclusively ultra-processed. However, Jamie's dreams of children feasting on diverse fresh meals (taking inspiration from his background at the River Café) quickly meets hard economic barriers. In one scene, Jamie is called into the headmistress's office for a telling off.

HEAD: The problem is, all three of your dishes came in over cost. The amount that's allocated [per pupil] is 37p. I mean, the Thai chicken and vegetable curry and noodles came out at a cost of nearly £1.10 per portion. The vegetable cannelloni came out at 70p. The vegetable soup and tomato bread at 62p. The pizza was the only one that came in at a good price. The problem with that is I'm not sure you actually realise that, if it goes over, the school bears the cost of it.

JAMIE [*looking suitably scalded*]: Right.

HEAD: So I've got to find where that money comes from, and that comes from either books or staffing.

But Jamie isn't a quitter. His campaign and his TV show – attracting over 5 million viewers – led to increases in central government funding for school meals and new regulation. In this instance, Jamie changed both individual tastes and the larger environment, such that these tastes became newly accessible.

Later, in *Jamie's Ministry of Food*, first broadcast in 2008, we follow the chef as he seeks to improve cookery skills among low-income people living in Rotherham, but this time his ambitious campaign fails to change the harder, material context of taste. The series kicks off with a meeting between Jamie, who turns up in Rotherham in his Range Rover, and Natasha, a single mum who feeds her children a diet of junk food. Jamie works closely with Natasha, who halfway through the series gains the confidence to cook a meal of fresh fish in front of a crowd gathered in the town centre. We see Natasha sautéing salmon in the market square wearing a pink T-shirt on which are printed the words: 'Before I met Jamie Oliver, I only ate kebabs.'

Several weeks later, Oliver pulls up at Natasha's house to check on the progress of his star pupil. Stood in Natasha's kitchen, Jamie receives another hard lesson in home economics.

JAMIE: How's things been going, have you been cooking much?

NATASHA: No. It hasn't been a good week if I'm honest. Well, it's been a crap few weeks.

JAMIE: Just other stuff, or ... ?

NATASHA: Yeah, nowt to do with the cooking, nowt to do with you. It's just, [*she pauses*] bills, debts, just embarrassing things really.

JAMIE: Money?

NATASHA: Yeah. I know it sounds a bit shit, but I can't see why I should waste the bit of money I have got on bus fare and that to go and buy meat and fish. And benefits are tight; really, really tight. So what do I do: go shopping or buy clothes or pay for electric? I haven't got the money to do the whole lot. And that's why I'm in a mess now. I've got nowt else to sell, nowt else to get rid of.

JAMIE: What do you mean?

NATASHA [*lights a cigarette and starts to cry*]: I'm sorry. I've got no jewellery left.

JAMIE: Oh, you've started pawning stuff?

NATASHA: I don't wanna do this ...

Speaking to camera after this episode, Jamie is sincere in his compassion and his desire to help Natasha change her family's diet. But this time he's confronting obstacles, including the benefits system, that the cook was unable to identify, never mind change. More recently, in 2025, Oliver has been criticised for discounting the cost of olive oil in the recipes featured in his *£1 Wonders* series (recipes in the series included pizza, spaghetti, gnocchi, risotto and minestrone, alongside more native-sounding staples like chicken pie).

Jamie has done more than anyone to take the rustic Italian trend mainstream. And he has evidently been successful in improving food standards in British schools. But traces of the River Café's idealism are combined with his distinctly Victorian-cum-New-Labour ideal of self-improvement and aspirational taste as the route out of food poverty.

Promoting his show *Jamie's Money Saving Meals* in 2013, the TV chef compared poor people in the UK with those on the Continent. Referring to people in England who are dependent on welfare, he said, 'I just want to hug them and teleport them to the Sicilian street cleaner who has twenty-five mussels, ten cherry tomatoes and a packet of spaghetti for sixty pence, and knocks out the most amazing pasta. You go to Italy or Spain and they eat well on not much money.'[27] Yet the person on unemployment insurance in England doesn't live in Italy or Spain, where the welfare system is in some ways more generous (and is certainly less geared toward directing public money to private landlords), and doesn't, by definition, have a job (i.e. isn't a street cleaner, or if they are their job clearly doesn't pay them enough to live on). There are no markets within walking distance of Natasha that will sell her twenty-five mussels and a handful of cherry tomatoes; Natashia cannot elect to live the life of an Italian or Spanish person in Rotherham – she doesn't have, as Elizabeth David put it, the 'luxury of authenticity'. Jamie's comment betrays the projection of a new middle-class romanticism that idealises an imagined poor person's exceptional quality of life in the rustic Mediterranean.

At root, Oliver's idealism stems from being the popular tribune of a utopian food culture, one presented in the guise of a collective, down-to-earth lifestyle and modelled on an idealised vision of humble Italian rurality. This self-image obscures the elitism of the rustic Italian trend – an elitism that is just as real as that of Restaurant X but which is concealed by the demotic qualities attributed to symbolic ingredients like olive oil.

Taste without equality

The genius of the River Café is its combination of luxury with a utopian ethic of non-hierarchical rusticity. This it achieves by referencing a largely imagined peasant cuisine, one that combines health concerns with Southern European Arcadia and a relaxed, almost austere, notion of life's simple pleasures – all of which tactfully masks its elitism. It is a cuisine that cultivates a way of seeing the world that, to reverse the old adage, knows the value of everything but price of nothing.

And yet there is a kernel of progressivism in the River Café. It shares with Restaurant X an emphasis on craft, sensuality and seasonality – all things that should be widely embraced. The River Café's ideals of gender equality, communality and informality are also virtues. The restaurant has helped to lighten the British palate, to give form to a broader shift in England from an almost exclusive focus on flesh towards the world of plants. While it's new-middle-class perspective emphasises the natural and down-to-earth, the restaurant in fact serves as a model for combining the artisanal with the modern.

But when the River Café's utopian spirit tries to mark out the borders of civilised life ('grow your own herbs', only use 'the best extra virgin'), then it is little wonder that olive oil, along with an appreciation for the many forms of artisanal food that are available today – from sourdough to hand-crafted sausages to farmhouse cheeses – ends up being rejected by many English eaters as 'posh', and hence becomes a fault line in the culture war over the nation's table.

The social exclusivity associated with campaigns to eat seasonally and only use the best extra virgin means that these campaigns can be self-defeating, insofar as they provoke a backlash in the form of celebrations of their opposite: of foods that are industrially produced and cheap, that are unpretentious and self-depreciating and yet also a marketing sensation. Or, to put it another way: owing to its class-blindness, the utopian spirit of the River Café can in fact lead to a joyful celebration of Greggs. This should come as no surprise; for ideals of good taste to become truly national, they must be part of a broader movement for the material enrichment of all.

Then again, to put aside craft, taste, nation and democracy, perhaps all food really amounts to is a personal, trackable requirement for calories?

6

Food as Fuel

TANK: *Here you go, buddy. Breakfast of champions.*

[...]

[Neo scoops up a spoonful]

DOZER: *It's a single-celled protein combined with synthetic aminos, vitamins, and minerals. Everything your body needs. We grow it in a vat.*

MOUSE: *Oh no, it doesn't have everything the body needs.*

[He sidles up to Neo.]

... Pay no attention to these hypocrites, Neo. To deny our impulses is to deny the very thing that makes us human.

Lana and Lilly Wachowski, *The Matrix*, 1999

I was hungover again when I decided it was time to get in better shape. I downloaded MyFitnessPal, a popular fitness app that allows users to track their exercise and eating habits. When you open the app for the first time you swish past all the small print and then check the boxes that give permission to the app's owners – a faceless investment firm called Francisco Partners – to store your bodily data. Then you select your goal. I selected an option labelled 'you want large, well-defined muscles, with a low percentage of body fat', which sounded great. I inputted my current weight and height, and I selected an option that described my lifestyle as 'moderately active'. The app instantly fed back that I needed to eat 2,830 calories a day, which broken down into macronutrients was 283 g of carbs, 248 g of protein and 79 g of fat. Micronutrients – that's vitamins and minerals – and fibre, plus all the other more scientifically murky aspects of food, like bacteria, aren't a primary focus of a MyFitnessPal regime.

The first stumbling block was inputting what I had eaten for breakfast. How to measure the splash of milk I had in my tea? There was an option to select thirty millilitres, but that seemed like more than a splash. And the handful of mixed nuts I ate: which nuts were in my handful, and how many were they exactly? How much butter did I spread on my toast, and what did each hand-carved slice of artisan sourdough weigh? Did MyFitnessPal know the nutrient profile of a Toad Bakery loaf of bread? Did Toad Bakery even know the nutrient profile of their bread? And what would I do during work, where on an almost breakless fourteen-hour shift my diet might consist of a handful of fried potatoes gone cold in a salty mixing bowl, innumerable teaspoons of purées and sauces (checked for their flavour and seasoning), a spoonful of risotto, an occasional fleshy bone carved from a grilled pork chop and a staff meal partly made up of leftovers. How would I track *that*?

I also realised that eating 2,830 calories (kl) of lean, high-protein food is hard work. After going to the gym on the first day of my new regime, I ate a can of tuna, an entire 300 g pot of low-fat cottage cheese and a bowl of lentil soup. I used the app's barcode scanner to input the tuna (74 kl, 18 g of protein) and the cheese (333 kl, 12 g of protein), then I made a rough guess as to the nutrient profile of the soup based on the data offered for a similar-sounding ready meal sold by Sainsbury's (170 kl, 7.1 g protein). I was completely full after this strange tapas and incredibly bloated. Yet, factoring in some guesswork as to my breakfast, I was still some 1,000 calories away from meeting my new goal.

One consequence of my beginning a digital fitness journey was that YouTube was now recommending me videos of bodybuilders. Endless reels of men who, sleeveless and moderately sweaty, explained their workout and dietary regimes in no uncertain terms: I was implored by one to drink a protein shake before I worked out, not afterwards; another told me that the latest science shows that seated leg curls are better than lying ones; still others that I should eat more, or eat less, eat proteins and no carbs, eat whole grains and plenty of carbs but no vegetables, or just red meat and salt, or endless pizzas, takeaways, milkshakes, ready meals *and* protein – the latter menu being what in gym speak is referred to as a 'dirty bulk'.

I spent longer than I care to admit watching the charismatic young bodybuilder Sam Sulek, including one video where he patiently devours a breakfast of six turkey-and-mustard sandwiches plus enough minced beef and broccoli to feed an average family of four. I watched a twenty-minute video of a giant of a man, Mark Bell, eating over 12,000 calories in a day. Discussing a 'quick meal' – consisting of eight scrambled eggs, two measured-out cups of Cinnamon Toast Crunch and a spoonful of peanut butter (calculated to be a total 1,180 calories) – Bell explained that while training is fun and might last only two hours, the eating never stops. 'It's a necessary evil,' he tells the camera. Scrambling eggs without oil in a non-stick pan to what he finds to be a 'palatable texture', Bell invites you to appreciate his method: 'We want the engine burning all day long,' he says.

The disenchantment of the world by calories

Pretty much every calorie count you have ever come across is wrong. The number of calories that you see listed on the side of a cereal box, on the lid of your cottage cheese, next to items on the menu of a restaurant or accessed through a database like the one used by MyFitnessPal is most probably based on estimates first worked out by an American scientist called Wilbur Olin Atwater at the end of the nineteenth century. Building upon the work of scientists in Germany, Atwater established the energy content of foods by burning them in a sealed chamber filled with pure oxygen, called a bomb calorimeter.

A calorie – from the Latin *calor*, meaning heat – is a unit that measures the heat required to raise the temperature of one gram of water by one degree Celsius. The bomb calorimeter ('bomb' here simply means a sealed chamber in which combustion takes place) was a device developed in the nineteenth century to measure the energy content of different fuels and chemicals being used in industry, although its origins can be traced to a tool used in the 1780s to measure how long it took a guinea pig to melt a block of ice. The innovation of scientists like Atwater was to use the bomb calorimeter to establish the energy content of different foods.

The human digestive system is not, however, a sealed chamber filled with pure oxygen. And so, in an to attempt to see how much energy a human actually absorbed through food, Atwater had a respiration calorimeter built at his lab at Wesleyan University in Connecticut. This device was essentially a big box that, according to Atwater's specifications, was made large enough for a person to live in for days at a time. Inside this box, Atwater fed a person food – the known calories of which were measured by burning them – while water flowing through the box's walls measured temperature changes caused by the person's body (much like a guinea pig melting a block of ice). The subject's breathing was also measured and their excrement collected and carefully examined.

The net result of hundreds of human tests conducted inside this big box was Atwater's general system for measuring the calorie content of food, the one we still use today. This system tells us that for every gram of fat, carbohydrate and protein, the human body absorbs nine, four and four calories respectively. All that food manufacturers have to do is work out the ratio of the macronutrients – the fat, carbs and protein – in their foods and then use this index to calculate the total digestible calories of their product.

One problem with this, though, and there are several, is that different combinations of fat, carbs and protein have different effects on the body's capacity to metabolise the energy contained within food. Knowing this, Atwater also produced lists of the available calories in specific common foods. But because the white bread given on Atwater's list is unlikely to be the same as the white bread sold to you by Warburtons, and because few manufacturers want to test all their products' exact calories, the 9-4-4 indexing method is used on the packet instead. Most calorie counts are therefore simply a best guess based on Atwater's original rule of thumb.

Other problems include the fact that not every fat, carbohydrate or protein is the same. Atwater divided proteins into plant, animal and dairy, but there are variations (in what we can digest and in how much energy is in each nutrient) within these categories.

Processing food also changes its calorific availability. In a previous effort to grow muscle I had taken to making protein smoothies: a blend of whey powder, bananas, peanut butter, oats, powdered greens and a mix of seeds, including flax. Ten grams of flaxseed is, according to Atwater's index, meant to contain fifty-three calories. Yet I could see unground (that is, unprocessed) seeds reappearing undigested in the toilet.

Then there's so-called ultra-processed food. In 2010, scientists ran a test where a group of healthy subjects ate two sandwiches with an identical calorie count and macronutrient breakdown; one of the sandwiches was made with processed cheese and white sliced bread and the other made with wholefoods. The experiment showed that the wholefood sandwich caused the subjects to passively burn more energy as heat immediately after eating – a result that points to the idea that ultra-processed food can slow down an eater's short-term metabolism, and that (as some scientists believe) can lead to metabolic issues over the longer term.

In fact, the complexity of our personal metabolism makes universal readings of food in terms of calories highly questionable. Just as different people have different relationships with food and appetite, your sex, your ethnicity, your muscle mass, your sleep patterns, the complicated state of your hormones and your gut bacteria, even your physical environment and the times and frequency of your meals can all affect your metabolic rates, meaning that a calorie is unlikely to contain the same amount of available energy for you as it did for me.

In truth, calories don't exist. There is nothing in the material world that you can point to and say: 'behold, the calorie!', just as there is no centimetre, gram, degree Celsius or gross domestic product. Yet we refer to the calorie as if it were a material thing when we talk about 'eating calories' or say 'that chocolate cake is bad for you, it contains far too many calories'.

A calorie is a unit of measurement, and yet, as we've just seen, it's not an objective one. Sure, when a slice of sourdough is burnt in a sealed chamber filled with pure oxygen we can measure it as a fuel; we can give the amount of heat emitted a number and say that this slice of bread contains so many calories. But what happens in a bomb calorimeter doesn't apply to *food*, i.e. things you eat rather than place in a sealed chamber and burn. The human digestive system is not a combustion engine. Your sandwich isn't burnt inside the body: it's converted by complex processes into usable forms of energy.

Atwater had an awareness of the difference between human digestion and a controlled combustion, yet he nonetheless viewed the human body as an engine fuelled by its food (recall that this is exactly how the muscle man Mark Bell views his body). By placing a 'typical' subject in a respiration calorimeter to provide us with 'universal' calorific measurements – the ones we still use today – the experiment transformed the metaphor of the body as a machine into a scientific fact. By accepting this transformation, we have underestimated the complexity of both the body and what we eat. Food scientists have had a habit of doing this, as we will see.

Calories don't exist, and yet they are everywhere: on packaging, on apps, in public policy and in the minds of many eaters. Far from being objective, the science of the calorie not only *reflects* the industrial metaphors of the age that produced it, but it has also helped to *constitute* our current dietary culture. Science, even what we often call hard science, has a social history.[1]

⁂

In the middle of the nineteenth century, not long before the invention of calories, animal-derived protein was seen by influential thinkers in the West as the chief pillar of good nutrition. This protein bias both reflected and constituted an imperial age dominated by the beef-eating British – the era we've already encountered earlier in this book. Men like the Victorian reformer of public health Edwin Lankester saw diets rich in 'animal food' as an explanation for Britain's power and productivity, particularly after the Napoleonic Wars. Eating meat, Lankester wrote, has produced 'the most vigorous, most moral, and most intellectual races of mankind'.[2]

Ensuring that meat was affordable could thus be seen as necessary to maintaining Britain's 'reputation for downright hard physical exertion' (we might recall here the French and British railway workers mentioned in chapter two: the productivity of the British was considered to be due to their greater consumption of beef).[3] One consequence of this protein bias was that Parliament often found itself under pressure to ensure trade routes that would keep the price of beef and mutton low, taking the former from Argentina, for example, and the latter from as far away as New Zealand. In contrast, populations from Naples to Bombay had their perceived laziness blamed on diets lacking in animal foods (the Southern Italians were known as *mangiafoglie* – leaf eaters – before becoming known as *mangiamaccheroni*. South Asians' inferiority was often seen by imperialists as deriving from a diet centred on legumes and rice).

In Germany, private industrialists, often with support from the state, saw the value of nutrition in terms of remaining productive in a competitive global economy dominated by the British. The logic of protein power was forcefully expressed by the German chemist Justus von Liebig, one of the first scientists to demarcate the three macronutrients in our food. Of these, Liebig saw protein as the 'master nutrient', or the 'only true nutrient'. Liebig's view of human biology – one that would be discredited in his lifetime – saw the body's consumption of its own muscles as being responsible for its 'mechanical' energy, which is why he thought the best fuel for human activity was muscle-building protein.

Liebig applied this view of nutrition, along with his great reputation as a scientist, to the promotion of his signature meat extract – a direct forerunner of the OXO cube – as a cheap, portable alternative to fresh flesh. According to the advertising, one ounce of Liebig's extract was the nutritional equivalent of two pounds of meat. From its appearance in the mid-1860s, rehydrated beef bouillon was seen as a wonder food capable of reviving the sick, nourishing the poor and powering armies – and, in turn, nations (this marketing is one of the reasons we still think of meat broth as healthy, even though its nutritional content is typically quite slim). The recipe won the support of British doctors, who administered meat extract in hospitals; even Florence Nightingale proposed that soldiers fighting in Crimea receive beef tea in their rations.

By the end of the decade, however, the nutritional benefits of Liebig's extract had been thrown into doubt. Even worse, Liebig's infant formula, malt soup, which was intended to mimic the macronutrients found in breast milk, killed the babies who depended on it. Yet this didn't prevent the idea of a 'master nutrient' from giving rise to a suite of products and dishes – from Maggi powder, to Fray Bentos pies, to Bovril, to katsu curry – that found a lasting foothold in our global diets (the OXO cube remained a part of British military rations up until the end of the First World War, while our current craze for protein is arguably another legacy).

The protein bias of the Victorian era, which affected scientists as much as anyone else, appeared to be confirmed by a series of tests conducted on dogs. François Magendie set out to see whether dogs, and by implication humans, required nitrogen in their diets. The first of Magendie's dogs ate nothing but sugar and all died after a month. Those fed on nothing but fat likewise perished. Tests were carried out to better understand gelatine, which, since it is high in nitrogen, was hailed as a kind of superfood in 1820s and '30s France, but here, confusingly, Magendie had landed upon another fatal diet for man's best friend.

Some of the same scientists, blinded by their commitment to protein, ignored older evidence that scurvy could be treated and prevented by way of regular consumption of citrus fruits; instead, it was typically supposed, all that sailors needed was more meat. Despite outbreaks of scurvy in British prisons during the famine in Ireland having a clear causal link to the withdrawal of potatoes from inmates' rations, it was only in the early twentieth century that scientists pointed to something they called vitamin C, thus admitting this quantity into the necessities of good nutrition.

Similarly ignored was the fact that many people in British society – many Irish and South Asian people, for example – ate little to no meat and (so long as there wasn't a famine) nonetheless thrived. A nascent vegetarian movement, which included a small number of workers as well as figures like the Romantic poet Percy Bysshe Shelley, seemed to contradict the view that large amounts of protein were essential. When further experiments with dogs late in the nineteenth century also seemed to refute the idea that our bodies need beef, scientists, still blinded by the bias of their era, performed feats of mental gymnastics in order to defend Liebig's muscle-centric view.[4]

Two German scientists, Adolf Fick and Johannes Wislicenus, stood apart from the consensus, however, when, in 1866, the pair put Liebig's master nutrient thesis to the test. Over the course of a day, Fick and Wislicenus climbed a mountain while subsisting on a diet of only fat and carbohydrates. If Liebig was right, the scientists would be able to detect the consumption of the protein stored in their bodies' muscles by measuring the nitrogen in their urine. Yet the amount of nitrogen they detected was incommensurate with the precisely calculated amount of energy needed to undertake the climb. Perhaps, the pair suggested, the energy driving the body wasn't stored in muscle; perhaps the body was instead akin to the steam engine, which did not consume itself but was driven by an external fuel. What was emerging with experiments like this was a new paradigm for understanding human respiration, one informed by the metaphor of an engine and eventually captured by the idea of the calorie.

While the protein bias persisted in scientifically derived dietary standards, as it did (and still does) in our culture, the special role of protein came to be seen in terms of building and repairing the body's tissue. But fuelling the body was now understood to be a matter of simple combustion. Calories, a unit first used to measure the coal that powered a steam engine, could now be deployed to analyse the human motor – the body as a machine powered by a loaf of bread.

As a practising Christian, it was important for Atwater to frame his research in terms of helping the ignorant and needy make decisions that would improve their welfare. 'If we will care for men's souls most effectively, we must care for their bodies also', he wrote, quoting a bishop in the opening to one of his popular essays for *Century Magazine*. In another essay, Atwater lists the most nourishing foods an American worker could acquire for 25¢: a quarter spent on beef neck with a fuel value of almost 4,000 calories, for example, was more economical than sirloin, where the same budget would only deliver 1,000 calories. Both these options, he points out, are less economical than corn and beans (in his essays, Atwater often seems to have a particular gripe with oysters, which for 25¢ yield the fewest calories and the least protein of all the items listed).

The problem, as Atwater saw it, was not that American workers were underfed. In fact, his studies of working-class diets indicated that if anything they were wasting their food and eating too much. The real issue was that workers were making bad choices. Atwater struggled to comprehend people like the poorly housed coal labourer he met who, instead of saving to buy a house or find himself better accommodation to rent, 'made it an article of faith to give his family the best of flour, the finest sugar and very best quality of meat' when the nutritional equivalents of these foods could be acquired at a fraction of the price.[5] It was all so needlessly irrational.

This concern for the economy of workers overlapped with a broader spirit of industry in America. A close collaborator of Atwater's, an industrialist called Edward Atkinson, saw the economic potential of his friend's nutritional research. Atkinson firmly believed that a worker required adequate food to achieve the greatest possible output. He also believed that adequate food was a matter of individual choice. With Atwater's advice, American workers could, for example, obtain good nutrition from milk and corn that, pound for pound, contained more energy than the beefsteaks and pork chops that they typically preferred. Atkinson combined national income statistics with the nutritional science of Atwater's calorie tables to paint an elegant vision of a rational society. For Atkinson this had the makings of a win-win situation: greater nutrition meant greater output, while efficient eating decisions meant that workers would be able to adequately subsist without receiving higher wages.[6]

The irrationalism of working-class eating habits had been bothering the scientist Max Rubner in Germany as well. In Berlin in 1913, Rubner purchased twenty-eight sandwiches and found that this popular working-class lunch only delivered adequate nutrition at great expense, or else poor nutrition at a price workers could actually afford. It would be far better if this 'unnecessary custom' were replaced by the purchasing of cheaper bodily fuels like potatoes, flour, rice and beans.[7]

In Britain, meanwhile, following the lead of Charles Booth's late-Victorian survey of poverty in London's East End, Seebohm Rowntree's *Poverty: A Study of Town Life*, published in 1901, deployed Atwater's dietary standards and his calorie tables to provide an objective measurement of deprivation. 'The labouring classes', Rowntree concluded from his hometown in York, 'upon whom the bulk of the muscular work falls, and who form so large a proportion of the industrial population, are seriously underfed.'

Like Atkinson in the US, Rowntree implored his readers to recognise just how essential adequate nutrition – as understood by Atwater's latest science – was for industrial efficiency, particularly in the context of international competition. 'The machine needs fuel,' Rowntree wrote in his study. 'Starch and sugar are burned in the body and yield heat and power, just as truly as does the coal which is burned in a stove to heat the house or under a boiler to drive an engine.' And yet, like Atwater, Atkinson and Rubner, Rowntree noted the irrationality of working-class eating habits: 'established customs and many prejudices would have to be uprooted', he proposed, in order for better, more nutritious and economical choices to be made.

As we saw at the start of this book, it was only when war arrived that such concerns found an audience within Britain's political establishment. In 1899 Britain sought recruits to fight for the Empire in Southern Africa, where important gold and diamond deposits had recently been found. Yet around half of those who signed up for the Boer War were deemed to be physically unfit for service, with many men having been crippled by inadequate nutrition. These findings prompted a voluntary national efficiency movement aimed at promoting health through exercise and temperance, as well as the formation of the Boy Scouts Association. Again, the problem was seen in terms of individual choice (or worse, for some elites, in terms of eugenics). Yet, growing out of these imperial concerns, and as a marker of what would emerge as the welfare state, Parliament legislated to allow local authorities to tax their residents in order to feed schoolchildren.

The limited extent of these shifts, however, was evident when, according to Lloyd George, the British fighting force in the First World War lacked a million extra men because of the nation's poor diet. 'A war, like sickness, lays bare the weakness of a constitution,' the prime minister said in a major speech in Manchester in 1918. Referring to the grades used by doctors to assess the health of potential recruits, George concluded his speech with a warning: 'you cannot maintain an A-1 Empire with a C-3 population'.[8]

Such concerns prompted the state to survey the bodily welfare of Britain's inhabitants, with good health being defined as the ability to bear arms. Nutritional scientists found a voice within Whitehall for the first time during the war and afterwards, combining Atwater's calorie indexes with native testing to determine suitable dietary standards.[9]

Although the importance of adequately feeding soldiers had long been recognised, Edward Cathcart and John Orr declared in the opening of their report on the subject, published in 1919, that 'there has been no serious investigation of the food requirements for the performance of military duties'.[10] This report included extensive tables accounting for the calorie expenditure of troops engaged in activities that ranged from standing to attention to bayonet fighting. The pair found that British troops, overall, needed to eat more calories. Under orders from Winston Churchill, the joint armed forces finally centralised their meal provision in the 1920s, partly to ensure that these scientifically determined standards were met.

Just as Liebig's science of protein took its cues from Britain's traditional dietary preferences at the height of its Empire, so too could the calorie both justify and amplify existing national diets, albeit now in an era in which industrial workers had taken centre stage. Sugar was everywhere in Edwardian England, providing around a quarter of all calories consumed.[11] Sweet tea, jam, condensed milk, boiled sweets, chocolate, biscuits, fizzy pop and cakes all rotted teeth, which were often dispensed with at an early age (a fact that drove a preference for soft, processed foods and an aversion to harder foods, as was evident from Britain's displeasure with heavy loaves of darker bread), leading to dramatic changes in the shape of the average British jawline. Contemporaries of this new era of nutrition began to see sugar as a wonder food. As per her love of the OXO cube, Florence Nightingale now viewed sugar as 'one of the most nutritive of all articles', while one Edwardian doctor claimed that sugar was the best fuel for children, causing their bodies to 'blaze with energy'.[12] William Beveridge, the man seen as the father of Britain's welfare state, thought sugar 'so well-suited to children' that it was 'practically irreplaceable'.[13] (Alcohol would likely have been seen in much the same way – Atwater had found that it served very well as a fuel, having made a man live off nothing but wine in one of his experiments – had it not been for temperance movements that combined religious moralism with concerns about the tendency of heavy drinking to lead to factory disobedience, worker absences and domestic strife.)[14]

In Britain's prisons, the modern science of calorific calculations could be used to administrate the traditional preference for punitively under-nourishing diets, while school and hospital catering developed with persistent reference to Atwater's index. By the outbreak of the Second World War, scientists, including Orr, had taken the lead in designing a plan for rationing based upon the science of caloric needs, an approach which by now dominated the state's thinking when it came to administering food.

For 'less developed' nations, where traditional foods remained a barrier to greater consumption of cheap calories and therefore to national progress, traditions could be altered and new ones invented. The modern moussaka – with its layer of béchamel in place of what was once a kind of yoghurt – is a dish created in such a vein. Famously, Gandhi resisted these calls to science and progress, advocating dietary abstinence instead.

In his *Scenes from the Life of the Future*, a collection of stories and essays reflecting on the modern culture of America, the French author Georges Duhamel despairs at the new world that was waiting in store for Europeans, particularly when recounting how a man whom Duhamel had dined with had said he should order oatmeal and cream rather than sweet potatoes, since 'it will give you two hundred more calories'.

'It will give me *what?*' Duhamel replied. 'I said two hundred calories. It's much richer in nourishment.' Duhamel looked again at his menu to find a definite number beside each dish. 'The idea of eating calories spoils my appetite,' the Frenchman told his American companion.

Mastery of the self

On the first Friday of my new regime I wildly overshot my calorie goal by drinking four pints of Stella, two small cans of IPA and a pint of Guiness. My cousin was in town with his band, the Reytones, and things got a bit out of hand. On Saturday morning, after a terrible night's sleep, I inputted the cursed data and MyFitnessPal told me that I would get fat if I carried on like this. Feeling embittered, I paused my new diet for the weekend to eat pizza and recover.

The following week went OK. I managed to keep up regular appearances at the gym, and I ate plain yet 'palatable' high-protein meals consisting mainly of cottage cheese, tuna, quinoa, vegetables and chicken. At the weekend I did a one-off shift at a trendy French bistro, during which I consumed a fried pig's ear, a spoonful of braised pork, a slice of cured ham, a chicken heart and several teaspoons of a heavily reduced sauce, in addition to drinking a glass of crisp white wine when the shift was finished. The following day I ate Turkish food in North London, sharing with my partner plates of hummus, fluffy white bread, pickles and juicy grilled lamb, plus a jug of wonderfully salty ayran. I was forced to accept the loss of another weekend's worth of data.

These first two weeks of calorie counting made me realise that the easiest way to conform to a MyFitnessPal regime was to eat things with barcodes, ideally weighing out the portions beforehand. But I'd already grown tired of raw-dogging cans of tuna, weighing my muesli and eating cottage cheese directly out of the pot with a spoon. I was also concerned about the expense and the suffering involved in eating so much fish and chicken.

It was around this time that the YouTube algorithm introduced me to Huel, a meal-replacement drink available as a powder to mix with water or in ready-to-consume elongated plastic bottles. One of Huel's founders is James Collier, a former bodybuilder and nutrition scientist who at fifty-two maintains biceps that are roughly equivalent in their width to that of my thighs. 'If you're a bodybuilder trying to gain muscle and you're struggling to eat as much as you need to, [Huel] can be your extra meal', Collier said in an interview.[15] I thought I would give this a go, and within twenty-four hours of ordering I had before me a large cardboard box containing my first two bags of powdered food. 'You're a Hueligan now', the legend printed inside the box told me when I opened it. 'You've made the right choice to be healthier, save money, and help our planet', it said, signed Julian Hearn, another of Huel's founders.

Huel – the name is a portmanteau of 'human fuel' – is a nutritionally complete and efficient way of eating, at least according to the marketing. I can vouch for the latter. All that is required to consume a portion of Huel is to place two scoops of the beige powder, which smells faintly of rice bran, in the branded beaker provided, add water, shake and drink. As to the claim of being nutritionally complete, I cannot say. Huel is a mix of oats, peas, rice, tapioca and sunflower oil, all converted to a powdered form, plus isolated vitamins, minerals and artificial emulsifiers – some of which I recognised from working in high-end kitchens (hello xanthan gum).

I've heard experts in nutrition vouch for Huel. But then, didn't experts in nutrition vouch for the superfood properties of gelatine that turned out, after research, to be functionally useless? Didn't they also claim that Liebig's beef extract would fuel the powerful and cure the needy, only for that, too, to turn out to be only slightly more nutritious than a cup of hot water with a spoonful of salt? And then of course there was Liebig's deadly baby formula.

I ordered two types of Huel: the one containing extra protein (40 g per portion) was totally plain, without artificial sweeteners or flavouring. Drinking this is an unmemorable experience, akin to gulping down a thin slurry of porridge. To be honest, I did not really mind it. My other bag was of 'Huel original', containing half the amount of protein plus sucralose and unspecified 'natural flavourings', which to me tasted faintly of carob.

I found drinking the flavoured, lower-protein version to be a more memorable experience, but not in a good way. After the initial grainy, oaty taste fades as the slurry glides down your throat, your palate is left covered by an enduring film of sweetness. I also found that consuming Huel original made me horribly bloated, which from a quick internet search seems to be a pretty common reaction. I put this down to the sucralose – some scientists think that the indigestible sweetener damages your gut microbiome. I emailed Huel and reported this experience, and they sent me another bag of their unflavoured option.

After some initial sampling, I decided to replace at least one meal a day with Huel for at least a month. Now working in an upmarket modern Mediterranean restaurant directly inspired by the River Café, I found that I could quickly mix a beaker of Human Fuel and drink it while deshelling a huge box of hand-dived scallops. I gulped down Huel mid-service while gently poaching wild sea trout and running tweezers through a pot of heavily seasoned Italian spinach, slick with a grassy olive oil. I enjoyed feeling efficiently full at work, and MyFitnessPal loved it when I inputted another two scoops of Huel, rewarding me at the end of the day with gratifying pie charts and dietary affirmations. I drank Huel blended with a banana before a workout and felt, on one occasion, the metaphor of the body as a machine come to life as I rowed against the clock.

On YouTube I watched men (it seemed to be exclusively men) in their late twenties and thirties document themselves as they subsisted on nothing but Huel for a month. A passionate rock climber enjoyed how efficient his diet had become, although he spent half a day during this experiment hugging his knees on the sofa as he suffered from painful stomach cramps. Another reported that Huel had allowed him to give up a diet of junk food. He was elated at having reclaimed his life from a weekday rhythm of supermarket meal deals and told viewers about his new-found energy, which he invested in further self-improvement in the gym.

The official story behind Huel goes that Julian Hearn, the man whose signature appeared on my Huel delivery box, invented the product after setting himself the goal of dropping from 21 to 11 per cent body fat. Hearn achieved this goal through a strict calorie-controlled diet, one high in animal proteins and wholefoods. Hearn carefully measured out all his ingredients and cooked his meals from scratch. But when friends – tech entrepreneurs like himself – wanted to know how Hearn had lost so much weight, they found his answer too expensive and laborious. 'I had the idea that there should be an easier way of getting this complete diet in a more time-saving way', Hearn told the *Guardian*.[16]

The bodybuilder Collier was hired to advise on the recipe while Hearn focused on the branding. Huel's simple logo is rendered in Helvetica, the clean Swiss typeface that once epitomised corporate blandness but which today is associated with a connoisseur's appreciation for good graphic design. The packaging – simply contrasting black and white – has the same ubiquitous elegance as products like the iPhone, as if intended to melt into the modern landscape. Huel's merch, its T-shirts and the beakers that come free with your first purchase, promotes the cultish idea, indicated on the box, of being a proud 'Hueligan'.

Huel's growth has exceeded its founders' expectations. Launched in 2015, the company claims to have enjoyed an average annual growth of 16 per cent. Its success is expected to continue, in part due to the growing popularity of appetite-suppressing dieting drugs like Ozempic.

Yet the originality of the product is overstated. To write a history of the many claims that humans have made about a single source of food providing all the body's needs we might start with the Ancient Greek myths, in which the gods feasted exclusively upon ambrosia, or nectar (think of how various cheap lagers today get described as 'the nectar of the gods'). Other historical forerunners to the apparently 'complete nutrition' of Huel include ship's biscuits, or hard tack, which was basically flour, water and salt; American K-rations, which were composed of canned meals, powdered drinks, sugar tablets and cigarettes; the space food that was developed by NASA and dispensed from squeezable tubes; dieting shakes such as those provided by Weight Watchers; calorie-dense famine foods like Plumpy'Nut; and the 'tube feeds' prescribed to hospital patients who are incapable of eating (as well as, historically, to imprisoned food strikers). Huel stands out from its predecessors not because it claims to be based on the latest (the latest, latest, latest) nutritional science, but because people like me are slurping down this replacement meal more or less by choice.

Yet the most obvious, direct forerunner to Huel is Soylent, a US company established in 2013 by Rob Rhinehart, who like Hearn was once an aspiring tech entrepreneur. Rhinehart was less proficient in marketing, however. Soylent is apparently named after a fictional soy and lentil product that appears in the sci-fi novel *Make Room! Make Room!*, which depicts life in a world crippled by overpopulation, but the name is far more reminiscent of the film adaptation of the same book, *Soylent Green*, in which the inhabitants of a dystopian New York eat a product made of human flesh.

The development of Soylent was wonderfully amateurish, even compared to other instances in the now-familiar genre of giant American corporations that were established by geeks in a garage. Rhinehart documented Soylent's creation in a series of now-infamous blog posts, beginning with one entitled 'How I Stopped Eating Food'. 'Food is the fossil fuel of human energy,' Rhinehart writes at the beginning of this post, using a somewhat awkward metaphor – surely food is the food of human energy? – but one which underlines his Atwater-esque view of eating as a mechanistic necessity. Rhinehart goes on to say that he 'resented the time, money, and effort [that] the purchase, preparation, consumption, and clean-up of food was consuming'. Food, for Rhinehart, is a waste, and, as he points out, it also produces waste ('Why else would the trash can always be in the kitchen?'). His sci-fi futurism is of an old industrial vintage. Wouldn't it be better, Rhinehart muses, if we could 'spend less energy getting energy'? Atwater, Atkinson, Rubner and Rowntree certainly thought so.

Rhinehart says that he set out to engineer a meal replacement that would, as he put it (apparently unknowingly paraphrasing a famous scene in *The Matrix*), provide him with 'every vitamin and mineral the body needs'. 'The first morning my kitchen looked more like a chemistry lab than a cookery [*sic*], but I eventually ended up with an [*sic*] thick, odorless, beige liquid. I call it "Soylent",' he wrote in his blog. Rhinehart studied human biology and government nutritional guidelines, bought all the isolated nutrients online, mixed them together and drank his potion. 'It was delicious! I felt like I'd just had the best breakfast of my life.' (Reading this, one must keep in mind that prior to drinking his nutrients Rhinehart was almost exclusively eating junk food, judged by him to be the cheapest way to get calories, plus vitamin C tablets to prevent scurvy.)

On day three of consuming Soylent, the blog continues, Rhinehart 'noticed [his] heart was racing and [his] energy level was suddenly dropping'. He realised that he'd forgotten to include iron in his recipe. Soylent 1.0 also contained almost no fibre, enabling Rhinehart to declare that he no longer needed to poo. Recently, however, scientists have found fibre to be far more important to our gut health than had previously been thought, and so Soylent, the product you can still buy today, have had to put it back in.

In a documentary made by *Vice* shortly after Soylent became available to buy online, we find Rhinehart and a merry band of bearded tech entrepreneurs in dirty sandals and tokenistic hairnets spooning sacks of powder into silver bags. The camera cuts to a rat scurrying away from the production area as a voice-over explains that, because regulators don't view Soylent as a food, they do not require the company to meet the usual standards. In the documentary, Rhinehart is dismissive of those who think the problem with food is over-processing and who call for greater harmony with nature: 'I think there's just an emotional attachment to culture and tradition,' he says.

There are comparisons to be made between Rhinehart and Steven Bartlett, another of the big names associated with Huel. Bartlett is a guy you might know. He's behind the chart-topping podcast *The Diary of a CEO* and the bestselling book of the same name. He appears on the TV show *Dragons' Den* and, like Rhinehart, considers himself to be a tech entrepreneur. While Rhinehart landed on Soylent after working without pause trying to develop a cheaper alternative to broadcasting towers, Bartlett made his first million via Social Chain, a social media marketing company (how much money Bartlett actually made from Social Chain has been disputed). Both men embody a productivist spirit of self-optimisation, as is manifest in their commitment to the efficiently consumable 'complete foods' Soylent and Huel.

After interviewing Julian Hearn on his podcast, Bartlett became an investor in and a board member of Huel, as well as becoming an important face of its marketing. Since then, Bartlett has told fans that he was gulping Huel (his favourite flavour is berry) throughout his time as CEO of Social Chain (although Social Chain predates Huel's launch by a year). His video advertisements are intended to make you feel as though Huel is a key part of his success.

Bartlett's book – subtitled *The 33 Laws of Business and Life* – is 'about the fundamental, enduring laws of building great things and becoming great yourself'. These laws, Bartlett claims, are universal and timeless, 'rooted in psychology, science and centuries of research', and, if that wasn't compelling enough, they are also validated by his personal survey of 'thousands of people across every continent, every age group and every profession'.[17] If that sounds hubristic, it's because it is. But so is thinking you can create a meal replacement drink after a quick bit of googling.

There are 'four pillars of greatness' proposed in Bartlett's book, the first of which is 'mastery of the self'. Comparing Bartlett and his self-help ethos to the science of welfare and warfare discussed above helps us see the extent to which responsibility for rational eating has been transferred from groups and states to individuals. In our current era in the West, a powerful narrative, one promoted by people like Bartlett, tells us that who you are – physically, emotionally, intellectually, in your careers and in your relationships – is largely down to you alone, to the decisions that you take, to the food that you consume. If there was anything that all the contradicting videos I watched on YouTube agreed upon, it was that. My fitness, my diet, *my responsibility*.

This move, from society to the self, or what in the technical jargon is called neoliberalism, has occurred over the past sixty or so years.

We can make out this shift by returning to the example of school dinners mentioned previously. When imperial concerns (about whether the population was fighting fit and able to work) prompted the British state to allow local authorities to raise the revenue needed to pay for school canteens, the 1906 Education (Provision of Meals) Act led to widespread concern that the pursuit of public welfare would have a detrimental effect on parental responsibilities and family life. Such concerns have long been used in Britain to resist the costs associated with social reform. That's why it was only when government money was made available for school dinners during the First World War that uptake came close to 10 per cent of all school children. This was to be a temporary suspension of the norms of 'free trade', however, with the rate falling back to around 1 per cent in the 1920s and '30s.[18]

The government again provided money for school meal provision during the Second World War, setting scientific standards that specified that each child should receive a 1,000-calorie meal containing twenty to twenty-five grams of animal protein and thirty grams of fat. The Education Act of 1944 put these standards on a legal footing, which appeared to mark a significant departure from the era of limited or non-existent government intervention. Centrally directed standards continued to develop along with the latest science, while the prices paid in canteens were also tightly controlled by the state. Improvements in school meals continued in the post-war era, as did improvements in childhood health. But this, too, was only temporary.

The dismantling of the school meal system began in the late 1960s under a cash-strapped Labour government, which was unwilling to push social control of the economy any further and instead favoured the gradual embrace of private ownership and market incentives. The reversal was then dramatically accelerated under the Conservative government of Margaret Thatcher. With the Iron Lady in charge, the war over the largely irrelevant Falkland Islands was carried out in a nostalgic register, for which was required all the available pomp and power of Britain's faded navy. It did not require wholesale conscription, however – far from it – and so the population's bodies were left alone.

Elsewhere, in France and Germany, for example, states have had a deeper history of intervening in their populations' diets, continuing to regulate the price of bread when Britain turned to free trade, for example, or in other nineteenth-century policies that have shown greater concern with the productivity and fighting capacity of their respective populations. The reasons for this have been hinted at in the last paragraph and elsewhere in this book: up until the mass slaughter of the First World War, Britain's global dominance had been based on its navy, which meant that, compared with the territorial focus of Germany and France, the management of large numbers of armed men was less of a priority. That same navy enabled Britain to benefit disproportionately from a system of 'free trade' that kept food costs at the heart of Empire among the lowest in the world. This, in turn, paid dividends in the relatively low cost of exports. Other nations could only hope to catch up with Britain, although the UK's peculiar model of 'free trade' development could not, in practice, be copied outright, meaning that greater state intervention was required. In this sense, Britain's naval supremacy once again casts a long shadow.

~

From society, then, back to the self. And if there is a self that Steven Barlett has mastered, it's the 'self' of self-promotion. Putting to one side his universal laws and his attribution of his success to factors like conviction, compulsive work, exercise, carefully monitored sleep patterns, supplement-taking and attention to diet more generally, his business model is straightforward. Barlett tends to find a consumable good that he can invest in, then he uses his influencer status to promote it. The richer Bartlett becomes, the more influential he is. The more influential he is, the richer he becomes. Bartlett has made a name for himself by telling you that certain character traits and habits are the keys to success, but in fact he is not really *telling* you anything; he's *selling* you something. Although it can be hard to discern what makes Bartlett so successful from his cosmic spew of self-promotion, he has never really hidden the fact that he works in marketing. He's a salesman, and he typically sells products that he has a personal stake in.

In 2023 Bartlett found another gig. Zoe is a company that offers personalised data on your health and diet by taking samples of your excrement and monitoring the sugar levels in your blood for two weeks. Once Zoe has built up a profile of your metabolism, its app (£300 for the initial subscription and £60 a month thereafter) can be used to monitor everything you eat, providing you with a score that is meant to tally with what is good for *you*. In this privatised health space we find that we are now a long way from Atwater's recommendations for calorie intakes, which were merely subdivided in accordance with the anticipated needs of different social groups (sedentary workers were told to eat less than stonemasons, for example).

The nature of work has changed since Atwater produced his tables. Physical exertion is now a far less fundamental factor in economic productivity. We have become concerned with eating too much and moving too little. Unless, like me, you are trying to gain muscle, calories are counted today with a view to losing weight, not to fuelling our bodies like coal fuels an engine. Our minds are increasingly likely to play the central role in our productive endeavours: picture men like Rhinehart and Bartlett slurping their powders while plugged into their laptops, with Rhinehart having managed to cut down the time he spends on the toilet to do so. 'If there was a way that I couldn't eat so that I could work more, I would not eat', Elon Musk once posted on X.

Our bodies are seen as barriers to greater productivity in the workplace, while outside of it they can become aesthetic objects – so much clay to be shaped in the manner of Greek statues, bleached of their weirder contextual markings and boasting the sculpted curves and flat stomachs that mark out an optimised self.

Zoe reminds us that science and society are still very much mutually constitutive. Awareness of the idiosyncratic aspects of our personal metabolisms is the cutting edge of modern nutritional research, hence the production of tools like Zoe, which in turn reinforce an individualised culture that has all but dispensed with dietary standards for distinct social groups. It is possible to conceive of a very different science of nutrition (one focused on enabling humans to feel greater empathy with animals, for example – or how about one promoting beard growth in women?), but it is hard to imagine such a science taking shape in the absence of the contextual factors that would favour its development (greater respect for animals, or a deep love for feminine facial hair). The science of vitamins was well advanced by the time of the Second World War, but scarcity meant that fruit was treated as a low public health priority by official nutritionists, and the old science of the cheapest calorie took precedence. Scientific concerns, then, both reflect and help to reproduce broader social concerns.

Zoe also shows that, while we live in new times defined by individual optimisation, our context is deeply layered by long-standing traditions. When Thatcher removed the duty of schools to provide students with any kind of meal, very few of them actually stopped serving food. What she failed to remove was the expectations that accompanied the brief golden age of the welfare state. Today, in Britain, we still think that everyone has a universal right to healthcare, free at the point of use. Yet living alongside the NHS are a growing number of elite, personalised services like Zoe.

Listening to Bartlett's podcast, you get the feeling that too much conflicting information has become a source of confusion even for the show's charismatic host. In several episodes Bartlett platforms crankish advocates of the ketogenic diet – the one where you eat no carbohydrates – and toys with giving it a go himself (his selection of guests and talking points seem to be inspired by other podcasts, especially American ones like Joe Rogan's). Yet in another episode Bartlett interviews the epidemiologist Tim Spector, a co-founder of Zoe, who says the ketogenic diet is unsafe. When Spector tells Bartlett that the value of dietary supplements is unproven, Bartlett seems disappointed, admitting that his kitchen cabinets are full of them. Six months later, he interviews a man called Layne Norton who sings the praises of supplements and who (surprise, surprise) owns a company selling them – a company that Bartlett has a stake in.

Perhaps Bartlett's gift is allowing us to believe that he, too, is navigating our strange secular world, a world in which there is no agreed-upon father figure to tell you how to eat or live. Or perhaps it's booking guests who are likely to say things that will get clicks. Late in 2024, a BBC investigation of fifteen health-related episodes of Bartlett's podcast found that fourteen contained claims that, if acted upon, were likely to cause harm. These included bombastic anti-vaccine statements, statements against conventional cancer treatments and claims that the ketogenic diet can reverse autism, all of which went unchallenged by Bartlett in the course of the episodes (in fact he justified anti-vax sentiments by comparing them to the civil rights movement and the movement for women's suffrage). Earlier in 2024, Bartlett put his money and his image behind 'ear seeds', a product he discovered on the show *Dragons' Den* and which dubiously claimed to aid recovery from ME.

Whatever personal confusion he might be feeling has not got in the way of business: Bartlett reportedly invested $2.5 million in Zoe, and this despite the fact that Zoe and Spector advise against ultra-processed foods, of which Huel is surely an example. But the UK's Advertising Standards Authority has been something of a barrier, forcing both Huel and Zoe to withdraw ads from Facebook that failed to make clear that Bartlett's reviews – 'this is Huel's best product', and 'Zoe … might just change your life' – were sales pitches made by a significant investor.[19] Despite all of this, at the time of writing, the former CEO-cum-insider-marketer continues to thrive.

As for Rob Rhinehart, here the comparisons diverge. Rhinehart stepped down as CEO of Soylent in 2017 and seems to have disappeared from public view. The most recent footage I could find of the Silicon Valley tech bro shows him with a wiry beard, living in a smallholding somewhere in the Midwest, promoting outlandish conspiracy theories and reading poems he has written to an audience of goats. One of Rhinehart's poems ends with the lines: 'I do not care what you have heard. Grains are good. Bread is the word', which is odd coming from a man who was once so militantly modern.

Escaping the matrix

After a month of drinking Huel and six weeks following a MyFitnessPal regime, I gave in. I was lifting increasingly heavy weights, I could row faster and my arms, chest and legs were noticeably chunkier, but so too was my belly. I'd put on over three kilograms, but I didn't feel great about it. This was not the lean, muscular body that I had flippantly opted for in the app. I must have been eating too much, including too much protein, an excess of which the body can convert into fat. But what really bothered me was all the tracking, all the data entry, all the time spent looking at my phone for a ping of gratification. My relationship with food – as a fuel for my workouts and as a means for achieving my bodily ideals – had become a sad, administrative one. Worse, I felt that were I to continue I'd come close to developing an eating disorder. I stopped. I logged off. I was on my own again.

I continued to drink Huel at work, but I started to eat a little more normally, unmonitored. I worked out in a less compulsive way. Eventually I returned to some sort of normal size – normal to me, anyway. I accept that the complex workings of my metabolism and my appetite tend to result in me being mostly slim. For a lot of people that is not the case. But the issue here is not yours alone. Whether it's an issue at all depends on how your weight relates to your broader health and our culture's view of human beauty standards. The extent to which we really have control over our diets is also hard to judge in an eating environment dominated by inequality and cheap processed foods. My parents, both vegetarians, are believers in wholefoods, albeit not dogmatically; my favourite meal as a kid was a smoky, meatless hot dog served in a supermarket pitta bread with olive oil spread and Heinz tomato ketchup. And for this culinary upbringing I'm grateful.

Food science reflects and reproduces the age in which it appears. Calories, as we have seen, belong to an age of industry, but it was empire and war that made them a matter of public concern in the UK. Elsewhere, in nations trying to catch up with British 'development', calories had already become a central focus of a more general concern with bodily productivity, as expressed in modern movements of culinary nationalism. We have since entered an individualised age, with services like Zoe being intended to tailor diets to specific needs. But the past doesn't simply disappear with each new development, and so the reign of the calorie continues, as too does our concern with protein.

Part of the trouble with seeing food in secular scientific terms is that the science keeps on changing. Vitamins were only discovered in the 1910s. The study of the gut, still in its infancy, is only the latest development. That makes scientifically informed eating a somewhat fraught endeavour. Humans keep finding out new things about our food, often things we did not know we did not know. And if this history tells us anything it's that we should be less hubristic when it comes to the question of what we should eat.

I'm far from being the first person to make this point. Gyorgy Scrinis's book *Nutritionism* presents a similar argument, a version of which was amplified by Michael Pollan in his bestselling *In Defense of Food*. Yet when it comes to alternatives to the dominant way of seeing things, I find myself troubled by these two authors. For both Scrinis and Pollan, it is the displacement of traditional food cultures that has given rise to problems in our diet, and it is to traditional food cultures, they argue, that we should now return.

But which tradition, exactly, are we talking about? Might such sentiments in fact be encouraging men like Brian Johnson, better known as the Liver King? Johnson is an ultra-masculine influencer with outrageously bulging muscles who advocates a 'return' to a carnivore diet and who markets branded liver supplements to his millions of followers while secretly taking steroids.

The world of male influencers that my diet and gym routine put me onto via YouTube is not the focus of Pollan's book

(*In Defense of Food* first appeared in 2008). But his contention that nutritional scientists have displaced the wisdom of our mothers overlaps with the arguments of populist dietary gurus like the Liver King. 'I speak mainly on the authority of tradition and common sense,' Pollan writes. 'Most of what we need to know about how to eat we already know, or once did until we allowed the nutrition experts and the advertisers to shake our confidence in common sense, tradition, the testimony of our senses, and the wisdom of our mothers and grandmothers.'[20]

Pollan's advice is simple: 'don't eat anything your great grandmother wouldn't recognise as food'.[21] And yet his great-grandmother was probably born around the time that Liebig was encouraging parents to feed their children a fatal baby formula, back when gelatine and beef tea were briefly considered superfoods, and back when bakers were adulterating their bread with bark and acorns. My paternal great-grandmother was apparently a strong believer in eating roast beef and boiled cabbage whenever it was available. Should I, then, eat meat and two veg at every meal? I'm pretty sure she never ate olive oil, lentils, pine nuts or kimchi, so should I cut these from my diet as well?

How far back should we go before we find a worthy tradition, one free of nutritional expertise? My maternal great-great-grandmother lived a simple rural life with her farm labourer husband. In all likelihood her diet consisted of little more than bread. Why, come to think of it, is no one arguing for a return to a panivore diet, one consisting solely of dense dark loaves and eight pints of beer per day (and no clean water)? According to Pollan, traditional food cultures endured 'only because they tended to keep people healthy'.[22] But I'm not so sure that's true.

Perhaps we should go back further? Perhaps my great-great-great … fifty-generations great-grandmother drank mead and feasted on free-range roasted pigs, although from the best of our knowledge about Anglo-Saxon culture she is just as likely to have scratched out an inadequate diet based on boiled grains and turnips. Perhaps if she had been married to a senior official in Roman Britannia, eighty great-grandmothers back, she might have eaten imported fermented fish sauce and drunk plenty of organic natural wine, but then again, as a woman, that was also unlikely. Ah, but the druids … about whom we know so very little.

No wonder many people today, like the Liver King, aim to adopt the diets of cavemen (cavemen who can shop at Trader Joes and eat a vast range of branded supplements). Pollan has positive things to say about the Neolithic diet, which apparently (and bear in mind we're talking about diets across the globe in a period spanning about 1,500 years) was low in carbohydrates and high in animal protein. Another version of what Pollan is saying is 'eat like an Italian', and yet, as we saw in chapter five, until recently for most people that meant not eating enough.

There is clearly a lot of romanticising at work when we talk about tradition. Did your great-grandmother shop for locally produced vegetables at farmers' markets? Did she bake sourdough loaves at home for her doting family? Did she treat her children to occasional meals out at Chez Panisse, California's equivalent to the River Café? The answer is probably no, but Pollan makes you think otherwise.

While it may be true that the master's tools will never destroy the master's house, they may be necessary to survive in it. I find myself agreeing with tech bros like Rhinehart when they make the case for replacing nutritionally deficient and often joyless meals with slurps of a low-impact, high-quality human fuel. Some meals, your supermarket meal deal or ready meal, for example, could be painlessly replaced in this way. I for one have no objection, so long as I eat interesting, lovingly made meals the rest of the time, with exceptional meals occasionally.

But perhaps what all the bloodlusting, Huel-drinking, weightlifting men on my timeline really want is direction and meaning. If so, these lost boys aren't going to find the daddy-figure they're looking for in men who, like Steven Bartlett, have almost nothing to say but plenty to sell. Health and gym influencers might tell you that a ketogenic diet has saved their life, but it's more likely to have shortened it. Invented traditions are a bit of a drug.

Perhaps what many of us need is an occasional break from the alienating effects of modernity. In an automated world of machines, crafting something physically takes on new meaning. So too do eating, feeling and relating to the world with one's senses. Sip a crisp glass of artisanal wine and think about those south-facing slopes. Isn't that what makes us human? Perhaps what we need is to get back to basics, and closer to the land where our food comes from.

7

Castle Howard Revisited

The barony goes on. When all of you are dead Julia's son will be called by the name his fathers bore before the fat days; the days of wool shearing and the wide corn lands, the days of growth and building, when the marshes were drained and the waste land brought under the plough, when one built the house, his son added the dome.

Lord Marchmain's deathbed speech from
Evelyn Waugh, *Brideshead Revisited*, 1945

When the MP and keen antiquarian Horace Walpole first visited Castle Howard, he was in awe. Walpole, the fourth Earl of Orford and son of Britain's first prime minister, Sir Robert Walpole, reported in a letter,

> Nobody had informed me at one view I should see a palace, a town, a fortified city, temples on high places, woods worthy of being a metropolis of Druids, the noblest lawn fenced by half the horizon and a mausoleum that would tempt me to be buried alive: in short, I have seen gigantic places before, but never a sublime one.[1]

This was in 1772. Plans for a new estate had been made at the end of the previous century by Charles Howard, the third Earl of Carlisle, whose father inherited the 13,000 acres in which Castle Howard now presides, and which was first parcelled up into noble ownership after the Norman Conquest. The Howards of Castle Howard can identify among their ancestors Thomas Howard, the third Duke of Norfolk, famed for matchmaking the Tudor king Henry VIII with his two beheaded wives, Anne Boleyn and Catherine Howard.

The third Earl of Carlisle hired the dramatist and amateur architect Sir John Vanbrugh to work with the more experienced Nicholas Hawksmoor (who had served his apprenticeship under Sir Christopher Wren) to realise the earl's dreams of a fashionable estate, combining a classical and ornate house with a radically naturalistic approach to the rural North Yorkshire landscape. Such plans embodied the proto-nationalist ideals of eighteenth-century country living. Indeed, a book of recipes from the fourth Countess of Carlisle, Isabella Howard, contains many of the new patriotic dishes from that era, blended with several more French-sounding meals that reflected her and her husband's cosmopolitan tastes.

When it was constructed, the estate gained the earl an important leg up in his political career. And in the spirit of agricultural 'improvement' that marked the turn of the century, the earl had the small family-run farms on his land replaced by newer, larger, more productive enterprises with irrigated fields and a waged workforce. A small village was cleared away along with its church, while the remains of a moated medieval castle were dispensed with and demolished, the sacks of stone and earth being carried on labourers' backs, in barrows and on mules. In place of the castle now stands the large symmetrically winged house with what in its time was a state-of-the-art dome: a cupola circled by busts of men cast in the manner of Ancient Greece, with a gilded lantern like a cherry on top.

Stone from the old castle was repurposed for a grand slab of medieval wall parked at the southern entrance to the estate, complete with fortified turrets and cruciform arrow slots, giving way on either side to rough fencing. This nostalgic folly is the first of several that visitors to Castle Howard encounter. It was features like these, in a setting complete with ancient woods and sculpted lakes, that so heated Walpole's imagination and that have since justified the idea that the Howard estate is home to one of the earliest and most striking examples of an English landscape garden.[2]

My reasons for wandering about in this 'sublime Elysium' on a clear, cold day in February were, in contrast to the setting, quite prosaic. I had been making a sourdough focaccia at work when I examined the sack of Wildfarmed flour I was using, curious as to what was meant by the oxymoronic brand name. Wildfarmed, according to the bright green packaging, is a 'life changing' product because the flour is made of wheat from regenerative farms in the UK and France, farms that the company 'knows by name'. Regenerative farms, the website continues to sermonise, are 'restoring soil and landscapes across the country. So yeah, lifechanging. For real.'

For real? I decided I'd find out.

From a quick look online it is hard to determine what proportion of Wildfarmed's mission is simply marketing and how much is a sincere interest in improving the sad state of soil health (along with a broader ecology, from plants and insects to birds and mammals) on modern English farms where intensive, chemical-dependent monocropping carried out since the 1950s has rendered agricultural land close to barren. One of Wildfarmed's founders is Andy Cato, co-producer of the band Groove Armada, who today grows wheat on his regenerative farm in France. Becoming concerned about the ways in which industrial agribusiness has undermined biodiversity, Andy put his money where his mouth is, selling the rights to his band's popular back catalogue to sustain his unconventional agriculture. Andy is a charming zealot for regen, but I wanted to know who else is part of what his company describes as a growing movement aimed at fixing our broken food system.

The Wildfarmed website lists 114 wheat producers in England that supply their flour. Working my way through this list, I counted twenty-two farms directly belonging to the traditional landed gentry. A further eleven are traditional aristocratic estates, including one owned by the Duke of Bedford, whose status as one of the largest private landowners in Britain can, like the original Castle Howard, be traced back to William the Conqueror. The remainder of the 'wild' farms are a mix of privately owned but relatively recently acquired land, including the farm belonging to the TV presenter Jeremy Clarkson, and other agrobusiness using rented land. It is famously difficult to determine who, exactly, owns land in England, but it would be reasonable to assume that the majority of the farmers in this latter group will be renting fields from England's highly concentrated pool of private landowners (according to Guy Shrubsole, less than 1 per cent of people in England own half the land).[3] Safe to say none of the wheat that goes into a Wildfarmed sack of flour is grown on land owned by the public.

How can England's traditional elites be so heavily represented in a brand-cum-food-movement that claims to be so life-changing? Has the aristocracy returned as a vital force in contemporary England, or did it never quite go away? And, from the point of view of creating a proud national food culture, why does any of this matter?

The persistence of the old regime

This book has argued that England's peculiar food culture is a product of its peculiar experience of modernity. And yet, in a sense, we have never been modern. This country's 'backwardness' can seem undeniable when we look at some of our political institutions: the persistence of a monarch who is head of both church and state, for example; the unelected House of Lords; or the custom, precedent and convention that operate in the space where other nations have formal constitutions.[4]

English history – and in this respect we resemble most other nations – is replete with examples of the old world persisting alongside the new. Marx and Engels's famous prediction in *The Communist Manifesto* turned out to be false: far from everything that was holy in Britain has been rendered profane by the advent of industrial capitalism.

Even at the point at which Britain was known as the workshop of the world, the bulk of the profits being made here were in commerce and finance. 'Manchester produced a mere handful of millionaires, less than Liverpool with its ship-owners, merchants and bankers', the historian Perry Anderson has written. 'Even within the manufacturing sector itself, it was not the pioneering industries – textiles, railways, chemicals – that generated the major dynasties, but those closer to pre-industrial activities: above all, food, drink and tobacco.'[5]

Traditional elites integrated themselves within the rising middle classes in Victorian Britain, just as the urban bourgeoisie took on some of the cultural and economic trappings of the ancien régime (recall the preference for French fine dining shared by many members of these two groups). For landowners in the nineteenth century, the realisation eventually came that there was money to be made from the modern world, particularly in the form of renting urban land for housing, infrastructure and business, as well as renting rural land for canals, railways and mines – more money, in fact, than might have been made from producing grain, a task that was now increasingly outsourced to the Empire. While the landed classes had resisted importing wheat earlier in the century, agricultural trade eventually freed up this class's inheritance for the obtaining of modern rents.

In fact, we can see how the presence of England's landed elites is sedimented within the broader experience of modernity by looking at the only dish in England that carries the national affix. The full English breakfast is today seen as something of a working-class affair, a meal consumed before a hard day of manual labour or medicinally after a night of drinking. But the full English has a distinctly landed ancestry. It combines the rural gentry's taste for a hearty, carnivorous late-morning meal – the elements of which would once have been laid out on a sideboard that displayed the best of the gentleman's rural estate, from fresh eggs to wild game – with a popular taste for bacon (the latter was for a long time a rare source of animal protein in the diet of Britain's lower classes; it has chiefly been provided by Denmark since the turn of the twentieth century). Then we find the inexpensive addition of toasted or fried factory-made white bread, tinned baked beans and, heaven forbid, Italian-grown tinned tomatoes and the distinctly American hash brown. HP sauce gives us a sense of the upper-class medieval palate and England's long love affair with spices, while a mug of tea with milk and sugar brings the outside in – tea being an Indian import, coming by way of the opening up of China with the forced trade in opium, and sugar finding popularity in England when it was the principal product of slavery. As the dish was gradually democratised and codified it became an urban English meal, yet one with these traditional rural roots.

Oddly enough, when in the 1960s Anderson began investigating what he saw as the structural limits of Britain's modernity, the UK was at its most national-industrial.[6] England's landed elite had suffered following the gradual enfranchisement of Britain's 'lower orders' in the late nineteenth century and into the twentieth. From 1894, death duties introduced by the reforming Liberal government meant large estates like Castle Howard faced a 30 to 40 per cent tax on their total value at the moment of inheritance. This rate continued to rise over the next half a century to fund wars and welfare as democratic politics in Britain continued down a path set out by New Liberalism.

Some of England's traditional elite were forced to respond to these threatening new times by auctioning off precious objects accumulated in their houses by their ancestors and by selling parts of their estates (Castle Howard was reduced in size from 13,000 to 9,000 acres over the course of the twentieth century). Between the turn of the century and 1975, some 1,200 stately homes were demolished by owners who wished to avoid the costs of staffing and maintenance. (The theme park at Alton Towers, built on the site of what was once a large manorial estate dating back to the Norman Conquest, is the most famous, and today quite surreal, example of these trends.)

In 1974, while a relatively equal Britain was still in the era of its national-industrial prowess, the incoming Labour government was formulating plans to further redistribute aristocratic wealth. This time meeting the threat head-on,

England's landed classes successfully framed their private wealth in terms of 'national heritage'. Groups including the Country Landowners Association and the Historic Houses Association joined forces with the British Tourist Authority, the Art Fund, the National Gallery, Tate and the British Museum to resist these potential wealth taxes.

A 1974 exhibition at the V&A entitled *The Destruction of the Country House: 1875 to 1975* captured a Brideshead-esque spirit of melancholia that was haunting members of the traditional upper class, a sense that all that was beautiful, distinctive and rural in the old world was being swept away by the dull, utilitarian 'age of Hooper'.[7] According to its curator, Sir Roy Strong, writing in the exhibition catalogue, 'death duties, and capital gains tax, let alone the threatened Wealth and Inheritance Taxes, spell the final ruin of these most precious works of art'. 'The historic houses of this country belong to everybody,' Strong asserted, 'or at least everybody who cares about this country and its traditions.'[8] Elsewhere, in the book *Heritage in Danger*, the Conservative MP Patrick Cormack pronounced that 'it is perhaps in our country houses and churches that one comes closest to the spirit of England'.[9]

Within a year, the Labour government's plans had been shelved, with traditional landowners emerging as the triumphant bearers of the nation's historical soul – a status that was confirmed by the furore over the flailing government's failure to either prevent or profit from the forced sale of the neo-Gothic Mentmore Towers in Buckinghamshire. When election time rolled around in 1979, and Labour once more hinted at a wealth tax to mobilise its base, Nick Howard's father, George Howard, then chair of the Historic Houses Association, campaigned against a government that he said would oversee the loss of England's heritage, i.e. country estates like his own. Evaluating the first three years of the Thatcher regime that followed, George Howard praised the new tax environment that, he said, 'has been pulled into more or less the right shape'.[10]

After what now looks, in the grand scheme of things, like a brief decline in the twentieth century, landed elites have made a comeback. In cultural terms, the growth of the heritage industry since the mid-1970s has ensured this class a place at the heart of a certain ideal of English nationalism. Our patriotic patricians are today seen as vital custodians of a common heritage, primarily in the form of their private estates, with their grand homes stuffed full of loot that has now been rebranded as national treasure.

In a minor key, the members of this old elite are also the custodians of 'traditional' ways of eating. Beyond the post-war dynamics that led to the creation of the heritage industry, the reasons for this culinary status are twofold. First, when food historians peer into the kitchens of the past they often do so through the written records available, and these records have for the most part been handed down to us by elites. This is why so many histories have reimagined distinctively upper-class foods as being representative of the national diet, as if everyone in the time of Henry VIII was eating roasted boar.[11]

Secondly, the landed classes have a long, sometimes unbroken, connection to the countryside – a unique position in our deeply urbanised nation. The rural landscape has often occupied a central, if contradictory, role in the self-narrations of 'green and pleasant' English nationalism.[12] That's why, for example, shooting grouse has an authentic, national vibe, despite being a relatively recent, and distinctly elite, invention, dependent on the shotgun and the systematic desolation of moorlands.

Rentiers have also returned to their dominant position within the UK in economic terms. During the period spanning the start of the First World War and the election of Thatcher in 1979, a vast amount of land was taken into public ownership. Economists and politicians, on both the left and the right, had long seen rents accruing from land as a form of unearned income and a barrier to greater modernisation (take, for instance, Churchill, who when he was a Liberal MP claimed that the landlord 'renders no service to the community, he contributes nothing to the general welfare, he contributes nothing to the process from which his own enrichment is derived'[13]). Today, the majority of the land that was briefly managed by the state has been sold back into private hands, while the progressive, pro-growth case against landlords has almost disappeared. No wonder that, in recent iterations of the *Sunday Times* Rich List, around a quarter of the entries state that property is the entrant's main source of wealth.

Nature safari

I decided to contact the aristocratic landowners who supplied wheat to Wildfarmed and see if I could arrange a field trip. To my surprise, I received a prompt reply from Castle Howard.

And so it was that, several weeks after baking a Wildfarmed focaccia, I found myself in an ornate library, sipping black coffee out of a China teacup as I interviewed a distant relative of the Tudor Duke of Norfolk.

Nicholas Paul Geoffrey Howard does not actually hold an aristocratic title, nor does he have a particularly long name. For a start, Nick's side of the Howard family tree is a minor (or *cadet*) branch. Indeed, it was this sense of titular insecurity that prompted the first Earl of Carlisle (Nick's nine-generations great-grandfather) to build a new estate. The line of first male heirs – the major, primogenital line – running from the Duke of Norfolk to the present brings us to Edward William Fitzalan-Howard, the most senior non-royal peer in England, himself a large landowner.

But Nick, well he's just an old hippy. At least, that's what he says. I find this hard to register as Nick addresses me in his deep, equestrian tone, wearing a chequered shirt and tweed gilet. Nevertheless, it's the hippy side of Nick's personality that motivates him to make his land biodiverse; he simply enjoys being surrounded by animals and flowers.

When England's old caste of hereditary peers found themselves under attack in the first half of the twentieth century, many were drawn into cities, with some finding jobs in finance. Others fled to the remaining corners of Britain's Empire, hoping to recreate the manorial experience abroad, as other Englishmen had done in the Raj. Among those who remained steadfast in the country, some found new ways of making money from their inheritance. The Duke of Bedford, for example, was among several traditional landowners who purchased lions and zebras and turned their estates into safaris. And it was to this latter crowd that Nick Howard's grandfather, George Howard, belonged.

When George returned from the war and reclaimed possession of Castle Howard (the house had been loaned to an evacuated school during the Blitz), he returned to a building badly damaged by fire. To help cover the costs of renovations, George opened the doors of his grand estate to a paying public, collecting the fees in person.

Today, 27 million people visit privately owned stately homes in Britain each year, making this branch of so-called heritage tourism a vital part of the tourism sector as a whole. And it isn't just because of its innovative grandeur that Castle Howard forms an important destination on the map of England's great estates, alongside the likes of Blenheim and Chatsworth. In the late 1970s, George Howard was approached by the producer Derek Granger about making his home the setting for what would become a famous and well-loved TV adaptation of *Brideshead Revisited*. The contract with Granada for the series immortalised Castle Howard as a noble arcadia within the grinding modernity of twentieth-century life.

More recently, the house has featured in the TV series *Bridgerton*, as well as forming a backdrop to the well-documented marriage of pop musician Jay Chou, who is arguably the biggest artist in the Chinese-speaking world. When I saw small groups of East Asian women taking selfies in peculiar places on the estate, it was explained to me that Jay Chou was the reason why. Today, Castle Howard receives some quarter of a million visitors each year, with 25,000 people paying £100 for an annual membership.

Regenerative farming at Castle Howard has as much to do with attracting these visitors as it does with producing wheat. In fact, when I visited, there were just three roughly-one-acre fields put aside for a trial for growing grain, and these, I was told, had mostly failed. 'The quality was there,' Nick explained, 'there just wasn't much of it.' The idea had been to grow beans as a companion species for the wheat, and then allow cattle to graze on the stalks after the harvest and so to manure the fields. Unfortunately, the beans proved to be too dominant, and sorting grain from legumes turned out to be an expensive task after the fact. The experiment only broke even thanks to a sustainable farming incentive payment from the Treasury. But these are early days, Nick said. He and his team have plans to keep trying.

Along with renting the land and its various properties to tenant farmers and households, and along with the produce acquired from the contract farmers operating on the estate (produce such as pork and beef), Nick's major line of business remains the same as his grandfather's. And here, Nick's hippy taste in nature is part of Castle Howard's appeal.

After my coffee in the library and a brief stop at the scraggy fields set aside for Wildfarmed, I'm taken to a part of the estate called Bog Hall, a 400-acre area of marginal, marshy farmland. In 2024 the site was selected for nature restoration. I was told of plans to introduce new plant species and a free-ranging herd of cows whose grazing and manure should ensure biodiversity while also restoring soil health. Eventually, Bog Hall will become home to a family of beavers, with maps already drawn up for safari tracks that will enable visitors to take in the newly natural landscape.

The inspiration for all of this comes by way of the Knepp Estate in Sussex, another traditional manorial property whose owners have made it a beacon for the 'rewilding' movement. The story goes that, in 1987, Sir Charles Raymond Burrell, tenth Baronet (a hereditary title ranking below that of 'Lord'), inherited the 3,500-acre estate, which came complete with an early nineteenth-century mansion built, like the slab of wall at Castle Howard, in medieval style. The estate was first acquired by Burrell's seven-times great-grandfather, who paid for it through returns on his investments in the East India Company. Sir Charles Raymond Burrell, who moved onto the estate with his wife, the writer Isabella Tree (whose family also contains several dukes), renovated the manor house and farmed the land conventionally for seventeen years until, in 2000, it was deemed no longer profitable.

Tree documents her husband's decision to end farming on the estate in her bestselling book *Wilding: The Return of Nature to a British Farm*. 'The farm workers were stunned', she writes of the scene. 'It was a black day. Eleven men lost their jobs.'[14] Despite local opposition, and through careful, hands-off management, with the introduction of wild pigs, longhorn cattle, ponies and beavers, Tree and Burrell have made their estate a celebrated sanctuary for wildlife, seeing the return of rare species of butterflies, bats, nightingales and turtle doves.

Knepp, like Castle Howard, now attracts tens of thousands of visitors each year, many of whom take the short drive down from London, with some staying over in Knepp's rustic cabins and bell tents, eating modern European dishes at the on-site restaurant. Safaris on the estate, conducted in an open-top Landcruiser, start at £75 per person (and perhaps remind Charles Burrell of his childhood spent in Southern Rhodesia). In these ways, the business has gradually become profitable.

The landscape created at Knepp is pastoral in the extreme. At the end of the seventeenth century, when Castle Howard was being planned, the fashion that would become known as the English country garden grew out of a preference for 'naturalistic' landscapes, in direct contrast to French formalism exemplified by Versailles. The gardener Stephen Switzer advised the third Earl of Carlisle that a manicured woodland at Castle Howard should be preserved as a monument to 'natural wilderness', writing of the forest in his *Ichnographia Rustica* that ''tis there that Nature is truly imitated, if not excell'd'.[15]

This history is illustrative of how the idea of 'nature' as something quite apart from human culture is a distinctly modern one, even as we witness this separation occurring on an aristocratic estate. The rewilding movement has inherited the perspective that informed the country garden trend, along with its socially elite context.

Central to Isabella Tree's vision for Knepp, and central to the arguments of her bestselling book, is the idea that at the beginning of our geological epoch, about 11,700 years ago, Europe was not a closed canopy forest, as scientific and popular consensus would have it, but was instead maintained as mostly open pasture by large herbivores such as wild oxen and horses. But this theory, known as the Vera hypothesis, is far from being accepted by scientists, and is an awkward fit with much of the available evidence. Tree's book on Knepp has inspired a generation of rewilders, yet this Eden in Sussex appears to be a case of invented tradition at the scale of geological time.

Like the scientists who see human nutrition in terms of our fixed, evolutionarily defined predispositions, Burrell and Tree appear to have made, or invented, their world as if from the prehistorical perspective of hunter-gatherers, projecting backwards over 10,000 years of human habitation (although even hunter-gatherers had complex and varied culture, as their cave paintings make evident). Or rather, theirs is not a land constructed from *within* the prehistoric perspective, but, instead, from without, as an extreme form of landscaping, traversable via safari. A kind of Alton Towers for 'hippies' like Nick.

It isn't just Castle Howard that Knepp has inspired. King Charles and the Prince of Wales have both shown a keen interest in rewilding, while beavers have become the latest must-have item for every landowner worthy of the name. A cluster of new-money billionaires have also got on board, including Anders Holch Povlsen, the largest private landowner in the UK, who made his fortune in fast fashion. Povlsen plans to rewild 89,000 acres of his 220,000-acre estate in the Scottish Highlands, which he visits from his native Norway by means of a private jet.

In fact, England finds itself in the odd position of having private landowners, led by some of the heirs of the country's traditional landed elites, being at the cutting edge of proposed solutions to the many problems of modern industrial farming. Is it therefore surprising that their vision of the future is a conservative, idealised interpretation of the past?

Modernity anew

Of course, not every large landowner in Britain is so benevolent, or at least not every landowner has adopted such a benevolent business model. Guy Shrubsole has estimated that a third of all the land in England, urban and rural, is owned by the traditional landed gentry and by aristocrats. A further 250,000 acres is owned by a non-traditional landed elite, i.e. those who made their money after the eighteenth century. Of this vast amount of elite-owned English land, a tiny proportion, probably less than 1 per cent, is being used for regenerative agriculture and 'rewilding'.[16] By contrast, a monumental 550,000 acres is given over to grouse moors. Might these moors, privately owned and managed for an environmentally destructive form of elite recreation, be better put aside as a haven for wildlife as well?[17]

Wildfarmed claims to be life-changing. And that's fine, because perhaps, on some small level, it might be true. Yet the barriers to a better food system will not be overcome by bold marketing prompting conscious consumption. There is the food system we already have, in which regenerative wheat constitutes a high-value product akin to the River Café's 'best olive oil', and in which 'rewilding' fits in mainly as a tourist attraction, and then there is the food system that we need and may, given the option, even want as a nation. But, as in the past, to get from one system to the other will require the demands of the people being expressed through the agency of the state.

Britain's post-Brexit *National Food Strategy* (the report authored by Henry Dimbleby, mentioned in the introduction of this book) proposed that England take a mixed approach to the rational use of its agricultural lands. This radical, ambitious strategy called for turning a small amount – around 5 to 8 per cent – of the most unproductive farmland into both a carbon sink and a habitat for nature. Under the same plan, the use of higher-yielding land for farming would have been incentivised by way of subsidies for those who continued to farm conventionally and productively while reducing chemical inputs. Then, at the same time, some proportion of farmers would have been encouraged to use innovative regenerative methods. Such a plan would have given real force to the demand for sovereignty articulated in the Brexit vote.

Elsewhere, in a book that is both profoundly pleasant and optimistic while also documenting the collapse of our wildlife and the existential threat of climate change, *Regenesis* by George Monbiot makes the case for a massive shift in consumption patterns such that humanity would get all of the protein and fat it needs from bacteria produced in factories (think here of Quorn). Monbiot clearly shares the 'hippyish' tastes of Nick Howard – the backdrop of the book is the author's delight in soil biodiversity, apple trees and wild animals – yet he is also an ambitious modernist. Land use, Monbiot claims, is the environmental issue of our times; it is the key that unlocks the problems of greenhouse gas emissions, ecological diversity, human health and animal cruelty. He is right to point out that land use was never mentioned in the campaign to leave the EU, despite 40 per cent of the EU's budget being spent on subsidies. This is ironic, since, again, what better example of sovereignty could there be than a nation determining for itself how it uses its land?

Monbiot is also right in saying that a large proportion of the protein that we eat (and which is used as animal feed, although he would rather we not raise animals for food at all) comes from almost featureless sources such as chicken and soy. Creating a low-impact, cheaper alternative, particularly if a way can be found to make plant- and bacteria-based nutrients behave a bit more like meat, could change our food system dramatically. Land used for farming would consequently fall, and so more space could be made for biodiversity. This is what modernity in the service of 'nature' looks like.

And yet I don't share Monbiot's faith (or perhaps it is a desperate hope) that bacteria are the future of all protein and fat consumption. There is a risk of nutritional hubris here, as raised in the previous chapter. But even if a truly nutritionally complete diet could be obtained by means of a bacterial gloop or powder, most people do not eat food solely in order to get their fill of nutrients (bodybuilders and gym fanatics are not representative of most people). Even the English still possess deeply ingrained patterns of eating, even if these largely (though not only) manifest themselves in a preference for unhealthy processed food.

It is in the domain of processed foods that lab-grown nutrients could most easily serve as an alternative to meat and dairy, assuming that a low price could be arrived at (such an outcome would still require rethinking our regulatory and subsidy system, plus, most probably, some form of state-private partnership capable of generating the alternatives in question). Yet it is probably only vegans like Monbiot, or hyper-modernists like the younger Rob Rhinehart, who would actually choose not to eat even an occasional 'traditional' meal – who would choose, for example, never to experience a bite of sharp and fruity Cheddar cheese again, or a juicy roasted chicken with perfectly crisp skin, or a steaming bowl of rich beef stew, braised in stout. As with the sourdough movement, or indeed Monbiot's love of apples, our connection with food anchors us – via the rituals associated with real and invented traditions – to the natural world and to a sense of ourselves as having a cultural home. And to my mind, that's an important part of what makes us human.

Monbiot's conception of a world in which new technologies will lead to fantastic new creations is to his credit. 'I can picture inventive chefs working with scientists to create, for example, a morsel that tastes like seared steak but with the texture of scallops. Or they might develop a mousse that breaks on the tongue like panna cotta but has the flavor of jamón ibérico.'[18] The trouble is that it's quite hard to imagine such a menu appearing organically in a world in which seared steaks, scallops and jamón ibérico already exist and their consumption is not outright banned. It is perhaps more possible, and in my view desirable, to imagine the incorporation of sustainable sources of nutrients into our diets alongside the rise of a renewed investment in artisanal agriculture, and in the craft-based culinary enterprises that regularly generate the kind of pride and pleasure we invest in special occasions such as Sunday lunch.

In any case, and whatever the detail of the changes we must make, it is clear that when the future of food and land is left to the market we find that creating desolate environments in which to shoot wild chicken can be a far more profitable enterprise than growing regenerative wheat. In the case of Castle Howard, efforts to grow wheat for Wildfarmed are little more than a sideshow, one tacked on to a larger rewilding project that reflects both the idealism and the economic needs of a benevolent aristocrat. If the implications of this are not obvious then let me state them clearly: leaving existing landholders to make decisions affecting England's future, in particular our relationship to the land and its produce, is a terrible way to go.

Just as bad is the effect that England's return to being a rent-seeking society is having on the rest of the economy. As was famously shown by Thomas Piketty in his book *Capital in the Twenty-First Century*, since the 1980s, Western economies have resumed their long-term tendency to reward existing asset ownership over entrepreneurial investment and labour. This has led to growing inequality, which, among other things, restricts the scope for a truly national food culture, in the sense that, while some may lay claim to the civilising effects of good olive oil, fresh herbs and regenerative wheat, many more of us – perhaps resentful at these exclusive claims, particularly when they are trussed up in an ersatz rusticity – will find that we rejoice in Greggs.

England needs a new movement for modernity: one that embraces alternative sources for our basic foods while also making space for a renewed artisanal food culture. Doing that requires at the very least that we displace the rentier from the centre of our culture and economy.

Epilogue: Sausage Rolls

The press release promised a bar designed according to a belle époque specification. Picture Leonardo DiCaprio wearing a tuxedo, lifting a wide-brimmed glass of champagne in a GIF scraped from *The Great Gatsby* – and then picture him with a sausage roll in his other hand.

Online videos made by influencers emphasised the grandeur of the offering, mostly without irony. One can order a bottle of Bollinger at the Greggs champagne bar, temporarily located in the Fenwick department store in Newcastle during the Christmas period. The fizz will accompany your order of a sausage roll, vegan sausage roll, steak, chicken, cheese and onion, baked bean or festive bake, each of which comes with a trendy-sounding accompaniment such as Brussel sprout kimchi. The pastries are cut into triangles by the solitary teenage chef and are served on large, heavy blue plates, each dish inexplicitly garnished with a pinch of limp cress.

The mild excitement I had before my arrival gave way to mild disappointment once I had taken my seat. The bar was in a corner of the food hall, opposite a coffee shop and a precarious pyramid of Lindt chocolates. It had some twenty bar stools lined up along a faux marble counter, the counter being at least a foot too tall, so that you had to unfold your elbows to reach up to the eating surface like a child. Aside from the champagne, the only belle époque gesture was a string of low-hanging lights – ornate glass fittings hung by coiled brown wire that seemed muted amid the brightness of the store.

Wizzard's 'I Wish It Could Be Christmas Every Day' was being played from a Bluetooth speaker on the working side of the bar, and before me, as I sat with my chin almost leaning on the counter, was a glass bell placed on a surprisingly dirty mat that read 'ring for service'.

~

I have become something of a Greggs expert. It all started when I walked into a Primark in Newcastle and observed a group of teenagers in a state of wild excitement over a range of Greggs-branded clothing: bucket hats and bum bags, plastic clogs and basketball vests, boxer shorts with a hundred little sausage rolls on. I decided to make a podcast episode about Greggs and found out that the bakery (although Greggs hasn't sold bread since 2013) sells some 3 million sausage rolls every week and persistently tops its rivals in public polling as Britain's best-loved high street food chain.

The following year I was asked to discuss Greggs on BBC Radio 4's *The Food Programme*. I met the crew at a Greggs in Leicester Square and a well-dressed woman, whom I took to be the show's producer, asked me what my favourite item was. None of it, I told her, if I'm honest. The woman turned out to be from Greggs's corporate PR team. I alleviated her horrified reaction by explaining in positive terms during the interview just why Greggs has become a national institution. It taps into a deep English tradition of eating buns, pies and sausages – seasoned, I pointed out, with a little cayenne, nutmeg and mace, a once distinctly elite flavour profile (in the medieval period) that had been taken up, I said, in the anti-French mode of eighteenth-century country cooking. It also speaks to our tradition of urbanised industrial-imperial eating; the imported palm oil that serves as the fat in the pastry and the filling recalls an approach we've taken to food in England for 150 years. The Greggs sausage roll, I said, is the closest thing we have to a national dish today, one that – and this is essential, I pointed out – everyone can afford. The PR person looked mostly relieved.

Not long after this interview I appeared on a Channel 4 documentary about Greggs presented by Dani Dyer where I was made to take a fat bite from a cold, almost stale jam doughnut in front of the cameras. Having prepared for this too, I now find I know more about Greggs than is reasonable for any one person to know.

The first ever Greggs was opened by John Gregg on Newcastle's Gosforth High Street in 1951. In 1968 he opened the firm's first factory. In 1972 Greggs began taking over other, less successful bakeries in Leeds and Glasgow, a process of expansion that peaked in the mid-1990s when Greggs acquired the national chain Bakers Oven.

In 2012, UK Chancellor George Osborne attempted to change the way food is taxed, but the changes were branded by the *Sun* newspaper as 'the pasty tax', and competing politicians were photographed eating at Greggs until Osborne backed down. The pasty tax was one of only a handful of policies in his austerity agenda that was successfully resisted.

At the time of writing, Greggs has 2,675 outlets in the UK, which is about 1,200 more than McDonald's. In Newcastle city centre – the city with the highest Greggs concentration in the known universe – I worked out you are never more than five minutes' walk from a branch of the bakery. Nationally, Greggs employs more than 20,000 people, it makes some £2 billion in revenue each year and it takes almost £2 of every £100 spent in the UK hospitality sector. It sells more sausage rolls than McDonald's sells Big Macs and more coffee than Starbucks.

The first Greggs VIP card was awarded to the rapper Stormzy in 2020, entitling him to a lifetime's worth of sausage rolls and steak bakes. Another card was given to the pop musician Ed Sheeran, who, in turn, gave it to LadBaby, the YouTuber responsible for no fewer than *five* Christmas number one singles about eating sausage rolls, all of them awful.

Experts in Greggs, such as myself, may be aware of an advert that is less well known than the stratospheric launch of the vegan sausage roll, Greggs' controversial depiction of the baby Jesus as a sausage roll, or the Christmas campaign featuring the plummy cookery writer and celebrity chef Nigella Lawson. The advert I'm talking about shows employees of Greggs going undercover at a 'gourmet food festival'. The plan, we're told, is for Greggs to pretend to be a grander-sounding company going by the prim name of Gregory and Gregory. 'We're here today to test Greggs's new summer range on some of Britain's most discerning palates,' a server dressed in the fake brand's muted tones tells us. The camera cuts to shots of clinking champagne glasses and expensive-looking food stalls, some run by Michelin-starred chefs.

Of course, the discerning attendees who appear in the ad love Gregory and Gregory's summer salads and wraps. The first person to be introduced is a man wearing a Sgt Pepper–style jacket, a flat cap and an ear piercing, who declares, unironically, that 'avocado is so *au fait* at the moment, it [the vegan wrap] definitely pops'. 'I'm not usually a vegan type of person,' another man in a checkered Ralph Lauren shirt tells us with his mouth full, 'but this is really good.' An older man with a signet ring and a navy sweater draped over his shoulders waves around a pot of salad, pronouncing it to be 'very well balanced'. When the server turns around the sign to show that the food is actually from Greggs, the discriminating foodies are shocked. 'Greggs?!' a white man with dreadlocks sporting a waistcoat scoffs. 'Dear God, you're joking,' says another in a Home Counties accent.

The stunt gets to the heart of Greggs's highly successful marketing strategy, and it also underlines a key point I have been making about English food culture in this book. The ad suggests, perhaps it even shows, that everything upper-class foodies eat is little more than an affectation, its ostensible quality being nothing more than a façade of pretence and expense. Being a foodie is, in a word, 'posh'. Since, behold: Greggs is just as good as the food these snobs are eating – the food sold to them at rip-off prices by Michelin-starred chefs and at middle-class establishments like the River Café.

And what is good food, anyway? Maybe there's really no such thing, or at least there's no such thing as food that's better than what you get at Greggs. The ad helps position the brand as a national cuisine, since it reinforces not only the idea that 'gourmet' food and discerning taste are posh, but also that, in fact, there's no such thing as 'gourmet' food or discerning taste. It speaks to the Dairylea-loving protesters we encountered at the outset of this book who think investment in food is a little more than a means for rich people to flaunt their wealth.

There are two additional ways in which Greggs speaks of our food traditions. The first, as I said in my Radio 4 interview, is its reference to the kind of post-medieval country cooking that was popular in England in the eighteenth century. The iconic Greggs sausage roll is faintly seasoned with spices in a manner that might have been familiar to Hannah Glasse and Elizabeth Raffald. Greggs also alludes, albeit to a very limited extent, to the kind of regional baking traditions that I referred to in chapter one. In North London, for example, you can buy Tottenham cakes, essentially sponge cakes with pink icing. Greggs in Newcastle sells stotties, the pleasingly round flatbreads that sometimes have a hole poked in the middle and which vaguely resemble oversized English muffins. I'm told that Glasgow has a handful of local offerings, including Scotch pies and Lorne sausages.

Secondly, and as I also mentioned to the BBC, Greggs speaks to our familiarity with industrially processed food, which – and this would be unfamiliar to Glasse and Raffald – has enabled people in Britain to regularly eat meals that were once the preserve of the wealthy. According to analysis carried out for a Channel 5 documentary, the sausage in a Greggs sausage roll is only 22 per cent pork, meaning that it legally cannot be labelled a *pork* sausage roll. Britain has a long history of lower-class foods being adulterated, and so this low pork content might itself be something of a long-standing tradition. The presence of modified maize starch, milk protein isolates, emulsifiers, stabilisers and regulators are all distinctly modern, industrial versions of this tradition, albeit ones that we came to accept some time ago.

A cork pops at the Greggs champagne bar in Newcastle. A woman sitting on the stool next to me receives her first course and, seeing it, remarks to the waiter – and this is a direct quote – 'Oh, it's very posh the way you cut the sausage rolls.' At a corner of the bar another woman bops her head to a Caribbean steel pan rendition of 'Hark the Herald Angels Sing'. Then, after the first bite of her festive bake, delicately eaten with a knife and fork, I see her dramatically mouth the words 'oh my lord!' to her dining partner, who keenly nods his agreement.

The belle époque setting is a reference to the era of Escoffier, a reference that has the same knowing quality as the Gregory and Gregory ad. In both cases we have some of the motifs of 'posh' culture, but – and because we know poshness is little more than a scam – they aren't taken entirely seriously. Like most of what Greggs sells you, it's really all a bit of a joke. There's a gesture toward the kind of environment one encounters at Restaurant X, yet here we are in a department store eating cheap pies.

I order a steak bake, which comes with a small pot of wet peppercorn aioli in which it is hard to make out either pepper or garlic. The experience of eating the bake, which comes with its signature unctuous gravy, is not dissimilar, I can't help thinking, to that of eating hot cat food wrapped in a claggy shell. Next to arrive is the sausage roll, which comes with an incredibly sweet 'hot honey chilli sauce', and then, shortly after, the mysterious festive bake (vegetable filling unknown) with Brussel sprout kimchi. To drink I have a glass of Gremillet brut champagne and, to end, at the recommendation of my friendly server, a cream éclair dessert cocktail, which is a refreshing, alcoholic chocolate milk. My total bill comes to £40.90, plus the service charge.

Food critics have the difficult task of judging meals while knowing that taste is highly subjective. And yet, as we've seen, taste is also deeply social. In that vein, here was a traditionally English pre-Christmas meal; all that was missing was the option of a pint of lager and a chicken balti pie.

The service bell and the coupe glasses of champagne are signs of a world turned upside down during the festive period, yet one that, by way of its contrast with the day-to-day, speaks of how the world appears when it is the right way up. Here we were, sat on stools, my fellow diners and I, cosplaying as members of the elite, except that we, the righteous sausage roll-munching classes, know what a decent plate of food *really* is.

For those of our countrymen who fail to personally identify with Greggs's working-class tropes, it is these qualities that lend the sausage roll a naughty or else comical frisson. It is Nigella Lawson taking a delicate bite of a festive bake in the Greggs advert, seductively eyeing the camera and announcing that this is 'the very flakiest of pastries'.

As a national pastime, eating at Greggs speaks of the ways in which English food was modernised by the peculiar experiences of urbanisation, industrialisation, empire and war. Greggs is what has emerged in the wake of our native baking traditions having been eroded and replaced by sliced white loaves and sourdough. Some of Greggs's offer lays claim to the pre-modern past, yet it is first and foremost a product of English modernity.

Our love of Greggs, our championing of it – even, or especially, when it is ironic – expresses our ingrained sense of food as something unworthy of refinement, artistry or serious concern. Greggs is the vast, popular bedrock of a functionalist English food culture, a culture that is as often counterposed to the smug, hypocritical elitism of the new middle classes as it is comically contrasted with the tradition of bourgeois fine dining.

There is surely scope today for a renewed English cuisine, and from the point of view of our bodily and planetary health there is surely a pressing need for one. Our nation is likewise in great need of a new, common sense of pride – an emotion that, when sublimated, can too often manifest itself as a flag-waving form of hatred. Xenophobia promises a refuge from modern alienation, but it is a fundamentally malign force. By contrast, artisanal culinary endeavour and the labour of human hands can provide a joyful, uplifting alternative, crafting objects that inspire both pleasure and respect.

When food and cooking become worthy of pride they also become something akin to an art form. But in order for such an art form to become the pastime of a nation, that nation must become more equal than ours is today. It is only a society of equals 'which can choose to forgo gross luxury and base utilitarianism in return for the unwearying pleasure of tasting the fulness of life' – so wrote the Victorian activist and artisan William Morris. 'It is my firm belief', Morris continued 'that we shall in the end realize this society of equals, and also that when it is realized it will not endure a vicarious life by means of machinery; that it will in short be the master of its machinery and not the servant, as our age is now.'[1]

It is not for individuals like me to write recipes for the cooks of the future. The birth of a new, democratic cuisine will be both a means and an outcome of a political movement that is serious about enriching society as a whole. It will be a means, because any movement that aims to restore the public realm will be technocratic and unpopular without cultural investment. A means, too, because any policy agenda aimed at redistribution will require an accompanying moral framework if it is to have a basis for consent. It will be an end of such a movement because there can be no proud national food culture so long as our society is as materially divided as it is now, or at least no national food culture beyond the likes of Greggs.

Acknowledgements

Leo Hollis and John Merrick had faith in this project long before we knew the shape it would take. Leo ensured it got over the line; without his steer I would have spent many more months in the library. I am grateful to the rest of the team at Verso and to the long health of a publisher whose intellectual tradition has long shaped my view of the world.

My thanks are of course due to the cast of characters who appear in this book, and to others whose insights I gleaned even where their names do not. These latter include Chris Young, Rebecca Spaven, Caroline Bennett, NEF's Chris Williams, Will McCallum, Robb Robinson, the family of the late Graham Doswell, the subterranean chefs of Restaurant X, the River Café family and the boys grafting away at Shababs, plus the marketing teams of Castle Howard (sorry) and Greggs (ditto). A special thanks to Wesley Jones, who endured a George Orwell–inspired research trip to Blackpool on New Year's Eve, the events of which never made the final edit, which is probably for the best.

The team at Llewelyn's and Lulu's, past and present, have been great company while I was engaged in this work. My job at these restaurants has been a relief from writing this book as well as an inspiration for it. Many years ago my Ph.D. supervisors Kevin Gillan and Ian Bruff guided me through a project that profoundly enriched some of the perspectives that underlie this work; I hope they see this book as a token of their investment. Jonathan Nunn helped kick-start this endeavour after I first approached him with an idea for a podcast on English food. David Webb, aka Forest DLG, helped make that podcast happen. I received invaluable feedback on ideas and drafts for this book from Evelina Gambino, Maia Holtermann-Entwistle and Joe Leigh, all of whom have also been essential companions. I'm grateful to Joe for constructively highlighting important weaknesses in my research and arguments and Maia for help sharpening my meanings. Angus Ledingham's copy editing has profoundly improved the clarity and accuracy of this work. The responsibility for the issues that remain is, of course, mine.

Eve has heard my thoughts on this book develop from their faintest to their fullest. She has been exposed to the smell of bait in my washing and to my many research-related hangovers. The hours we have shared reading, writing and talking together are woven throughout these pages.

This book is dedicated to the restaurant lifers, to the cooks, cleaners and servers, and to all those whose labour turns the wheels of our culinary culture.

Notes

Introduction

1 Barry M. Popkin et al., 'A Policy Approach to Identifying Food and Beverage Products That Are Ultra-processed and High in Added Salt, Sugar and Saturated Fat in the United States: A Cross-Sectional Analysis of Packaged Foods', *Lancet Regional Health: Americas*, 32 (April 2024).

2 Eric Hobsbawm and George Rudé, *Captain Swing* (Pantheon Books, 1969), 23.

3 For example: Robin Mann, '"It Just Feels English Rather than Multicultural": Local Interpretations of Englishness and Non-Englishness', *Sociological Review*, 59/1 (February 2011); Ross Bond, 'National Identities Among Minority and "Majority" Ethnic Groups: Evidence from the 2021 Census in England and Wales', *Journal of Ethnic and Migration Studies*, 51 (2025).

4 Sunder Katwala, John Denham and Steve Ballinger, *Beyond a 90-minute Nation: Why It's Time for an Inclusive England Outside the Stadium* (British Future, 2021).

1. Sourdough

1 See Elizabeth David, *English Bread and Yeast Cookery* (Allen Lane 1977), 90.

2 Anatoly Liberman, 'Returning to Our Daily Bread Part II', *OUPblog*, 24 October 2018.

3 Eric Pallant, *Sourdough Culture: A History of Bread Making from Ancient to Modern Bakers* (Agate, 2021).

4 Ruth Goodman, *How to Be a Tudor: A Dawn-to-Dusk Guide to Everyday Life* (Penguin, 2016).

5 Ibid., 128.

6 Gervase Markham, *The English Huswife* (McGill-Queen's University Press,1986 [1615]), 210.

7 Ann Hagen, *A Handbook of Anglo-Saxon Food: Processing and Consumption* (Anglo-Saxon Books, 1992), 15.

8 Conan Doyle, 'Beer and Ale in Early Medieval England: A Survey of Evidence', in *Beer and Brewing in Medieval Culture and Contemporary Medievalism*, eds John A. Geck, Rosemary O'Neill and Noelle Phillips. (Palgrave Macmillan, 2022), 40.

9 Herbert Monckton, *A History of English Ale and Beer* (Bodley Head, 1966), 75.

10 Walter T. Banfield, *Manna: A Comprehensive Treatise on Bread Manufacture* (Maclaren & Sons, 1947), 235.

11 Karl Marx, *Capital* (Penguin, 1992 [1867]) i. 358. Marx cites H. S. Tremenheere's 1862 Royal Commission report on the baking trade, which states: 'there is probably no branch of trade supplying a vast and constant demand which has so completely remained in the primitive condition of ministering to that demand from a multitude of small and isolated sources as the baking trade'.

12 Derek J. Oddy calculates that pre-modern bread contained around 20–30 per cent water. A loaf made at Quince was much closer to 50 per cent water. In *From Plain Fare to Fusion Food: British Diet from the 1890s to the 1990s* (Boydell Press, 2003).

13 David, *English Bread and Yeast Cookery*, 296.

14 Diane Purkiss, *English Food: A People's History* (HarperCollins, 2022).
15 Sylvester Graham, *A Treatise on Bread, and Bread-Making* (Light & Stearns, 1837), 61.
16 There is also evidence that the French had better technique and equipment when it came to milling and sifting their flours, producing a lighter bread. See John Le Couteur, *On the Varieties, Properties, and Classification of Wheat* (H. Payn, 1836), 92.
17 According to the industry group the Federation of Bakers, 85 per cent of all bread consumed in the UK comes from large factory bakeries producing mostly sliced white bread using the high-speed Chorleywood process. Twelve per cent of our bread comes from supermarket in-store bakeries, and these loaves are usually pre-made in the same factories as the sliced white stuff and then re-baked to a golden crust in-store. If this data is accurate, that means that only 3 per cent of the bread consumed in Britain comes from high street and artisan bakers. Market insights from Mintel broadly confirm this.
18 David, *English Bread and Yeast Cookery*, 35.
19 Cited in John Burnett, *Plenty and Want: A Social History of Food in England from 1815 to the Present Day* (Routledge, 1989) (first published1966), 18.
20 See Christian Petersen, *Bread and the British Economy, c.1770–1870* (Routledge, 1995).
21 Burke took white bread's popularity among early industrial workers as evidence that their lives were improving. See *Thoughts and Details on Scarcity* (F. and C. Rivington, 1800), 5.
22 Quite simply, the Assize required that a local measure be taken of the price of grain, to which was added a predetermined wage for the baker as the formula for the price of a loaf of bread. While simple, this calculation became hard to enact owing to an increasingly complex market in wheat as well as variations in measuring and enforcement. Among other issues was the government's efforts to disincentivise the consumption of refined wheat, which resulted in bakers producing the fixed-price brown loaves at the lowest possible quality. This was another reason why workers demanded white bread.

23 The committee responsible for its abolition declared that 'more benefit is likely to result from the effects of a free competition… than can be expected to result from any regulations or restrictions'.

24 The persistence of the Assize of Bread (which even after it was abolished went on to some extent in the self-organisation of bakers via their guilds) was one reason why the baking industry remained industrially undeveloped: since profits were limited, so too was private investment.

25 Petersen, *Bread and the British Economy, c.1770–1870* (Routledge, 1995), 157.

26 During the war, 'the British Isles produced only one-fifth of the wheat, two-fifths of the butter and cheese, three-fifths of the meat and bacon, and none of the sugar that they required. Only in respect of fish, potatoes, and milk were they self-sufficient, and even the consumption of liquid milk was eked out by importation of condensed varieties.' Oddy, *From Plain Fare to Fusion Food*, 71.

27 David C. Fouser, *The Global Staff of Life: Wheat, Flour, and Bread in Britain, 1846–1914*, Ph.D. diss. (University of California, 2016).

28 Petersen, *Bread and the British Economy*, 11.

29 Eric Hobsbawm, *The Age of Empire, 1875–1914* (Weidenfeld & Nicolson, 1987), 34.

30 Oddy, *From Plain Fare to Fusion Food*, 11.

31 Despite this, Britain remained dependent on America for more than half of its flour in 1918. It also needed America for 84 per cent of its bacon and ham, over 31 per cent of its meat overall and almost 38 per cent of the dairy produce consumed in Britain. See Oddy, *From Plain Fare to Fusion Food*, 86.

32 Oddy, *From Plain Fare to Fusion Food*, 96.

33 Angus Calder, *The People's War: Britain, 1939–1945* (Pantheon, 1969), 384.

34 Eric Hobsbawm, 'The Invention of Tradition', in *The Invention of Tradition*, eds Eric Hobsbawm and Terence Ranger (Cambridge University Press, 1983), 4.

35 See Kimbell's website sourdough.co.uk

2. Les Rosbifs

1 See for example Bill Burford's popular books on French and Italian cuisines.

2 Stephen Mennell, *All Manners of Food: Eating and Taste in England and France from the Middle Ages to the Present* (University of Illinois Press, 1996).

3 A giant ball he must have been indeed, since 'when Louis XIV died in 1715, doctors noted upon conducting his autopsy that his stomach was three times the size of that of the average adult'. Melissa M. Wittmeier, 'The Art of the Table in Eighteenth-Century France', *Journal of the Western Society for French History*, 38 (2010).

4 Barbara Ketcham Wheaton, *Savoring the Past: The French Kitchen and Table from 1300 to 1789* (Simon & Schuster, 1983).

5 Among the first of the new restaurants in Paris was one named La Grande Taverne de Londres.

6 According to Mennell, the way in which the Revolution spurred the development of restaurants had less to do with the evacuation of cooks whose patrons had fled or been decapitated than with the ending of the guilds, which were a fetter upon cooking individual restaurant-style meals (*All Manners of Food*, 138).

7 Rachel Rich et al., 'Self-Fashioning, Food, and Masculinity in George III's Monarchy', *Historical Journal*, 38 (2025).

8 Gervase Markham, *The English Huswife* (McGill-Queen's University Press,1986 [1615]), 4.

9 John Wilmot, 2nd Earl of Rochester, 'Satyr', in *The Poems of Lord Rochester*, eds Keith Walker et al. (Penguin, 1984).

10 Elizabeth Raffald, *The Experienced English Housekeeper* (Southover Press Historic Cookery and Housekeeping, 2009 [1769]), 14.

11 Hannah Glasse, *The Art of Cookery Made Plain and Easy* (L. Wangford, 1747), iii.

12 Ben Rogers, *Beef and Liberty: Roast Beef, John Bull and the English Nation* (Chatto & Windus, 2003), 17.

13 Anson Rabinbach, *The Human Motor: Energy, Fatigue, and the Origins of Modernity* (University of California Press, 1992), 216.

14 Luke Barr, *Ritz and Escoffier: The Hotelier, The Chef, and the Rise of the Leisure Class* (Bantam Books, 2018).

15 'So rustic a dish can hardly, [Escoffier] realises, be offered to the fine ladies and gentlemen who frequent the elegant restaurant over which he presides. From force of habit he banishes the garlic and adds sliced truffles.' Elizabeth David, *French Provincial Cooking* (Penguin, 1964), 29.

16 Indeed, it was in this decade that the American sociologist Thorstein Veblen published his treatise on the conspicuous consumption of a new leisure class, one that had grown fat on investments.

17 Barr, *Ritz and Escoffier.*

18 Eric Hobsbawm, *The Age of Empire, 1875–1914* (Weidenfeld & Nicolson, 1987).

19 Oxford English Dictionary, oed.com, accessed 2025.

20 E. Charles Vivian, *The British Army from Within* (Hodder & Stoughton, 1914).

21 Albert Barrère and Charles Godfrey Leland, *A Dictionary of Slang, Jargon & Cant: Embracing English, American, and Anglo-Indian Slang, Pidgin English, Tinkers' Jargon and Other Irregular Phraseology* (The Ballantyne Press, 1889).

22 Amy B. Trubek, *Haute Cuisine: How the French Invented the Culinary Profession* (University of Pennsylvania Press, 2000), 63.

3. Whelks

1

The farmer has his rent to pay.
Haul, you joskins, haul.
And seed to buy, I've heard him say.
Haul, you joskins, haul.
But we who plough the North Sea deep,
Though never sowing, always reap
The harvest which to all is free,
And Gorleston Light is home for me.
Haul, you joskins, haul.

Cited in Arthur Michael Samuel, *The Herring: Its Effect on the History of Britain* (John Murray, 1918), 21. Samuel writes that '"joskin" is a jesting name used in East Norfolk to describe men who work on the land in summer, and go to sea "a-fishin'" in the autumn and winter'.

2 Rachael Laudan, '10 Reasons Why Fish Has Been So Suspect as Food', rachellaudan.com, 2017.

3 Unsurprisingly the metaphor doesn't appear in Mandarin or Japanese, i.e. in languages belonging to environments where cattle have, until recently, been rare.

4 'A good example of structural design', according to Dorothy Hartley in *Food in England* (Macdonald General Books, 1954), 247.

5 Diane Purkiss, *English Food: A People's History* (HarperCollins, 2022), 151.

6 Soyer includes a recipe for battered and fried fish in his cookbook *A Shilling Cookery for the People* (1854).

7 The above figures are from Panikos Panayi, *Fish and Chips: A Takeaway History* (Reaktion, 2014).

8 'Would it not be better if [the unemployed] spent more money on wholesome things like oranges and wholemeal bread or if they even, like the writer of the letter to the *New Statesman*, saved on fuel and ate their carrots raw? Yes, it would, but the point is that no ordinary human being is ever going to do such a thing. The ordinary human being would sooner starve than live on brown bread and raw carrots. And the peculiar evil is this, that the less money you have, the less inclined you feel to spend it on wholesome food. A millionaire may enjoy breakfasting off orange juice and Ryvita biscuits; an unemployed man doesn't. Here the tendency of which I spoke at the end of the last chapter comes into play. When you are unemployed, which is to say when you are underfed, harassed, bored, and miserable, you don't want to eat dull wholesome food. You want something a little bit "tasty". There is always some cheaply pleasant thing to tempt you.' George Orwell, *The Road to Wigan Pier* (Victor Gollancz, 1937), 88.

9 These estimates are from John de Witt, *A Representation of the Wholesome Political Grounds and Maxims of the Republic of Holland and West Friesland* (1669), accessed online.

10 More specifically, Dutch merchants were killed by Portuguese merchants when attempting to trade in Macau. Dutch privateers then robbed a Portuguese ship, the *Santa Catarina*; Grotius's tract formed the basis on which Dutch courts claimed that their piracy was a legal response.

11 Up to this point, French wine, mostly claret, had been a popular drink in London's taverns, but these Acts made it prohibitively expensive, such that beer then became the dominant drink to consume out of home. This development accelerated the decline of the tavern and the rise of the ale house, a legacy that is with us still.

12 1956 saw the peak of Britain's distant water landings, when the fleet brought 8.5 million tons to market, a figure that has since then trended downward.

13 Eleanor Ford and Bryce Stewart, *Building a Bridge over Troubled Water: An Analysis of Fishers' Trust in UK Fisheries Management* (Marine Ecosystem Management Report, University of York, 2019).

14 Rick Stein, *English Seafood Cookery* (Penguin, 1988), 17.

15 Craig McAngus, *Fishermen and the European Union: Report on Initial Analysis of a Survey of UK Fishermen Ahead of the Referendum on the UK's Membership of the EU* (University of Aberdeen, 2016).

16 Sourced from the now-defunct Fishing for Leave website: ffl.org.uk.

17 European Union (Withdrawal Agreement) Bill, Second Reading debate, 20 December 2019, *Hansard*, House of Commons, vol. 669.

18 This relationship – where some countries in the EU have resources while others have markets – underlies the architecture of the Common Fisheries Policy and explains why the common pooling of fisheries was decided after only six hours of negotiations. See Ernesto Penas Lado, *The Common Fisheries Policy: The Quest for Sustainability* (Wiley-Blackwell, 2016).

19 The UK is the world's second largest market for canned tuna (the USA is first). In 2018 we bought nearly 800 million tins of the stuff – equivalent to thirteen cans for every person in the country.

20 Ruth H. Thurstan, Simon Brockington and Callum M. Roberts, 'The Effects of 118 Years of Industrial Fishing on UK Bottom Trawl Fisheries', *Nature Communications*, 1/15 (2010).

4. Curry

1 Dorothy Hartley, *Food in England* (Macdonald General Books, 1954), v.

2 Pat Chapman, *Balti Curry Cookbook* (Piatkus, 1993), 1.

3 Andy Munro, whom we're about to encounter, verified this story by visiting the steel fabricator who made the first balti bowls. See his *The Balti: Its Birth, Its Boom Years, and Beyond* (Fonthill Media, 2025), 19.

4 See 'Robin Cook's Chicken Tikka Masala Speech', *Guardian*, 19 April 2009.

5 'People like me who came to England in the 1950s have been there for centuries; symbolically, we have been there for centuries. I was coming home. I am the sugar at the bottom of the English cup of tea. I am the sweet tooth, the sugar plantations that rotted generations of English children's teeth. There are thousands of others beside me that are, you know, the cup of tea itself. Because they don't grow it in Lancashire, you know. Not a single tea plantation exists within the United Kingdom. This is the symbolization of English identity – I mean, what does anybody in the world know about an English person except that they can't get through the day without a cup of tea?

'Where does it come from? Ceylon, Sri Lanka, India. That is the outside history that is inside the history of the English. There is no English history without that other history.' Stuart Hall, 'Old and New Identities, Old and New Ethnicities', in *Essential Essays, Volume 2: Identity and Diaspora* (Duke University Press, 2019) (first published 1991), 48.

6 David Burton, *The Raj at Table: A Culinary History of the British in India* (Faber and Faber, 1993), 2.

7 Ibid., 13.

8 I provide only two examples in what follows, but there are many more. See Nupur Chaudhuri, 'Shawls, Jewelry, Curry, and Rice in Victorian Britain', in *Western Women and Imperialism: Complicity and Resistance*, eds Nupur Chaudhuri and Margaret Strobel (Indiana University Press, 1992).

9 Eliza Acton, *Modern Cookery for Private Families* (Longmans, 1845), 296.

10 Susan Zlotnick, 'Domesticating Imperialism: Curry and Cookbooks in Victorian England', *Frontiers: A Journal of Women Studies*, 16/2–3 (1996).

11 This point is made by Lizzie Collingham in *Curry: A Tale of Cooks and Conquerors* (Vintage, 2005).

12 Quoted in Collingham, *Curry*, 114.

13 Cited in David Gilmour, *The British in India: Three Centuries of Ambition and Experience* (Allen Lane, 2018).

14 For the figures in this paragraph see: Homa Khaleeli, 'The Curry Crisis', *Guardian*, 8 January 2012; Malcolm Moore, 'The Great British Curry Crisis', *Financial Times*, 8 January 2016; Panikos Panayi, *Spicing Up Britain: The Multicultural History of British Food* (Reaktion, 2008). Andy provided me with the number of balti restaurants.

15 Chinese food in England, or more accurately the food of Hong Kong and what we call the Canton region, has a comparable history to that of curry, Hong Kong having been a British possession from the first Opium War in 1841 until 1997. But the fact that, until recently, nothing comparable to the curry club tradition has existed in England for Chinese food reflects the smaller extent of British colonisation in China and the racialised hierarchy discussed below; so-called East Asians were often confusedly understood and were engaged with to a lesser extent than South Asians.

16 British soldiers stationed in India, almost half of whom were Irish, had less choice when it came to avoiding local foods, and often topped up their basic rations of beef, bread and ale with whatever else was on offer.

17 Collingham is one such historian. See also Gilmore, *The British in India*, although he provides evidence, presented below, that at the very least this was not total.

18 Gilmore, *The British in India*.

19 As Francis Hutchins observed, 'India seemed to offer the prospect of aristocratic security at a time when England itself was falling prey

to democratic vulgarity.' Cited in David Cannadine, *Ornamentalism: How the British Saw Their Empire* (Oxford University Press, 2001).

20 Madhur Jaffrey, *An Invitation to Indian Cooking* (Jonathan Cape, 1976), 11.

21 Ibid., 12.

22 Ibid., 15.

23 The sketch, called 'Going for an English', can be seen on YouTube.

24 See Elizabeth Buettner, "Going for an Indian": South Asian Restaurants and the Limits of Multiculturalism in Britain', *Journal of Modern History*, 80/4 (December 2008).

25 Jaffrey, *An Invitation to Indian Cooking*, 17.

26 Quoted in Buettner, '"Going for an Indian"'.

27 Madhur Jaffrey, *Madhur Jaffrey's Ultimate Curry Bible: The Definitive Curry Cookbook from the Queen of Curry* (Ebury, 2003), 8.

28 The story is brilliantly told in Collingham's *Curry*, Chapter 8.

29 Arjun Appadurai, 'How to Make a National Cuisine: Cookbooks in Contemporary India', *Comparative Studies in Society and History*, V30/1 (January 1988).

30 The video, titled 'Stuart Hall on Cosmopolitanism', is available on YouTube.

31 Rose Prince, *The New English Kitchen: Changing the Way You Shop, Cook and Eat* (Fourth Estate, 2005), vii.

32 Such an appeal is part of the motivation for Colin Spencer's book *British Food: An Extraordinary Thousand Years of History* (Columbia University Press, 2003).

5. Olive Oil

1 Jonathan Meades, '*A Place for All People* by Richard Rogers Review – Architecture and the Elite', *Guardian*, 8 September 2017.

2 Richard Rogers, *A Place for all People* (Canongate, 2017).

3 Raphael Samuel, 'The SDP and the New Middle Class', in *Theatres of Memory* ii*: Island Stories: Unravelling Britain* (Verso, 1998).

4 Richard Rogers agonised before accepting a peerage from Tony Blair

(he had similarly brief reservations about accepting a knighthood), but he made a point of saying that while he would conform to the formal dress code at the House of Lords, he would leave his tie on a peg at Westminster and would not wear it otherwise.

5 Adam Gopnik, 'River Rennaissance', *New Yorker*, 15 July 1996.

6 Nigella Lawson, 'Italian on the Tongue', *The Times*, 13 May 1995.

7 Rose Gray and Ruth Rogers, *The River Cafe Classic Italian Cookbook*, 2017. I never saw any such Pugliese bread during my week at the River Café; the restaurant seems to have given in to the popularity of focaccia. Anna Higham, whom we met in chapter one and who was briefly the River Café's head pastry chef, tells me that she never saw it either.

8 Hugh Fearnley-Whittingstall, 'How I Shared a Stove with Rose Gray', *Guardian*, 1 March 2010.

9 Rachel Kelly, 'Peasant Food for the Well-heeled', *The Times*, 25 September 1995.

10 David Hencke, 'Chance Chat over Dinner Led Blair to Order U-turn on Private Beds', *Guardian*, 28 July 2000.

11 Quoted in Artemis Cooper, *Writing at the Kitchen Table: The Authorized Biography of Elizabeth David* (Faber and Faber, 2011), 129.

12 Quoted in ibid., 132.

13 Elizabeth David, *A Book of Mediterranean Food* (John Lehmann, 1950).

14 Elizabeth David, *A Book of Mediterranean Food* (Dorling Kindersley, 1988 [1950]).

15 David's experience in post-war Britain was in fact similar to that of Richard Rogers's mother, Dada Geiringer, who served as a key source of culinary inspiration for both Ruth Rogers and Rose Gray. Dada, who was raised in a professional middle-class family in Trieste, only took up cooking when forced to, having had to flee fascist Italy for Britain and making do with local ingredients, deficient cookware and the lack of hired help.

16 Elizabeth David, *Italian Food* (Macdonald, 1954).

17 Elizabeth David, *English Potted Meats and Fish Pastes* (Grub Street, 2023 [1968]).

18 Although arguably such 'rusticism' had a precursor in Italian fascism, where at times the consumption of pasta (made of wheat imported from America) was opposed in favour of a diet based upon that of an idealised national peasantry.

19 Despite being both gay and radically left-wing, the director and writer Pier Paolo Pasolini, for example, lamented the passing of the pre-modern world: an 'agricultural universe' with its 'church, country, family, obedience, order, savings [and] morality', replaced by 'the power of consumption' that was 'deforming the conscience of the Italian people to the point of irreversible degradation'. See 'L'Articolo delle lucciole', *Corriere della Sera*, 1 February 1975.

20 Alberto Grandi and Daniele Soffiati, *La cucina italiana non esiste* (Mondadori, 2024).

21 Ibid.

22 Kelly, 'Peasant Food for the Well-heeled'.

23 John Dickie, *Delizia!: The Epic History of the Italians and Their Food* (Hodder & Stoughton, 2023), 7.

24 Quoted in Tim Adams, 'Take Me to the River', *Observer*, 30 April 2000. This utopian atmosphere is also captured in the following from Richard Rogers:

> A subsidised canteen at Thames Wharf enabled us to eat together like an extended family...and we are planning something similar in our new offices. In the summer we play softball against other architects every Wednesday; in the winter we hold parties and play football. We take an annual trip together to see one of our newly-completed buildings and spend a weekend eating and drinking, and thinking about our future. Everyone can use the shared holiday home. (Richard Rogers, *A Place for all People*).

25 The quotes above are from the River Café's 'Blue' and 'Green' books (Ebury, 1996 and Ebury, 2000), plus *River Cafe 30: Simple Italian Recipes from an Iconic Restaurant* (Ebury, 2017).

26 This 'mockney' accent is often seen as a marker of Jamie's authentically working-class roots, but in actual fact his parents owned and ran a successful pub. This contrast between cultural markers of class

in England and economic status (i.e. ownership, wealth and income) reveals the sociological poverty of viewing class simply in terms of culture, as has long been a widespread tendency in England (and not helped by the popularity of Bourdieu). Combined with deindustrialisation and globalisation, the new middle class has, to some extent, dislodged these cultural markers insofar as its taste is for the demotic – meaning that today many members of the middle class sport chore jackets, own whippets and prefer to live in houses that resemble bare brick barns.

27 See Tony Bonnici, 'Jamie Oliver asks: "How can poor buy huge TVs but eat so badly?,"' *The Times*, 27 August 2013.

6. Food as Fuel

1 The now ubiquitous use of scales to weigh the body has a social history that illustrates this point. The practice first appeared in London in the mid-eighteenth century among merchants, who required measurements of their goods. It then spread to agricultural fairs, train stations and chemists, long before it eventually made its way into household bathrooms. Weighing one's body – a public practice transformed into a private one – both reflected and helped to shape a rational, profit-making age of definite calculation.

2 Quoted in Mark R. Finlay, 'Early Marketing of the Theory of Nutrition: The Science and Culture of Liebig's Extract of Meat', in *The Science and Culture of Nutrition, 1840–1940*, eds Harmke Kamminga and Andrew Cunningham (Rodopi, 1995).

3 Ibid.

4 Kenneth J. Carpenter, *Protein and Energy: A Study of Changing Ideas in Nutrition* (Cambridge University Press, 1994), 97.

5 Wilbur Olin Atwater, 'Pecuniary Economy of Food', *Century Magazine*, January 1888.

6 'The best coal for a locomotive', Atkinson wrote in one of his many popular essays, 'is that which will enable it to haul the greatest number of tons over the longest distance. The best food for man is that which

will enable him to do the most work in a given time and keep him in perfect condition for further work.' Quoted in Steven Shapin, *Eating and Being: A History of Ideas About Our Food and Ourselves* (University of Chicago Press, 2024).

7 Quoted in Corinna Treitel, 'Max Rubner and the Biopolitics of Rational Nutrition', *Central European History*, 41/1 (January 2008).

8 This logic was, again, the same as that which informed the writings of Atkinson, who, in an 1885 address to the American Association for the Advancement of Science, stated that in an era of global competition 'the underfed cannot compete with the well-nourished'.

9 David F. Smith provides details of just how entangled the science of nutrition was with Britain's economic, colonial and military goals; it was even seen as a solution to gender inequality. See 'Nutrition Science and the Two World Wars', in *Nutrition in Britain: Science, Scientists and Politics in the Twentieth Century*, ed. David F. Smith (Routledge, 1997).

10 Edward Cathcart and John Orr, 'Energy Expenditure of the Infantry Recruit in Training', *Journal of Physiology*, 96 (1919).

11 This estimate is based on data presented by Chris Otter, who states that between 1909 and 1913 the average Briton obtained 395 calories from sugar per day. *Diet for a Large Planet: Industrial Britain, Food Systems, and World Ecology* (University of Chicago Press, 2020), 74.

12 Ibid., 281.

13 Ibid., 284.

14 In 1899 Atwater found that his subjects obtained enough fat and carbohydrates to function with only a bottle of wine a day. The finding was quickly taken up by alcohol advertising, and Atwater, a committed Christian, became a discredited figure within the Church. In his essay 'Time, Work-Discipline, and Industrial Capitalism' (in *Past and Present*, 1967), the social historian E. P. Thompson discusses the tradition of Saint Monday (*Blauer Montag* in Germany, *le lundi chômé* in France), wherein artisans, not yet beholden to factory discipline, would extend the weekend by a day to drink and/or recover from drinking. Hence my claim that alcohol was not sought out as a cheap source of calories capable of driving capitalist

productivity, in contrast to Atwater and Akinson's promotion of corn and beans.

15 Miranda McMinn, 'Eight Tips for Men to Stay Fit at Every Age (by the Man Who Created Huel)', *Daily Telegraph*, 16 January 2025.

16 Carole Cadwalladr, 'Could you Stomach Huel, the Food of the Future?', *Guardian*, 31 July 2016.

17 *The Diary of a CEO: The 33 Laws of Business and Life* (Edbury Edge, 2023), 4. Bartlett's previous book, also a bestseller, is called *Happy Sexy Millionaire* and promises a 'practical set of scientifically proven and unconventional ideas' to achieve happiness. Although what follows therein is neither peer-reviewed nor unconventional.

18 In 1917, the head of the newly created Ministry of Food, Lord Rhondda, accepted that war meant 'the free play of economic laws' had to be suspended. Yet 'under normal conditions', Rhondda claimed, such interventionist policy would 'prove very harmful'. Likewise, Lord Devenport, Britain's first food controller, appointed late in 1916, strongly disliked the bureaucracy involved in rationing, seeing it as un-English. See Otter, *Diet for a Large Planet*, 204 and 259.

19 The ASA's ruling may also explain why Bartlett quietly stepped down from the Huel board in 2025.

20 Michael Pollan, *In Defense of Food: The Myth of Nutrition and the Pleasures of Eating* (Penguin, 2008), 13.

21 Ibid., 148.

22 Ibid., 133.

7. Castle Howard Revisited

1 Quoted in Lance M. Neckar, 'Castle Howard: An Original Landscape Architecture', *Landscape Journal*, 19/1–2 (2000).

2 John Dixon Hunt, *Gardens and the Picturesque: Studies in the History of Landscape Architecture* (MIT Press, 1992), Chapter 1.

3 Guy Shrubsole, *Who Owns England? How We Lost Our Green and Pleasant Land and How to Take It Back* (William Collins, 2019).

4 We should see these institutions as being distinct from their ritualistic casings. The Palace of Westminster was built at the time of the Great Exhibition, but it was designed in a Gothic, medieval style. Likewise, Black Rod and the royal regalia, which form parts of the ceremony used to open Parliament each year, may recall the English Civil War, but the origins of these rituals are likewise Victorian. They are invented traditions, much like sourdough.

5 Perry Anderson, 'The Figures of Descent', *New Left Review* (Jan–Feb, 1987).

6 See David Edgerton, 'Why the Left Must Abandon the Myth of British Decline', *New Statesman*, 5 October 2021. Anderson's famous analysis of the historical limits of British capitalism arguably overlooks the extent of novelty and independence in the culture of the urban bourgeoisie, which can be seen when contrasting the trappings of that culture with the beef-eating preferences of the mostly non-urban elite, as presented in chapter two.

7 Corporal Hooper is the cheerfully crude working-class figure in Waugh's *Brideshead Revisited*. Hooper shows a casual and impious lack of interest in aristocratic tradition and culture.

8 Quoted in Robert Hewison, *The Heritage Industry: Britain in a Climate of Decline* (Methuen Publishing, 1987), 31.

9 Patrick Cormack, *Heritage in Danger* (Quartet Books, 1978), 13.

10 Quoted in Shrubsole, *Who Owns England?*.

11 Elizabeth David was well aware of this. 'It has to be borne in mind', she wrote in *Spices, Salt and Aromatics in The English Kitchen* (Penguin, 1970), 'that until the late-seventeenth century, recorded recipes, in England as elsewhere in Europe, were predominantly those of the royal households, of the nobility, the great land-owning barons, the princes of the Church, and the prosperous merchants' (30). For examples of this elite version of national culinary history, see, for example, Constance Anne Wilson, *Food and Drink in Britain: From the Stone Age to the Nineteenth Century* (Constable, 1973).

12 This is even, or especially, true for those who have known little of the countryside; for example, the urban men fighting in the First World War were encouraged by patriotic images of rolling hills, thatched

cottages and smallholdings. See Martin J. Wiener, *English Culture and the Decline of the Industrial Spirit, 1850–1980* (Cambridge University Press, 1981).

13 Speech delivered at the King's Theatre in Edinburgh on 17 July 1909.

14 Isabella Tree, *Wilding: The Return of Nature to a British Farm* (Picador, 2018), 40.

15 Quoted in Neil Levine, 'Castle Howard and the Emergence of the Modern Architectural Subject', *Journal of the Society of Architectural Historians*, 62/3 (September 2003): 332.

16 This estimate comes from Fiona Burns et al., *State of Nature 2023* (State of Nature Partnership, 2023).

17 The same might be said of sheep farming, which, as George Monbiot points out, is a romantic national pastime because it is a simply unprofitable way to use land; the rearing of sheep is probably better understood, he observes, as a kind of subsidy farming. See *Regenesis: Feeding the World Without Devouring the Planet* (Allen Lane, 2022).

18 Ibid., 190.

Epilogue

1 William Morris, 'The Revival of Handicraft', *Fortnightly Review*, November 1888.

Index